The

BOB
VERDI

Collection

ALSO BY BOB VERDI
McMahon! *(with Jim McMahon)*

SPORTSWRITER'S EYE

The
BOB
VERDI
Collection

Introduction by
MIKE ROYKO

TAYLOR PUBLISHING COMPANY
Dallas, Texas

Published by Taylor Publishing Company
1550 West Mockingbird Lane
Dallas, Texas 75235

Library of Congress Cataloging-in-Publication Data

Verdi, Bob.
　　The Bob Verdi collection.
　　(Contemporary American sportswriters)
　　Includes index.
　　1. Sports.　2. Newspapers—Sections, columns, etc.—
Sports.　I. Title.　II. Series.
GV707.V47　1988　070.4'49796　87-33612
ISBN 0-87833-608-7

Printed in the United States of America

0　9　8　7　6　5　4　3　2　1

To my parents, who thought I
would outgrow listening to
five ballgames a day, and to my
co-workers at the *Chicago Tribune,*
who now have to put up with
me trying to cover one.

Introduction

When I was a kid, the first thing I turned to in the newspaper was the sports page. I sought great truths. Would Joltin' Joe get a hit in every game forever? Could the Splendid Splinter really count the stitches on the ball as it sped toward the plate? Did the Brown Bomber's kayo punch travel only a mere three inches?

Looking back, I'm not sure if my questions were ever fully answered. In fact, I may have been fed a line or two. The way the sports columnists told it, all athletes played for fun, drank milk, and ate Wheaties, and spent the off season hunting, fishing, and tilling the soil on their farms.

It never occurred to me that some of my heroes might have been drunks, gluttons, skirt-chasers, greedy, or in violation of even one of the Ten Commandments. What I read was what I believed. And what I read was that they were all okay guys.

That was the style of sportswriting in those pre-TV days. The jocks were bigger than life and they all spoke in complete sentences. I actually believed that grown men said: "As soon as I laid the wood on the old pea, I knew it was a circuit clout."

I believed, I believed.

Times changed. The tube zoomed in. We started hearing new and shocking words from the locker room and sidelines. And with it came a change in the sportswriting craft.

Editors said: "We must have the truth. We must tell the readers the story behind the story."

So we left the era of fantasy behind and entered the age of hard-eyed realism. A new wave of sportswriters took over. They stood back and took a hard look and gave us the truth. Jocks, it turned out, were just like the rest of us, with maybe a little better hand-eye coordination and foot speed. They had weaknesses beyond not hitting the curveball. They drank, sniffed, snorted, chased lewd women.

And worst of all, they were greedy. They actually wanted money, as much of it as they could get, and they hired agents. If anything shocked the new sports literati, it was the greed.

Even in a capitalist society, who would have thunk it? Say it ain't so, J. Pierpont Morgan.

The new wave of sports scribes became even more remorseless than the Woodwards and Bernsteins. They not only felt it was their duty to bring us all the warts of our heroes, many of them forgot that, hey, there *is* some artistry in a Gale Sayers run, a Mickey Mantle home run.

But you wouldn't know it by the stories. We had entered the age of the professional sports grump. You want to start your day with a smile? You had a better chance reading the obits. The sports grumps were busy telling us why the players and their agents were avaricious, the owners power-mad, the fans stupid. There were days when Richard Nixon's antics were light reading compared to a sports grump's blusterings about a contract negotiation.

And it lingers today. Some of the most dyspeptic souls in journalism tell us why it's all a sham, a fake, a fraud. Somewhere near the bottom, they might give you the final score.

Now and then, though, we have a Bob Verdi with his head screwed on straight.

Sure, he knows it's a business. He knows that, wow, the athletes want to be paid for their box-office appeal like everyone else in show biz. He knows the owners want to make a return on investment. But unlike so many of his contemporaries, he's managed to survive the trauma of knowing we are in a real world and that jocks are real people.

So he does something unusual for a modern sports columnist. He writes about the games and the way they're played. The fun, the thrills, the joy, and the humor. He gets inside the players' heads and finds something worth telling us about. Sure, there are agents, unions, owners, and contracts. But when the ball hits the bat and the center fielder lopes toward the fence, who cares about binding arbitration?

What he does isn't easy. The tube gives us the moment. But as sports nuts, we want more. We want to know what went through the mind as the body stood over the ten-foot putt of a lifetime. And we want it without the distraction of a sneer.

Verdi isn't a throwback to the days when they told it the way we wanted it to be, but really wasn't. Nor does he insult us with the obvious and irrelevant, as the grumps do.

What he does is use his words gracefully, wittily, concisely, and honestly. He reports and writes the way a fine athlete performs, by making it look easy, although we know it isn't.

He tells us how much fun it can be. And that, plus a cup of coffee, is a good way to start the day.

Mike Royko

Contents

CONTENTS

Golf / 93

Basketball / 127

Boxing / 149

Hockey / 171

Horse Racing / 189

Olympics / 203

Miscellany / 235

Preface

I don't remember the exact date, only the precise feeling.

I had just covered some sort of boxing match in Las Vegas a year or so ago, and was thinking I'd written a pretty good column for the *Chicago Tribune*. Concise, entertaining, funny and all that pertinent stuff, and I beat the deadline by about seven minutes, too.

So I fly on to my next assignment in Los Angeles in an excellent frame of mind until I land there and pick up a copy of the *Los Angeles Times*. My sense of accomplishment turns into a gripping, creeping humility as I read a column by Jim Murray, who covered the same boxing match that I attended in Las Vegas. Murray's version of what happened was not only infinitely better, it made mine read like his rough draft, his leftovers, the out-takes. It was as though he'd written what I'd written, then crumpled the whole thing up and said to himself, "I can do better than that."

I sought a taxi, and headed for the hotel, properly contrite after being the victim of a TKO.

I resurrect the incident above to make two points about this book and this business of sportswriting.

First, Jim Murray is a giant, as are Blackie Sherrod of the *Dallas Morning News* and Edwin Pope of the *Miami Herald*—all of whose efforts are part of this set of collected works brought to you by Taylor Publishing. For yours truly to be included in the same breath as Murray, Sherrod and Pope, let alone placed on the same shelf, is positively frightening.

The ultimate test in the newspaper racket is, after all, the test of time. Anybody can crank out a good column once in a while, but to ring the bell three or four times a week is to be a home-run hitter in the mold of the Murrays, Sherrods, and Popes.

You've seen those displays of historic front pages past? I encountered one of those recently at the airport in St. Louis (we spend a lot of time in airports). There was the *Dallas Times Herald* from November 23, 1963, the day after the tragic assassination of President John F. Kennedy in Dallas. Naturally, the newspaper was devoted to blanket coverage of the event, but there was Blackie on the sports page, great then, as he is great as ever now. The test of time.

Equal time here for Edwin Pope. I have watched the man labor for hours over a column, for instance, in the press facility at Augusta National Golf Club, site of the Masters. He writes, he rewrites, he fine tunes, he restarts, and finally, he sends his column to the newspaper early in the evening. Is he finished? No.

"Want to go for a beer, Eddie?" you ask.

"Maybe later," he says. "I just sent the office my piece, but it's bad. Gonna go back to the hotel and fix it."

I doubt that Pope's original version was broken enough to require fixing, but the professionals are never pleased. And the essence of sportswriting doesn't allow for much self-satisfaction, anyway. As Murray has remarked on numerous occasions, just when you think you can enjoy what might be a pretty good effort for today's newspaper, you start fretting about tomorrow's newspaper and the day after tomorrow's.

I began working at the *Chicago Tribune* in 1967, and, shortly thereafter, wrote hockey on a regular basis. Then I moved to the baseball beat, then the column. In that short time frame, I've traveled extensively and read enough different newspapers to start a bonfire, and I'm forever amazed at the high quality, the improving quality, of sports journalism in the United States.

The job has become increasingly more difficult and more competitive. Television and radio take care of immediate facts and figures as never before; thus, it is up to sports sections and sportswriters throughout the nation to supply deeper analysis, more interpretation, and better writing. As a rule—and I might be biased in this opinion—sports sections have succeeded mightily. Not just in the major markets, but in smaller, one-paper towns, too. There is excellent sportswriting everywhere, and what separates the journalist who works before a huge audience and the journalist who aspires to the "big league" job can be a matter of opportunity (there are only so many plums around) and, again, consistency (is he or she able to sustain a high level of work?)

As a child interested in sports, but able to hit only .200 with a high school baseball team, I suppose my heroes were the Mickey Mantles. Since then, however, my admiration has shifted considerably. Journalists' relationships with athletes have become more distant bordering on adversarial, which is fine. They are the performers, we are the critics, the reviewers. My "heroes" now are the Murrays and Sherrods and Popes— the craftsmen who attend a dull game and make it sing in print.

I'm not much for the assassination school of journalism. You can call a guy a lousy ballplayer for effect, or you can say that a ballplayer had a lousy day at the office. With rare exception, I find the latter approach preferable. In an era of Star Wars and 508-point "corrections" on Wall Street, I don't think the reader picks up the sports section to be overwhelmed by venom. This is not war, these are games, and a light dusting suffices. Accent on the light. Having fun with a subject is more difficult than making fun of a subject, and, too often, the latter ceases to be fun or funny at all. What was that they said about the late and wonderful Red Smith? His surgery was performed with a scalpel instead of a hatchet and was more effective, anyway. In the end, the subject might even chuckle at himself, which isn't all that bad.

What's a sports column? I'm not positive that I know, or that I'll ever know. For sure, it's you talking to the reader, asking the reader to agree or disagree, just to come along for the ride, but, above all, to listen. The power of the printed word is so great that we shouldn't diminish the effect or influence of what we do. We also should remember that, just because our picture might be in the newspaper every day, there's a chance the readers will be more interested in what we write about than us. In a sports column, viewpoints are a must. But whether readers want us to pontificate day after day, whether they are interested in state of the union messages, whether they pay their quarters to digest column after column written from the "I" formation, I'm not sure. I'm only sure that it's a fun line of work, and the day we don't reflect that in what we write is the day we should close up shop.

Bob Verdi
October, 1987
Northbrook, Illinois

Baseball

UECKER LAMENTS LOST RICHES

MAY 5, 1980

It is a hopeless proposition. Bob Uecker tries to hide his emotions, but, always, bitterness gets the best of him. This syndrome is common among retired ballplayers during this crazed era of free agents, but, in Uecker's case, the pain is acute.

"It tears me up," Mr. Baseball pouted Sunday, moments before donning a chartreuse sports jacket for the telecast back to Milwaukee of the Brewers' game against the White Sox. "Here I am, a lousy announcer, when if I were just a little younger, I could be the object of a bidding war.

"I would play out my option, and 26 teams would be drooling. I'd probably have to take my phone off the hook. Can you imagine what the market would be for a defensive catcher who had a career lifetime average of .200? Modestly, I'd say I could command a salary of $150,000 as a backup playing 60 games. Of course, if the team I signed with was deep in catching and only needed me for 30 games, I'd be worth $200,000. Fewer games I played, less chance for me to screw things up.

"And that doesn't include all the money I could make on the side. I see your paper has a Dave Kingman column. Well, I would do one, too. It would be strictly instructional, of course. Tips on how to put pine tar on bats, how to stay awake in the dugout during games. Important stuff that youngsters who want to grow up like me would need to know."

Before Uecker was a hit on the *Tonight Show,* he was, of course, a miss with several major-league teams. After his best season—the one when he played the fewest games—he was awarded his best salary, $23,000. Nowadays, naturally, that is tip money.

2

"As much as I know that I was underpaid, though, that doesn't mean I didn't have a lot of thrills in baseball," admitted Uecker, getting sentimental now. "Probably the biggest was when I started my first game for the Braves right in my hometown of Milwaukee back in 1957. My folks, friends, everybody was there. And they were all cheering. Wasn't until the third inning that the manager pulled me aside in the dugout and said, 'Kid, you're doing good, except that up here in the big leagues, most of us wear our athletic supporter on the inside of our uniforms.'

"Then there was the time when I hit a grand slam off the Giants' Ron Herbel. The manager, Herman Franks, came out of their dugout to lift Herbel and he was carrying Herbel's suitcase. For some reason, other teams took me lightly. I remember one time I'm batting against the Dodgers in Milwaukee. They lead 2-1, it's the bottom of the ninth, bases loaded for us, two out, and the pitcher has a full count on me. I look over to the Dodger dugout and they're all in street clothes. No respect.

"But the biggest thrill a ballplayer can have is when your son takes after you. That happened to me last summer. My Bobby was in his championship Little League game up in Milwaukee. He's only 14, but he showed me something. Struck out three times and lost the game for his team when a ball went through his legs at third base.

"Parents were throwing things at our car and swearing at us as we left the parking lot. Gosh, was I proud. A chip off the old block. I took Bobby for a big dinner that night. He was first named Sidney when we had him, but when I saw he had no coordination, we changed it to Bobby Jr.

"My other son, Steve, is a different story. He upsets me. He has talent. But he might be coming around. He went to Colorado skiing last winter and broke a leg. In time, he may become what I was. Sporting goods companies paid me to not endorse their products."

Just then, White Sox General Manager Roland Hemond walked by and turned pale at the sight of Uecker talking to a reporter.

"Roland goes through life scared, you know," allowed Mr. Baseball. "He's had a fine career, but one thing nobody is aware of is that he was the guy to sign me to a first major-league contract with the Braves. I can't imagine why he wouldn't be proud of that. Milwaukee signed me for a $3,000 bonus. That bothered my dad at the time, because he didn't have that kind of dough to lay out. Finally, he scraped it up and got me to leave home.

"In the end, though, the signing ceremony was one of the great athletic events in the city's history. The Braves officials took me to one of the finest restaurants. I had to have my dad with me for the occasion, but he was very nervous. He rolled down the window of the car after we were there 10 minutes, and the hamburgers fell off the tray."

Being released was a traumatic experience for Uecker. Back for a second time with the Braves in 1968, he walked into the clubhouse at spring training and General Manager Paul Richards kicked him out, saying no visitors were allowed. Then Manager Lum Harris happened by and promised Uecker a job in the organization. Coaching second base.

"Look, I know I wasn't a great hitter," says Uecker, "but I had a theory about guys who batted .350. What did they have to look forward to? Me, I hit .180 with four RBI every season, and they could always say I had a lot of potential. Baseball hasn't forgotten me, though. I go to Old-Timers games now and I haven't lost a thing. I sit in the bullpen and let people throw junk at me. Just like old times.

"I'm a little surprised that Cooperstown hasn't gotten a hold of me. I admit every year around Hall of Fame voting time, I get a little nervous. I sit by the phone waiting for the big call. I know it's coming. I'm out of the limelight now, my number's not unlisted anymore. It's in the book."

The transition to broadcasting baseball, either for the Brewers or ABC's Game of the Week, has not been easy for Uecker.

"Hardest thing I've ever had to do," he confesses. "There's a great temptation, being a former ballplayer, to be overly critical of the athletes on the field now. But, I just have to catch myself sometimes. Not fair for me to expect these guys to do things the way I did them. Just not fair."

KUENN COMES THROUGH

MAY 12, 1980

MILWAUKEE—Harvey Kuenn, who still is reaching for all the gusto in life, insists nothing really has changed.

"As far as I can tell, it's just like old times," he says. "When I walk home from having a few beers with the boys, I've got one foot in the street, another on the curb."

Obviously, Harvey Kuenn has survived his latest crisis rather well. They have cut off part of his right leg, true; they have cut off none of his vital signs, however.

"I just go around telling people what a lot of retired ballplayers tell people," he grins. "I've lost a step."

For 15 major-league seasons, Harvey Kuenn apologized to no one. After being named rookie of the year for the Detroit Tigers in 1953, he carved a .303 lifetime batting average with five clubs, including the Cubs in 1965–66. He was seven times an All-Star, a student of swat, a ballplayer's ballplayer.

Since retiring, he has been tested by physical breakdowns. Four years ago, a heart ailment required a quadruple bypass. Two years ago, kidney failure left him at 139 pounds. Neither time, thankfully, did the physical problems beget mental problems. Ditto last January, when Kuenn, a coach for the Milwaukee Brewers, took his dog for a walk at the team's spring training base in Sun City, Arizona.

"I felt a little pain in the back of my right calf," recalled Kuenn. "I didn't think much of it. Thought I might have stepped in a hole or something and pulled a muscle."

After a subsequent round of golf, though, he sprawled out on a living room chair, and his wife Audrey noticed that his right leg was chalk white. He dropped it down, as though to expedite blood flow, but the next time he propped up the leg, it was more blue than white.

"The doctor, who I went to right away, took X-rays," said

5

Kuenn. "I went right to the hospital. It was no pulled muscle. There was no circulation from the knee down. I had four operations to get the blood going again, but it never worked. It would flow for a few hours, then cut off. Finally, the doctors told me what I sort of expected all along. Amputate."

Audrey was there when the prognosis was rendered. She could not camouflage her fears.

"I thought to myself, 'Here is a man, my husband, who for all his life has excelled in everything he did physically,' " she mused. "If he bowled, he bowled better than anyone else; if he golfed, he golfed better than anyone else. And now, they are cutting his right leg off. I didn't know what to think. But the way he came out of it, he has become my true hero."

Harvey Kuenn came out of surgery like a trooper. He looked down to see nothing beyond his right knee, gazed up at the surgeon, and spoke.

"First of all," he said. "I'm starving. Will you get me something to eat? Second, how long will it be before I can play golf on this thing?"

Harvey Kuenn played golf here the other day. He shot an 87.

"Not bad," he said. "It's early, and I'm still a little cautious about those uphill and downhill lies. I don't want to go out there and swing and fall on my butt. I'm still getting used to it."

"It" is Harvey Kuenn's new right leg, or half leg—a prosthesis, attached to the stump, which leads to a rubberized foot that allows considerable mobility and flexibility. Once the swelling abates from his real leg, he will be fitted again for another prosthesis that will fit flush.

"If you weren't really looking for it, you couldn't tell the difference between the fake leg and what's left of the old one," he said. "It's flesh colored. I have a slight limp, but again, unless you were looking for it, you wouldn't notice."

The other day, Harvey Kuenn went to County Stadium to resume his coaching duties with the Brewers. He wasn't in uniform yet, but just the sight of her husband returning to his milieu was all Audrey really needed to see.

"He's been unreal through this whole thing," she said. "This has been a difficult winter for us. A couple days after Harvey came home from the hospital in March, my father passed away. Between that, and wondering whether Harvey could cope . . . but he never got down, never.

"He adjusted so well. He was supposed to use canes for a while when he started trying to walk again. But he was off them in three days. We don't know yet why it happened. It might have been related to the heart operation he had. The doctors explained it like this—the arteries going down into the leg are like an eight-lane highway. His went from that, to four, to nothing. Pretty soon, the cars had to back up. They had to amputate."

But Harvey Kuenn listened intently to the doctors, who told him he would be as good as he wanted to be.

"There was never any doubt in my mind that I'd make a go of it," he says. "Only thing I'm not doing yet is driving, and I'll start that soon. I'm really very fortunate, all the good things that have happened to me in life. Some of the guys—especially a couple players on the club—have had a tough time coming up to me. They feel sorry, and they don't know what to say.

"Then there's Bob Uecker. He told me he wants to play golf next week, and if I beat him, he's going to take my leg and just leave me sitting out there on the course. Hah.

"It was difficult having this happen. But not as bad as the time I was traded to Cleveland for Rocky Colavito in 1960. That was something. Now that's what you call a real shock."

DODGERS' FORTITUDE

OCTOBER 29, 1981

NEW YORK—Well, at least we won't have to hear about how the 1981 World Series was decided in a Los Angeles hotel. If the New York Yankees had won, surely owner George Steinbrenner's alleged fight seven floors above sea level would have been chronicled as the turning point.

But the Yankees didn't win, and after observing their rancid closing act Wednesday night, even the heavyweight elevator champion of the world admitted as much. After the Dodgers' 9–2 conquest at Yankee Stadium, one of the first guests in their bubbly domain was none other than old sore hands himself.

"We weren't very good, but that doesn't mean you didn't deserve it," King George allowed, hugging Los Angeles Manager Tom Lasorda. "Now, I'll try to get even with you on the golf course."

First, however, King George will want to get even with the Yankees. Having made his perfunctory political announcement, Steinbrenner will call for the moving vans. For years, the American League battle cry has been to break up the Yankees. Not to worry. George will see to that himself. The Yankees are aging and, unlike wine, they are not getting any better.

Bob Lemon, the poker-faced manager, may be Exhibit A. Lemon hadn't piloted a team without a designated hitter since 1972 at Kansas City. He tried this last week, and nearly every decision boomeranged. His fourth-inning gamble Wednesday, lifting starter Tommy John for a pinch batter with the bases loaded and score tied 1–1, may not live in infamy, but it won't die quickly. Certainly not as quickly as the Yankees expired in this tournament that they had half-won.

But the Yankees did not lose four straight games because Lemon lost his cool. They lost because they left too many men on base, because important people such as Dave Winfield swatted a rousing .045 in 22 at-bats, and because, beyond Goose Gossage, the bullpen that brought them so far came up so stunningly shy. Lemon danced with those who got him here and got his toes stepped on.

"I feel sorry for Lem," Lasorda said. "I left Fernando Valenzuela in Game 3 Friday night at Los Angeles. He didn't have much going for himself except heart. If that had backfired, they'd have cut my head off and rolled it down Wilshire Boulevard. But what Fernando had we all had. Never seen a team with heart like this. Never."

Because baseball's fractured season bent the product beyond recognition, you can stand on the argument that the better team didn't win the World Series because the two best teams weren't in it. But the Dodgers played by Bowie's Rules of Order, and they prevailed. To the victors of a spoiled summer go the spoils.

"I hope we don't have to read that the Yankees choked," said Ron Cey. "I hope that we get the credit we deserve. There are a lot of organizations in baseball, you know, which are happy to finish in the first division or happy to escape the cellar or happy just to get in the Series. Our objective has never been anything less than to win the whole thing."

Cey, a plucky third baseman, had been crowned Sunday by a Gossage fastball in Game 5. First, Cey was concerned about living. A distant second was being able to participate in Game 6. He reported to Yankee Stadium five hours before Wednesday's opening pitch to take laps in the outfield. He pronounced himself ready to play. When he singled on John's first offering in the opening inning, the Dodger bench became electrified.

"That one incident was a cue for us," said Steve Garvey. "The courage he showed was a tremendous inspiration for us. There wasn't a whole lot of talk in the room before the game tonight, but there was a whole lot of feeling. Ron did something out of the ordinary, but the whole team did in the end. I guess nobody really believed in us except us."

The Dodgers, for all the games they have won, had not won a World Series since 1965. They had failed four times since, twice to their albatrosses, the Yankees. The Dodgers, too, are overstocked with venerability. This will be the last hurrah for many of them. And if management makes the mistake the Philadelphia Phillies made last year, falling in love with players who should move on, Los Angeles' wait for another title could be long indeed.

"A few of us old guys were sitting in a sauna on the road a few weeks ago," recalled Davey Lopes, the error-prone second baseman. "One of us mentioned that we should get one of these for Dodger Stadium. Then we all realized that none of us may be back."

Cey shared most valuable honors with Pedro Guerrero, who will be a star, and Steve Yeager, the Dodgers' part-time catcher. How voters didn't stuff the ballot boxes for Steve Garvey is another of baseball's mysteries this season. Garvey failed only to bat in runs. But he hit .417 and anchored a Dodger infield which, on any given ground ball, can be an adventure. The man hasn't missed a game since 1975, and even when his personal life becomes disjointed, he never fails to comport himself splendidly. It has been said behind his back that Garvey is a phony. Perhaps he is the least phony of them all.

"We aren't machines," Garvey said. "We make a lot of money, and we enjoy a certain amount of fame. But that doesn't mean there isn't any sentiment attached to this. We've played together so long, some of us, that we know it can't go on forever. I don't think you doubt a team's character after it's done the things we've done—first against Houston, then against Montreal, now this. I felt that the perfect World Series was Yankees versus Dodgers. And as far as I'm concerned, it had the perfect ending."

As Garvey spoke, Steinbrenner left the celebration for his own clubhouse. We'll be hearing from him again soon. Can't wait, can you?

BASEBALL AGAIN REIGNS SUPREME

OCTOBER 5, 1982

ANAHEIM, CALIFORNIA—Baseball is king again. But, really, was there ever any doubt?

Winter sports, such as basketball and hockey, are about to start. And autumnal endeavors such as pro football will restart if and when Ed Garvey and his billionaire adversaries decide that issues demand answers, not egos.

But, after the summer of '82, the sports fan needn't dally in that tedium. And surely, you can wait awhile to learn whether Moses Malone is earning his $13.2 million in Philadelphia, or which 5 of 21 teams will avoid the NHL playoffs, or when the next illiterate college running back will get pinched for taking a U-turn at the classroom door.

All the sports fan need remember is the summer of '82, when baseball became king again, proving that it not only is the best game of all, but also is the most indestructible. One year after the strike that was supposed to be a death knell, baseball outdid itself. And the World Series is yet to come.

More fans paid to watch the game than ever before in the summer of '82, and, what's best, more fans than ever seemed to comprehend that it was only a game that they paid to watch.

When 51,642 customers in Baltimore can pay homage to their manager after their Orioles were clobbered 10–2, something is very right about the national pastime. And because Howard Cosell—who once called baseball dull—resists a director's plea to cut away from the picture of Earl Weaver crying before his public, you'll remember the scene long after you've forgotten the score.

Some 2,500 miles away, the integrity of the game was being

upheld by the San Diego Padres, who played hard to beat Atlanta, even though their least favorite team is the Los Angeles Dodgers. And, up the coast, the San Francisco Giants had nothing at stake except pride, but they put the Dodgers to sleep, anyway.

Still, if the defending world champions felt that all was lost, they soon realized there really were no losers in the summer of '82. Thousands of fans greeted them at the airport in Los Angeles. They didn't come to say thanks to the Dodgers for finishing first this time. They just came to say thanks.

After all, nothing in athletics matches the daily drama of baseball in September, and if this season's homestretch didn't captivate you, then have your pulse checked, my friend. It was electric from wire to wire, and if you looked the other way, you missed all the fun. There is room for cynicism in sports these days, yes, but this was neither the place, nor the time.

Baseball was supposed to be destroyed by the free-agent mentality, but since it came to be, the game has flourished, not floundered. Every year, the races get closer, and in the summer of '82, the later it became, the better it became.

Two division champions won by three games; two others won by one game. Fourteen teams finished within eight games of the top, and the formulas for success changed. The New York Yankees, World Series finalists one October ago, couldn't buy their way in. They wound up a game out of last place. The Cincinnati Reds, who had baseball's best record in 1981, couldn't fake their way in. They lost 101 times.

Unlike some other sports, baseball didn't need to create rivalries by synthetic means. Until the last day of the schedule, all you needed to create vibrations were a bat, a glove and a ball. The possibilities were as endless as they were delicious.

It might have been an all-freeway World Series, between the Dodgers of Hollywood and the Angels of Gene Autry. Or an all-Missouri World Series, between the Kansas City Royals who fired Whitey Herzog and the St. Louis Cardinals, whom Whitey Herzog rebuilt. It is said that the Baltimore Orioles want San Francisco's Frank Robinson as their next manager; they might have had him as their opposing manager in the fall classic.

Weaver, who idolized the Cardinals as a kid and wore Marty Marion's number on his back, will not be able to take his ballclub back home to St. Louis. But there's a decent chance that all the Brewers who became Cardinals and all the Cardinals who became Brewers will shake hands and come out swinging next week.

Perhaps, though, irony will best be served if the showdown means the Atlanta Braves against the Milwaukee Brewers. It was 25 years ago that Milwaukee was baseball capital of North America, because Spahn and Burdette and Mathews and Aaron had brought home a world championship.

But seven years later, a front-office harlequin named John McHale issued that infamous lie—"we will be in Milwaukee today, tomorrow and for as long as we are welcome." Soon, the citizens of that great city realized they had been framed. Their Braves were moved to Atlanta on account of greed and stupidity.

It wasn't that the Southeast didn't deserve to gain baseball. It was that Milwaukee didn't deserve to lose it.

"It was one of the worst things that ever happened to our game," says Allan "Bud" Selig. "A disgrace, a travesty of justice. The entire community was bitter. We could only hope for a better day."

Selig dumped his automobile business, and, in 1969, he brought baseball back to Milwaukee, where it belonged. Though performing in the major league's smallest market, the Brewers have outdrawn the Atlanta Braves for the last eight seasons. And, Tuesday night, the Milwaukee Brewers begin the American League playoffs here against the California Angels.

"A better day," says Selig. "A dream come true."

Baseball has mended another wound. Truly, it is the most indestructible game of all. And the best.

GLORY OF THE TIMES

OCTOBER 21, 1983

For baseball purists, the glorious summer of '83 couldn't have ended on a more proper note than it did on Sunday.

There they were, the Baltimore Orioles, world champions. And there was pitcher Scott McGregor, a former Yankee, trundling off the mound in Philadelphia to hug catcher Rick Dempsey, a former Yankee. Soon they were joined by another celebrant, manager Joe Altobelli, a former Yankee.

Through nine postseason games, the Orioles had been defeated twice—by Chicago's LaMarr Hoyt, a former Yankee who is likely to be the American League Cy Young Award winner, and by Philadelphia's John Denny, who probably will be paid similar homage in the National League.

What, you ask, is the connection between Denny and the Yankees? A brief and broken one is what. A couple years ago, the Yankees had budgeted for his services, too, but he chased them off while they were chasing him. Didn't like the hassle, Denny recalled.

Time out here. Do you think Yankees' owner George Steinbrenner, whose team payroll probably exceeds the gross national product of several countries, might just be sitting quietly at his desk in New York wondering what went wrong?

Actually, nothing at all. Baseball, the best sport known to man, woman and child, continued to thrive in 1983, not just survive. The seers who forecast stormy weather took another beating this year, a year when it was proven again that you don't need a clear day to see The Game going on forever.

When the Messersmith Decision made history in 1975, nervous nabobs predicted that baseball soon would be history, too. Free agents would destroy the fabric of The Game, parity would perish, the rich would get richer and so yawn.

In fact, baseball never has been better. Business improves

14

every season, not only at the bleacher ticket wickets downstairs but also in the board rooms upstairs. Ten years ago, Steinbrenner purchased the Yankees for $10 million. Five years ago, the Boston Red Sox went for $15 million. Two years ago, if you had $21 million, you could have the New York Mets.

Last week, the Detroit Tigers changed hands in a $43 million transaction. Those are the same Tigers who rarely stick a toe in the free-agent pool, the same Detroit Tigers who finished with the third best record in 1983. Baltimore, which doesn't like to buy players either, was second best. The White Sox, who had to go to market and did, finished first. Before the Orioles finished them.

Clearly, the warning sirens of 1975 were not worth a listen. There is more than one formula. Calvin Griffith, who pinches his nickels until the Buffalo groans, has parted with 10 times the talent than he has cared to keep for the Minnesota Twins. Yet, at a huge profit, he could sell his club to Tampa tomorrow morning.

Those who envisioned baseball chaos during the last decade didn't know how right, or wrong, they would be. Nothing is safe anymore, especially a dynasty. Since divisional play began 15 years ago, 20 different teams have participated in playoffs. The last six World Series have produced six different champions.

Often, this year's champion establishes next year's trend. On that note, the Orioles probably proved that a club needn't have 10 players making $1.5 million a season fighting for nine places on the lineup card. There is room, in the well-planned formula, for a Tito Landrum and a Benny Ayala.

The Orioles, by acting humble and together, offered a nice change of pace to Yankee pinstripes and to Tommy Lasorda's "Great Dodger in the Sky." The Baltimore throwbacks didn't need to get angry to win, but they got angry, anyway, when they took one smell of the high-falutin' Phillies' cavalier attitudes.

"Frankly," Baltimore pitching coach Ray Miller said, "we thought they acted a little pompous toward us."

And in an era when the bunker mentality threatens to invade sports of all sorts, the Orioles hugged each other like they meant it. Ask about their most trying moment of the season, and they just might give you a shocking answer. When Terry Crowley, one of the family, had to be cut, it hurt everybody.

But Baltimore management had best not fall in love with the current flock of Orioles because, according to the ways of The Game, today's crown is tomorrow's dunce cap. Ask the St. Louis Cardinals and Milwaukee Brewers. Last year's October finalists finished a total of 22 games out of first place.

In 1983, baseball gave us Tar Wars, starring George Brett; Ron Kittle; the Blue Jays on top at All-Star time; and the American League on top in an All-Star Game. A commissioner resigned, a first-place manager was fired, Dave Winfield reduced Canada's seagull population by one and the Cubs traveled all over the country for six months but went nowhere.

Johnny Bench, maybe the best catcher ever, and Yaz, perhaps the most durable player ever, said goodbye in the same towns where they first said hello. Another era, Gaylord Perry, put his wet one away forever. And Pete Rose is on the ropes but still trying to fight his way out of the twilight zone.

Like most of us, Pete's love for The Game knows no winter.

TOAST OF THE BLEACHERS

Dry-land training, it isn't.

Shortly before 1 p.m. Tuesday, from a tunnel beneath the stands, Harry Caray emerges, followed closely by a cooler full of his favorite medicine in pop-top cans. He is dressed in powder blue and looks not unlike a 200-pound Easter egg.

"HAR-EEE! HAR-EEE!" yell the customers in Wrigley Field's left-field bleachers, where Harry Caray, singer-announcer-raconteur of the Cubs, will do his work this splendid afternoon. "HAR-EEE! HAR-EEE!"

He is 64 years old now, going on 20, and he's never met a neon sign he didn't like. But, for all of his nocturnal meanderings, Harry Caray has not missed an inning, or an at-bat, since he entered the business with a bang rather than a whimper. They don't make digestive systems like his anymore.

"Closest I came was in spring training with the White Sox a few years ago," says Caray, filling out his lineup card. "My good friend, Jim Janek, got lost driving me to an exhibition game in Dunedin, Florida. We made it, though. Unbroken record, since 1945."

That year, of course, carries special significance in these tattered parts. Last time the Cubs won anything. Next time is any time now, which is why Tuesday's lawn party is a special day in the sun for Harry and clan. There is something in the air, and it's not the aroma of a cigar.

"I miss you, but not that rotten thing you smoke," Harry says to WGN-TV analyst Steve Stone, who is back behind home plate with the saner types, Lou Boudreau, Milo Hamilton and Vince Lloyd.

"Now that Princess Di has named her son Harry," counters Stone, "the poor kid will be reduced to a life of decadence like you, searching out the British equivalent of Rush Street."

The mood is festive along Aisle 153, where Harry has settled in, but the no-collar crowd is no problem. They obey Caray's every request, including one to unsalt the language when the camera's red light goes on. There's no seven-second delay here, folks. Whatever you say, Harry. It is that way with a cult figure.

"Where's Bill Veeck?" inquires Caray of Joe Cornejo, WGN's associate director for Tuesday's madness. Veeck, a bleacher creature who resides in right-center, sends word that he's staying put. Veeck doesn't invade Harry's turf; why is Harry invading Veeck's?

"Aahahagragah," laughs Harry, casting lascivious eyes on a girl who asks for an autograph. "You're how old? Only 17? Aahahagragah."

Left field, of late, belongs to popular Gary Matthews. When he trots out for the first inning, he shows the folks four fingers—the Cubs' magic number before Tuesday's game against Pittsburgh. The fans go bonkers. "Who's in charge? Sarge!" they chant.

"Arne, can you hear me?" Caray asks Arne Harris, WGN's executive producer-director at control center. "Which earphone is the right one? Boy, nothing like modern technology. This Bud's for me. Aahahagragah."

The gifts pour in. Beer, hats, sunglasses, a shot glass, cigars, a "Dallas Green for President" button. "How times have changed," remarks Harry. But mostly he is besieged with scraps of paper, business cards and torn-off program sheets. Grandmother's watching, please say hello, and so on.

"They're here from Kalamazoo," chirps Harry, "which, spelled backwards is, Oozamalak. There's a drive by Lee Lacy. It might be, it could be i-i-it i-i-s. Tie ballgame 1–1."

Occupants of right-field bleacher seats return the souvenir in disgust, but when Johnny Ray follows with another Pirate solo home run to left-center, the ball is not thrown back. This act of treason creates problems. The fan wants it as a keepsake; the surrounding melting pot will have none of it. The miscreant, under duress, chucks the ball back to the field an inning later, but better than never.

"Ahhh, ya' can't beat fun at the old ballpark," Harry warbles during a commercial break, sipping often. "What an advertisement this is for day baseball. Get a million-dollar tan for three bucks. Beats the time we were out here two hours in the rain a couple months ago. This is fun. When it isn't anymore, I'll get out.

"I see where WGN is talking to Brent Musburger. Well, they should make every effort to get him. All of us, except Steve, are in our twilight years. What's wrong with new blood? I know I can't go on forever, although, right now, every day is like the Fourth of July."

"Paaahhped it up!" crow the bleacher types, imitating Harry when a Cub skies one on the infield. Caray, meanwhile, grabs his fishnet in anticipation of a Ron Cey homer that is not to be.

"Aaaahright, everybody, ah-one, ah-two, ah-three," roars Harry as 30,721 vocalists turn toward Pavarotti in Aisle 153. Great moments in music, it's not, but it's Harry. Even the final score—Pittsburgh 6, Cubs 2—can't spoil this bash, because any day now, it will happen. And when it does, Chicago, like Harry, will studiously avoid sleep.

"Harry," says a bleacherite after Caray has wrapped up his broadcast. "You're the greatest."

"Aahahagragah," bellows the voice of summer, departing Aisle 153 with a wave. And with his cooler.

'HARD TO DEAL WITH'

OCTOBER 8, 1984

SAN DIEGO—Rick Sutcliffe spoke in a whisper and still could be heard. It was that quiet, that shocking, that final.

"They're going to the World Series and we're going home," he said. "This will hurt me for a long, long time. It will stay with all of us for a long time. It's hard to deal with. Very hard."

Keith Moreland's eyes were redder than his hair. Dallas Green stared through the hole in the top of a beer can. And Jim Frey's voice cracked for the first time all season. The Cubs had gotten beaten up for 39 years, and now they had picked a most untimely occasion to beat themselves.

It wasn't supposed to turn out like this, this American dream for America's Team. Not after the Cubs won the first two games in Chicago. Not after Thursday night's defeat. Not even after Saturday night's thrill theater, as delicious a game as was ever played.

Because Sunday, for the National League pennant, the Cubs had the big guy on the mound. Rick Sutcliffe. You could feel the great expectations in the bus going to Jack Murphy Stadium and during batting practice. You could sense it through five innings, when the lead was 3–0 and the destination Detroit.

"Instead, now we go home and pack our bags and pick up the pieces," said Sutcliffe (17–2). He had lost his first game in three months, but three months from Sunday, when the San Diego Padres beat him 6–3, that's what the big guy will be thinking about. Whether he has a fishing pole in his hand, a book or a child.

A lesser man might have hidden from the crush of interrogators wondering what happened. A free agent who should win the Cy Young Award and double his $900,000 salary could have pinned the donkey's tail on Leon Durham, who waited for

20

the ball to come up, or Ryne Sandberg, who thought the ball would stay down.

But Rick Sutcliffe, elegant in depression, blamed himself. For not holding a lead, for yielding a leadoff walk to Carmelo Martinez during the Padres' four-run seventh inning, for letting Steve Garvey get around on a fast ball.

"I take the responsibility for this," he said. "It's my fault. These guys have been great behind me all year. The key wasn't Durham's error. The key was the four pitches to Martinez. It was my loss. My loss. And I don't know quite how to describe the hurt."

A big crash landing, this was, with the big guy taking the blame. He said what he did during the regular schedule didn't matter now, and before he wills his body to the highest bidder in the off-season flesh market, he's got to rectify Sunday in his head. Where it went wrong, and why.

Sutcliffe maneuvered comfortably through five innings, surrendering but two hits. His breaking ball wasn't the best, and his location was less than pinpoint. But he's gotten by before, and Sunday, he was getting by again. Until the summer turned to winter.

Now, many people will try to unravel the cosmic significance of Sunday's comeuppance. People who have lived, but mostly died, with the Cubs. And people who just discovered baseball within the last two weeks. And people who maintain that tagging up on a deep fly has deep sociological impact.

Forget it, whether you're a season-ticket holder or one of the millions of dilettantes who joined the parade. Failure is letting a kid go hungry, not letting a pennant slip away. The Cubs won 98 games during a year when most experts figured they'd be fortunate to win 78. They were entertaining, energizing and, above all, promising.

In the end, as Rick Sutcliffe was saying, the hurt comes because the Cubs got a taste and never swallowed. This was a better team than anybody expected from April to Wednesday but too good a team to allow what happened from Thursday to Sunday.

If anything, it wasn't the four pitches to Carmelo Martinez that killed the Cubs; it was the euphoria surrounding them. They came here with one game to win but with thousands of friends, relatives and fans assuring that it was only a formality.

Nobody can look into an athlete's head; let it just be said that the possibility for distraction was everpresent.

"I know what you're driving at," said Green, "The celebrating before the job is finished. I don't know if that happened here. But I do know that at a time like this, you need all 25 guys to sacrifice like they've never sacrificed before."

And so, Sunday evening, there was nothing left to celebrate and even less to say. Frey shook every hand of every player but made no speeches. He had a suspicion that he could talk until he was blue and still not be heard.

"It was my loss," said Sutcliffe, repeating the lie. It was everybody's, not to rationalize or to dwell on, but to rectify and build on. Sunday's gloom has nothing to do with 1969, but 98 wins from April to Sunday doesn't guarantee that next year will be better. Chemistry, the White Sox proved, is a fragile item.

"39 More Years" the banner proclaimed as the Padres danced about Jack Murphy Stadium Sunday afternoon. Not likely. But not this year, either.

Ticket scalpers in Chicago will be sad; Las Vegas bookies will be relieved; there's a big election next month; and the in-laws still want to come over for Thanksgiving dinner.

STRUCK DOWN AGAIN

MAY 23, 1985

You're a fan, a baseball fan, and if it's Thursday, you're depressed, annoyed, waiting for the other shoe to drop—the other shoe you were assured would never drop again because everybody learned from the last time we went through this foolishness and everybody realized it couldn't happen again. At least that's what they said.

But talk is cheap, maybe the cheapest thing left in our national pastime, and it's Thursday, and it's happening again. The major league baseball players will meet at O'Hare, and they will vote on when to strike, when to destroy another summer, when to take their argument with management to its outer, most repugnant limits.

You've always heard that it's you, the fan, who makes this game what it is, the most perfect and beloved game of them all. You've always heard that if the best players in the world got together and played the best game ever on the prettiest afternoon ever, it wouldn't matter if you weren't there to watch it. With your kid, your wife, your girlfriend, a bunch of buddies or just by yourself. Without you and yours, there would be no games.

You've always heard it, and believed it, but now you're beginning to wonder. You were willing to accept the tradeoff, that if you made baseball go, baseball made you go, too. However, now you're wondering whether this sport really deserves all this devotion of yours. It is one thing to be loyal and another thing to be loyal to a fault. But is it fair to ask that you care about these people anymore if they give you another July without box scores?

"Baseball has endured its biggest crisis since the Black Sox scandal of 1919." That's what one owner said in 1981, after a 50-day layoff, after 712 games were canceled. The man who said it wasn't proud, he was ashamed, as well he should have been. So were most of his fellow owners, and so were the players, and when it was all over, the two sides had one thing in common. They agreed, never again. But never again might come again in 1985. How is it these people can repeat their mistake after only four years?

When it happened in 1981, they begged you to forgive them, and not forget them. And being the fan you are, you gladly obliged. You put up your money and stalled in traffic and waited in hot dog lines and came back. In record numbers you came back. But now, unless I'm mistaken, what these people are saying is insultingly simple. Don't ever forget us, they're saying, but we might forget you again. That doesn't seem fair, but that's baseball.

When you were growing up, breathing this game, you thought only of baseball's beauty, not the beasts trying to ruin it. All along, Coke was part of lunch in the bleachers, not an illegal substance. All along, a cap was something you bought for your child on a shiny day, not some mechanism proposed by owners to control themselves. All along you assumed this was a game of inches, not grinches.

When you smuggled that transistor radio into study hall during the World Series, you didn't do it to hear about meetings at O'Hare. When you rushed for the morning newspaper in the driveway, you didn't do it to read about rich owners crying poor. When you drove your son to his first Little League field, you didn't do it with the idea that he'd become a free agent who could hire an agent who could explain annuities.

Your gut reaction is to blame the players for this mess, because they're the most visible, because they're the ones meeting at O'Hare Thursday. But think again. It's not them. Listen to Pete Rose, the quintessential gamer, the 44-year-old boy who still runs to first base when he walks. If anybody could provide an ounce of sanity, or a pound of understanding, it would be him. Except Rose, who only wants to play, shakes his head, too.

"I've been through it," he says. "I've been in negotiations with owners when they've offered me horses and oil wells and beer distributorships. And then they say they're broke. And then they pay $1 million a year to a utility shortstop. And then they say they're losing their shirts. What's going on? Why do they only talk to us at the 11th hour? Where were they all winter?"

They drive their luxury cars and their stubborn bargains, but if they ran their other businesses the way they run baseball, they would be driving pushcarts. You wonder what ails these owners. Is it their fortunes that are depleted, or their egos? Is it true they can't break even, or do they just want to get even? Is it too much to ask that they open their books for once, instead of their mouths?

"Never." That is what the Cubs' Keith Moreland says when asked about the logical strike date, and how right he is. There is no logic to it. But, major force in the Players Association that he is, Moreland also says: "My optimism about avoiding a strike diminishes every day. I didn't think there was a chance in spring training. Now there's a chance."

You, the fan, can only hope that Peter Ueberroth, baseball's progressive new commissioner, will halt this madness. He doesn't want a strike in his rookie year, so maybe he's the answer. Maybe, in Ueberroth, labor and management will meet their match at last.

You, the fan, hope these people realize their sport is fun but it's not a vital occupation. If there are no games this summer, again, you hope they realize there will be lots of fishing holes for you to try, lots of picnics to be staged, lots of sand traps to visit, lots of lakes that would look nice next to your blanket.

You, the fan, hope they understand that as much as you need this game, this game needs you more. And next time you might forget these people rather than forgive, because you, the fan, have had it right up to here with this stupidity.

Baseball fever. . . . lose it?

FOR PETE'S SAKE

SEPTEMBER 12, 1985

CINCINNATI—In his 45th year, after his 13,768th major-league at-bat, during his 3,476th game, following his 4,192nd hit, Pete Rose finally showed his first sign of weakness on a baseball diamond Wednesday. They called a timeout so he could cry.

Riverfront Stadium was rife with passion and ripe for history this crisp evening—exactly the 57th anniversary of Ty Cobb's last swing. So it was that Rose, in his first crack at San Diego right-hander Eric Show, obliged by reaching out at a 2–1 pitch and reaching back into the sport's storied past.

That Rose would break Cobb's record was inevitable, but that didn't tarnish the drama a bit. Pete, a master of the unrehearsed, lashed a line single to left-center, and his beloved hometown hugged him from afar. And as 47,237 customers stood firm, the Cincinnati Kid buckled.

Rose is oft-remembered for bowling over catcher Ray Fosse in a bygone All-Star Game here, for wrestling with Bud Harrelson during an angry playoff match at New York, for arriving at the plate in ill humor, anywhere. But Wednesday night's snapshot for the ages is that of Pete Rose, after waving thanks, after embracing dozens of admirers, dipping that craggy face beneath the brim of his batting helmet to hide the tears. At last, the game he breathes had done him in.

"I was awful lonely out there at first base after it happened," a relaxed, relieved Rose admitted afterward. "I didn't know what to do. I was okay until I looked up in the air. Then I saw my dad and Ty Cobb. I wasn't so good after that."

The temptation is to think that on Wednesday night, September 11, 1985, Pete Rose showed he was human. Actually, he has been doing that all along, since he first hopped on the minor-league bus in 1960, whispering to himself, "I can't be-

26

lieve these people are paying me $400 a month to play ball."
What's more human than to grasp one's fantasy, then see it
through?

He's no angel, but even his first wife Karolyn attributes their
failed marriage to baseball. Pete never ducked that issue, any
more than he has ducked beanballs, interviews or dinners that
became autograph sessions. He's an American hero, one of the
last, who's not afraid to get his elbows dirty.

If only other athletes would take Rose's cue, that being successful doesn't have to mean being blasé. Rose arrived in the big
show as a bundle of energy and was branded a curiosity. He has
survived several trends, from short hair to long contracts, but
his devotion hasn't changed, and neither has his position in
sports. Only now, he's more unusual than ever, for he's in a
class of one.

Predictably, achieving 4,192 hits will not create a goal-less
vacuum for Rose, the man-child Mickey Mantle first tabbed
"Charlie Hustle." Rose is closing in on the 2,000-victory
mark—"nobody's done that before"—and he's among the elite
in total bases—"not bad for somebody who's supposed to be a
Punch-and-Judy hitter," Rose pointed out.

"I'm only behind four or five guys," he said. "And all those
guys got monuments. I'm right on Babe Ruth's heels. If I have
any kind of finish here this season, I hope to be back playing
next year. Only time I'll consider retiring is when I don't enjoy
it anymore, or I can't contribute. I'm not there yet."

Rose, who studies other hitters in both leagues, believes
Wade Boggs is as good as any. But the Boston star already is
making $1 million a year. Though Rose concedes it's possible to
play longer now than ever for two reasons—the designated
hitter rule in the American League, and the year-round physical fitness fetish—he realizes it's also possible to enjoy shorter,
yet still profitable careers.

"I mean, if Boggs is making that kind of money in his fourth
year," Rose theorized, "what's he going to be worth if he plays
23 years? Will he want to play 23 years? Robin Yount's nearing
2,000 hits, and he's only 30. But 3,000 hits? Heck, that's easy.
(Laugh). Somebody gave me a stat the other day. Only three
players got 2,000 hits after their 30th birthdays—Stan Musial,
Ty Cobb and me."

Probably, Rose can rest comfortably atop the baseball world, tacking on however many hits to his record booty—all the better to let someone else take a shot. Whoever tries, whenever, Rose's talent will not be the only blockade. Durability has been perhaps his greatest asset; he stared Father Time in the eye and turned him into a Cincinnati Reds' fan.

Witness: After Rose earned Rookie of the Year honors in 1963, teammate Tommy Helms won the award the next season. Helms, not a bad ballplayer, now a Reds' coach, quit eight years ago. Another example: Current White Sox coach Eddie Brinkman, a year younger than Rose, his high school pal from this town, logged 15 respectable summers in the major leagues. And he retired in 1975.

But Pete Rose, throwback, trucks on, thinking now only of his next game. What Eric Show, modern day athlete, thought about Wednesday night, who knows? Who cares? He called the Rose celebration a "media creation," then slinked into the night.

Show argued in the dugout with Carmelo Martinez, loudly criticizing the Padres' left fielder for not catching Dave Parker's bloop single after The Hit. Show, in his pique, doesn't comprehend that Wednesday night probably will be his closest brush with greatness.

Someday, perhaps Eric Show and his ilk will learn what it's all about. Which is the beauty of Pete Rose. He never had to be taught.

GIVE THE MAN A HAND

SEPTEMBER 25, 1985

When Peter Ueberroth became commissioner of baseball about a year ago, he dispensed with all the pretense. The game's deepest dilemma was not sagging attendance in San Francisco, or the logjam between leagues on the designated hitter rule, or the specter of territorial invasions by superstations from Atlanta, Chicago or New York.

No, if baseball were about to crack, to alienate its perpetually captive audience, to tarnish its image beyond repair, the reason would be drugs. If baseball was a release for much of society, then cocaine was an outlet for too much of baseball, and Peter Ueberroth would have none of it.

Tuesday, the commissioner acted. By requesting each major league player to accept voluntary and random testing, he has given them the ball, either to bobble or run with it toward a solution. We can only hope, after this summer of grim disclosures, that the athletes will realize their list of alternatives has been reduced to one.

"It's time to say, 'That's it, folks, we want this thing behind us,'" Ueberroth was saying Tuesday night from his New York headquarters. "It's time to say it's over, we want to be clean, we will be clean."

Because Ueberroth is a courageous administrator with a sparkling track record, he will forever be subject to criticism—on the grounds that he is a grandstander, an egomaniac, an erstwhile travel agent who is in over his head. Already, his proposal has come under attack by Donald Fehr, the director of the Major League Players Association. No surprise here. Ueberroth would be chided if he endorsed green grass and blue skies.

But if Ueberroth were interested in currying favor with a quick fix—to use an expression that several of baseball's affected surely will comprehend—he could have dealt merely with the seven players who were implicated during the federal trial in Pittsburgh, a trial that revealed an insidious drug culture throughout the sport, from the dugouts to clubhouses to hotel rooms.

Rather, Ueberroth has opted to attack the mountain instead of the molehill, and he should be applauded for it. His plan is aimed at treating and curing, not punishing and penalizing. It might be shot down; so might it also offer tremendous promise. Already, it is said, several teams have voted unanimously to comply.

"I would hope that the players will rally around this and create a groundswell," Ueberroth continued. "We have to remove this cloud over the game, because the game is in trouble. And the only people who can do it are the players. Not the commissioner, not management, not the union. The players. I want to see the players do it.

"In the military, this process has resulted in sharp decreases of drug use. In the minor leagues, same thing. It has worked. It's a deterrent. And there was absolute confidentiality at all times. I'll bet there isn't one player on the Cubs or White Sox who knows of a player in the minor leagues whose name came up positive for the drug tests on that level. Ridiculing the users is not the purpose. The few who can't stop, we want to get them help."

Ueberroth chose a representative of each major league franchise to relay his message Tuesday. His surrogate at Wrigley Field was Dallas Green, the Cubs' imposing general manager, who is as opposed to drugs as he is to scoring 15 runs and losing. Ueberroth said the implementation of his poll was up to each delegate—voice vote, written ballot, show of hands, whatever. Results, Friday.

"I don't know what they'll be, or how I'll deal with them when they come in," Ueberroth said. "I would hope there's some peer pressure here, naturally. If 80 percent say yes, they'll submit to testing, and 20 say no? If it's 80 percent against? If only one club says they'll do it, that's something. That's a start. Baseball must do something, and it's up to the players to do it."

Whether Ueberroth used such strategic allies as Green with each team, he wouldn't say. He mentioned only that he contacted someone in each location "who cared about the game."

During his rookie season, Ueberroth had indicated strongly that's his posture. He is a strong commissioner who doesn't need this job; baseball, however, needs a strong commissioner, and Tuesday, Ueberroth was his usual bold self.

There is some speculation that an upbeat response by the masses will bode well for whatever action Ueberroth takes concerning the Pittsburgh Seven. Not so, Ueberroth assured. "The two issues are not bound in any way," maintained Ueberroth, who is still studying that episode, its documents, its implications.

Ueberroth, however, will devote a lot less time on Fehr's charge that Tuesday's proposal is a deliberate attempt to bypass the union, and that it might even be unlawful.

"I have absolutely no problems with the union in all of this," Ueberroth promised. "If the players want to get involved as a union to clear baseball's name, that's fine. But, as I said before, it's the individual players who have to take this step. Not anybody else. As for Donald Fehr's remark that it's illegal, I'm not concerned with that. I don't believe it is. I've talked with lawyers, and I'll talk with more if I have to."

It is time that players comply with voluntary testing, lest they tempt even higher authorities than Peter Ueberroth to impose mandatory testing. After all, even if the commissioner's plan is illegal, it's not as illegal as cocaine.

SEASON REALLY HITS FAN

OCTOBER 23, 1985

KANSAS CITY, MISSOURI—John Tudor wore that cold New England stare of his, befitting a man who always appears to have a headache. But now, he also had a towel wrapped around his left hand and splotches of blood about his gray uniform. Seems he had attacked an electric fan, which was the only thing the St. Louis Cardinals hit all week.

These National League champions, bearing the name of a franchise with rich tradition, had pinged aggravated foes into submission throughout a wondrous summer, slapping singles and stealing bases, then calling on a deep bullpen to perform closing ceremonies.

But Sunday night, having had their feathers more than mildly sheared, the once-proud Redbirds were a source of annoyance only to themselves. They had lost the game 11–0 and the World Series to the Kansas City Royals, and, in the process, had created a new standard of regression in North America's premier sporting event.

Not only had the Cardinals batted a wan .185, the worst ever for a team that took the tournament to its limit. Not only had they become the first team to avoid capturing the championship after winning the first two games on the road. Not only had they managed but 13 runs and two stolen bases. In the end, the Cardinals completed the pratfall with an exit that included kicking and screaming.

"I'm sorry we couldn't have put on a better show tonight, Mr. President," Whitey Herzog was saying. "We kind of stunk the joint out."

By the time the White House called, the Cardinals' manager had cooled down somewhat. He had been dismissed from the premises, along with his fifth of seven pitchers, Joaquin Andujar, a 21-game winner who was a postseason bust, and a churlish one at that. Tudor, whose pride had been wounded even before his paw, beat them to the clubhouse, where it took only minutes for all to realize the totality of the humiliation.

"We got 13 runs in seven games? That's almost a disgrace," Herzog pondered. "I didn't think we'd ever get handled like that. In many ways, we were fortunate to get this far, to win three games. But in another way, I thought we should have gone home last night, and I think my players felt the same way."

Saturday night, two outs away from their second World Series title in four years, the Cardinals were wronged by an egregiously bad call from Don Denkinger, first-base umpire, American League. Sunday night, Denkinger was behind the plate, judging balls and strikes, throwing Herzog and Andujar out of the game.

"I didn't say anything to him when I took out the lineup card except, 'Try to have a good night,'" Herzog allowed. "Well, he had a better night than we did. I don't think the Royals could win our division. I don't think the Royals could win the American League East. But they whipped our butts.

"If they're that good, they'd have won 130 games in that weak division of theirs. But they beat us, and give 'em credit. And the umpires had nothing to do with it tonight. Last night, yes. But tonight, no."

Andujar, mopping through a hopeless situation, contends "I was misunderstood" during the Royals' six-run fifth. He claims he motioned toward the plate for catcher Darrell Porter, at which point Denkinger took offense. Before it was all over, Herzog and then Andujar were ejected. It would also be safe to say they were dejected.

"I had seen quite enough at that point," Herzog related. "I was hoping they'd invoke the 10-run rule. But I was just going out there to protect my pitcher.

"I think we were all a little frustrated at that point, and probably the umpire was a little on edge, too. I don't want to use him as an excuse, though. Don's a good umpire. He blew a play last night, but we should have put Kansas City away at home. We just couldn't. Couldn't hit. I mean, we're a contact team that shouldn't go through a thing like this. But we just couldn't do anything. I'm not embarrassed about what went on there with Denkinger. I don't like the way we played, though."

Tudor was no match for either Bret Saberhagen or his own temper. A veteran who relies on working the fine lines, Tudor betrays a lack of stuff by twitching with his neck on the mound. Sunday night, first inning, he was squirming. With one out in the third, he was gone, his earliest knockout of the season. Tudor did not react kindly, punching a metal fan en route to a moment of peace. He took stitches and his lumps.

"I made a stupid mistake, and it's my business," he said. "I'm okay. I let the team down. There's no defense against home runs and walks, and all year long, I let the guys make the plays behind me. I didn't do that tonight.

"If I was nervous before the game, that would have been one thing. But I wasn't. I felt I was okay warming up. The umpire had nothing to do with my problems. I just didn't pitch well.

"The Royals did everything they had to do. They outpitched us, outhit us. I never thought I'd see our team shut down like Kansas City shut us down. Even if we'd have won the game tonight, I don't know whether I'd have been ready to admit that we're a better team than they are. We didn't win, and now we've got to live with it."

That will be easier said than done for Herzog, who lives only two and a half miles down the road. As Kansas City manager, he suffered, thrice winning division titles, thrice losing pennants to the Yankees before he was fired in 1979. But Sunday night, after his Cardinals showed an amazing lack of grace, "the White Rat" was last seen stare-fighting the ceiling in his office.

"Like I told Mr. Reagan," Herzog repeated. "We stunk."

MARIS A VICTIM OF TIME, PLACE

DECEMBER 19, 1985

There are lessons to be learned from the mistreatment of Roger Maris, but none more important than these: Treat an athlete for the person he is, not the person we think he ought to be; and judge what he accomplishes according to his era, not another irrelevant time-frame of reference.

Maris, who died Saturday at age 51, forever will be remembered as one of the most uncomfortable sports figures of our generation. When he clubbed a record 61 home runs for the New York Yankees in 1961, he should have savored the feat. Instead, he became a dour man, given to fits of depression and nervousness. He lost some hair, and if it weren't for family and friends, he might have lost his wits.

But, unlike too many other athletes who can't seem to enjoy a glorious occupation, that was not Maris' nature. When later traded to the St. Louis Cardinals, he was a human being again, a ballplayer who just wanted to play ball and was allowed that luxury. Until cancer finally grounded him, Maris was hardly a recluse. Though wife and six children remained his top priorities, he was a public figure, and a decent one.

What, then, caused his demeanor in New York? Too many insensitive fans, certain segments of a jaded press and Maris' reluctance to massage either faction. He probably could have relaxed a lot more during his quest of Babe Ruth's hallowed mark had he been even a little more phony. But that wasn't his style, he wouldn't alter it, and he suffered the unfair consequences. He was born to play ball, not to debate.

Though Maris had some values far superior to those of Mickey Mantle, the latter was a people's choice. The Mick, a

Yankee blueblood, had his moody moments, especially with the media. But he was the hero, while Maris, who came to New York by way of the Cleveland Indians and Kansas City A's, was made to feel like some interloper—not only on Mantle's turf but on Ruth's legend.

Mantle, to his credit, didn't partake in such pettiness. He was Maris' pal and roommate. When Mantle incurred a leg injury during their chase, he turned to Maris one evening and said, "I'm done. It's all yours now. Go get it." Maris got it, but on the last afternoon of the season, when he stroked No. 61 off Boston's Tracy Stallard, only 23,154 fans attended.

Had Maris achieved this milestone in a smaller city, or any market where he was not bucking both a current and deceased demigod, he might have been better appreciated. Likewise, if Maris had received attention as warmly as does Pete Rose—who greeted last September's "Cobb Watch" masses with a big grin and a new array of *bon mots* every day—it might have worked out more peacefully.

But there is only one Pete Rose and, at last check, only one Roger Maris. Only one man has hit 61 home runs in a single season. Observers who couldn't fathom Maris effecting such a breakthrough incorrectly branded him a fluke. Well, it was history in a surprise package. However, Maris earned Most Valuable Player honors a year before his summer of misery, and he was a complete player who could throw and run, and he also hit 214 other home runs during the other 11 years of his career.

Maris was so wanting for positive mementos that he had his own batch of "61 in '61" T-shirts printed. Not until George Steinbrenner, the not-all-bad Yankee owner, invited Maris back to New York for an Old-Timers' fete in 1977 did he feel appreciated, though it was too little, too late. At least Steinbrenner realized the deed for what it was—magnificent—and the author for what he was—an athlete, like so many then and now, who feel that playing a good game needn't include talking a good game.

But because Maris didn't kiss the right people in the right places, he was kicked for it, and nobody hit him harder than Ford Frick, a clerk of a commissioner. He ruled during the pre-proliferation mentality, and when Maris beat The Babe it was the first season after expansion. The American League had grown from eight to 10 teams, the schedule had swelled from 154 to 162 games, and the talent, presumably, had gone from excellent to diluted.

Something had to be done to qualify Maris' mark, so Frick unfurled his asterisk. Not only was the commissioner's brainstorm unwarranted; it was pretty much accepted by the public. If Frick were still in office, we could assume that he would have interrupted the giddy proceedings at Cincinnati's Riverfront Stadium last September 10 to inform the world that Pete Rose's 4,192nd hit—while a lovely line drive, indeed—would have to carry a barnacle of a notation. Ty Cobb, after all, required many fewer at-bats.

Such folly. What Kareem Abdul-Jabbar does tomorrow does not diminish, nor should it be diminished by, what giant predecessor George Mikan did yesterday. Wayne Gretzky's 73 goals last year don't dwarf what Bobby Hull's 58 meant in 1969. That Walter Payton needed to rush the ball more than Jimmy Brown to become the NFL's all-time leader requires no apologies on either side—from Payton for taking longer, or from Brown for running at linebackers of the 1960s who were built like defensive backs of the 1980s.

Superior athletes, just as superior salesmen or superior airline pilots, encounter enough pressures each morning. They needn't be artificially compared with other people in other decades. If we so honor records that are made to be broken, we should respect whoever breaks them, whenever, however. Achievers are achievers, and that is the only equitable barometer. If only life had been so fair while it lasted for Roger Maris, who will be buried Thursday. They should bury the asterisk and the hatchet, too.

SURE SMELLS FAMILIAR

OCTOBER 9, 1986

BOSTON—To a whiplashed observer of baseball, Chicago style, the game wasn't nearly as strange as reactions to it. People were actually puzzled by what they saw at Fenway Park this lovely autumn Wednesday afternoon. Tell me, are they new to our national pastime? Is this an expansion city? Either that, or some fans simply can't appreciate the finer points, the nuances, the intricacies of the sport.

Why was everybody scratching their heads after this American League playoff contest? Don't pitchers always lose ground balls in the sun? What's the big deal about three errors by the same infield in the same inning? Aren't coaches supposed to keep their hands folded when runners round third base? And if a guy swings and misses at a dropped third strike, isn't he taught to stand at home plate while the catcher throws the ball to the third baseman before the third baseman throws the ball to the first baseman for the out?

"Crazy," said Don Sutton, who will pitch Game 4 for the California Angels Saturday against the Boston Red Sox unless the commissioner decides it should be the Skins against the Shirts. "The last time I saw anything like this, our coach took us for Tastee-Freeze milkshakes after it was all over."

If there was a moral to this cartoon, it was that a perfectly decent and honest soul, Lawrence George "Moose" Stubing, will be remembered only as a man who doesn't allow adversity to affect his appetite. For a while there, Stubing's version of directing traffic made him look like the worst cop this side of Inspector Clouseau. But because his Angels compounded his gaffe and turned this thing into a full-fledged miscalculation, he will not be blamed for a 9–2 defeat. And not because he didn't try.

It was the sixth inning, Red Sox leading only 3–2, when Bob

Boone lined a hard single to left. Bobby Grich, perched on second, took off as though he knew what he was doing. Which was fair and square, until everybody in the stadium realized that Stubing was either out to lunch, or dreaming about dinner. Moose, all 250 pounds of him, is the California third-base coach, at least until further notice. He did the reasonable thing to do. He tried to talk to Grich while only 32,786 fans were screaming in the immediate vicinity.

"My one thought there is to score," said Grich, a highly intense type. "And if I'm not going to be able to score, I need some emphatic signal by the coach. I can't read lips."

By the time Grich decoded Stubing's message—Please stop, Bobby—it was all over. Grich was several strides down the third-base line, his feet about to go under, and left fielder Jim Rice—who is paid well to handle those chummy environs—had fired the ball to Wade Boggs, Boston's cutoff man. Grich was ambushed while groveling back to the bag, after which he threw his helmet down and screamed at Stubing. Grich punctuated the tantrum by raising his arms in disgust, a much-belated show of hands on the play. The rally was extinguished, but not Stubing's pursuit of culinary goodies.

"Made a bad decision," he said, inhaling a piece of pizza afterward. "I didn't see Boggs slip in there. I thought the throw by Rice was going through to the plate, that Grich might have a chance to score. I screwed up. I didn't give him the right sign, and by the time I tried to yell him back, it was too late. I tried to make something happen and I made something happen, all right."

According to a couple of anonymous Angels, Stubing's reactions aren't traditionally cat-like in these bang-bang situations. Then again, in defense of the Moose, his major-league career consisted of five at-bats, four of which resulted in strikeouts. Chances are, he never even saw third base until he became a coach there.

"I can take the heat," said the portly Stubing, still nibbling, not about to leave any snacks behind. "I'm a college basketball official on the West Coast in the winter. No harm, no foul."

Grich apologized to Stubing for showing him up on national TV, which was swell of the veteran second baseman. There was no record, however, of Stubing going bananas when Grich permitted a routine pop-up by Dwight Evans to fall for a double one inning earlier, allowing what would be the winning run to score. That Grich booted a grounder to ignite Boston's three-run seventh was just another compelling reason to imagine that, after everybody wakes up, all of this was a replay of something that really took place in Chicago, say, around mid-July. Name your year. Name any year.

"We play 162 games at either 1:30 or 7:30," Grich said. "Now, when you get to the playoffs and World Series, because of television, they switch all the times around. That was a high sky today, and the shadows were as bad as I've ever seen them. Guys were up there swinging against a background of shirtsleeves. And trying to field was an adventure."

Grich's points were valid and endorsed by athletes on either side, which still doesn't clarify how a guy who plays in California and lives on the beach can lose a ball in the sun. But Wednesday at Fenway wasn't supposed to make any sense, starting right with the Angels' lineup that benched Reggie Jackson in favor of Rick Burleson as designated hitter. The appearance of George Hendrick, the sleepiest of the sleepy, taking tepid cuts and making nonchalant grabs in the outfield also didn't mesh with this Angels' chant, that they want to win so badly, that they never, ever beat themselves.

"I don't understand a lot of what I saw out there today," said California manager Gene Mauch, who wasn't alone.

But the Red Sox shared in the seance, botching potential big innings into small innings until they couldn't avoid taking what California gave them. A personal favorite involved Rich Gedman, who wailed at a ball in the dirt for strike three, apparently concluding the Boston fifth. Boone, the Angel catcher, threw to third where Don Baylor was breaking off the base. There, Doug DeCinces fired across to first to nail Gedman, who didn't need nailing. He never moved from the batter's box. If you're keeping score at home, that strikeout goes 2–5–3.

Come back, Cubs and White Sox. We miss you, wherever you are. Or did you never leave? Wasn't that really you out there?

SOMETHING'S LOST IN TRANSLATION

OCTOBER 23, 1986

BOSTON—It's not been an easy World Series to comprehend, and it's not going to get any better, folks. The more things happen, the more people from the participating cities will try to explain these things, and that's the problem. It's difficult enough to figure out why players play the way they do, but comprehending what the fans are saying is next to impossible.

Honest now, have you ever heard a New Yorker argue with a Bostonian about baseball? Don't try it, unless you travel with a translator. No wonder the rooters for the Red Sox hate the rooters for the Mets and vice versa. They can't understand each other. No matter what happens, this Fall Classic will go down as the first ever with a language barrier. Here we are, in two of America's communication centers, separated by 45 minutes on hourly shuttle planes, and we're dealing with two foreign accents.

Can't anybody please speak English this week?

Take Wednesday night's pitcher for Boston in Game 4, Al Nipper. He's been in the Red Sox system since 1980, and the tweedy types up thisaway still call him something else. Specifically, Nippah. Oh, they have some other names for him, but most of those are a result of his winning only two games in the last two months and building his earned-run average into a hefty 5.38. Little wonder that he was kept out of the American League playoffs by his manager, John McNamara, who's got his rotation exactly where he wants it for the rest of the World Series.

"Strange," a Met fan was grousing to a guy from The Hub.

"McNamarer goes with a guy like Nipper in a big game like tonight's, but McNamarer got rid of the guy who pitched so great for us last night, Bob Ojeder."

"Bob who?" the Boston fan queried. "You mean Ojedah?"

They were both wrong. Says here that it was Bob Ojeda who won Game 3. But so it goes here in Fenway Pahk, where Red Sox fans booed Gary Carter for three hours during the Mets' 7–1 triumph Tuesday night before he realized he was the object of their disaffection. The reason, of course, is that he thought they were razzing somebody else.

"You stink, Cahtah!!" a guy in a Red Sox hat yelled.

"Cahtah?" corrected an antagonist from Manhattan. "You mean Cawta?"

Confusion reached epidemic proportions in Tuesday night's first inning, a first inning that began with a home run by Lenny Dykstra, a gritty little center-fielder whom the Mets will have to make a regular soon. Same, probably, with second baseman Wally Backman. Anyway, there was this ground ball struck by New York's Ray Knight with Keith Hernandez breaking toward home from third base, where Boston's Wade Boggs fielded the ball. The Red Sox could have had two outs, absolutely should have recorded one, but wound up with none when Hernandez scrambled back safely, as did Carter at second. The Red Sox botched the elementary rundown play something awful.

"How could youse guys blow dat?" laughed the grateful Metnick. "Youse should have tagged out da man at thoid."

"Where? Who?" replied the disgusted guy for the Red Sox. "You mean Cahtah?"

"Who?" the Met guy said. "Hoinandez was at thoid. Your pitcher must be angry now. What's his name? Dennis 'Earl Can' Boyd?"

"Who?" said the Boston fan. "I know one thing. You ahen't going to leave heah without losing at least one more game. Thursday night, we're coming back with the guy who beat Dahling in New Yahk on Saturday night, the night New Yahk was shut out."

"Hoist?" asked the Met fan. "Youse mean Bruce Hoist? The guy who beat Dawlink?"

"Who?" said the Boston fan, shaking his head.

They are different breeds, for sure. Red Sox fans know all

about broken hearts. Met fans are more partial to broken heads, windows, appliances, you get the idea. Red Sox fans are thrifty; Met fans throw golf balls at opposing outfielders. Red Sox fans are used to seeing The Wall in left field; Met fans at Shea Stadium look over the left-field fence and find a runway. Fenway is full of history; Shea ia an annex of LaGuardia Airport.

"We're going back to Shea," the Met fan said after the Mets scored three runs in the fourth inning Wednesday night, two on a homer by Carter. "Youse guys will never get out of there alive this weekend. If it goes to Game 7 Sunday, we got Dawlink coming back. What's da story wid him, anyway? He comes from around here, but he still talks normal. What's wid Dawlink?"

"Who?" said the Red Sox fan, who went on to defend McNamara. The Boston manager was chided for taking a gamble on starting Nipper in Game 4. Fact is, though, now the Red Sox will have their three top pitchers ready and rested if necessary—Hurst for Thursday after working Saturday, Clemens for Saturday after working Sunday and Boyd for Sunday after working Tuesday. If the Red Sox lost this tournament, they'll do so with their best arms. Or so the Red Sox fan figures.

"Youse mean you would dare want to have Earl Can pitchin' da clincher in Shea?" chirped the Met guy. "McNamarer is gonna wind up in da Chawles River if he blows dis."

"Hold your hahses," said the Red Sox guy. "We'll take our chances. This team of ours has been doubted all year. They picked this team for fifth, and look where it is now."

"In trouble is where youse are," said the Met guy. "It's a new ballgame now. New Yawk is gonna be the baseball capital of the woild."

"Baseball capital of . . . what?" asked the Red Sox guy, shaking his head.

RED SOX BURST OWN BALLOONS

OCTOBER 28, 1986

NEW YORK—There were balloons in the clubhouse of the Boston Red Sox, who had wanted so much to end their season with a party for a change, but now was not the time. So Rene Lachemann, the third base coach, took it upon himself to pop them, one by one.

So much for noise in the only quiet place at Shea Stadium Monday night. Wade Boggs was already brushing his teeth to go home, Dennis "Oil Can" Boyd was nervously rocking back and forth on his chair and Bruce Hurst was pacing. Outside, you could hear screaming fans, but not here.

Star-crossed before, star-crossed still, the Boston Red Sox. Put to bed for another season without a full meal. So close to scratching that 68-year itch, yet so silent now. So new, yet so old. In this same room where champagne had been brought Sunday morning, there were only balloons without air, players without expressions, bats without anymore balls to hit.

It was over, you could tell, in the top of the ninth inning. The police on horseback were poised in the outfield bullpens, the people in the stands were up to welcome the title they had expected since April and the Red Sox were clapping in the dugout out of habit and desperation. But they were never heard from again, because the New York Mets beat them 8–5 to win the World Series.

"How do I summarize what happened? I summarize it that we had a great season," said catcher Rich Gedman, picking at his toenails. But there wasn't much spunk in his monotone, because it was as though he knew that he and his teammates would have to deal with this problem for seasons to come.

It wasn't just that the Red Sox had become only the second team in World Series history to lose the tournament after winning the first two games on the road. It was that the Red Sox had Game 6 all but in the bag Sunday morning, and held a 3–0 lead in Game 7 through five innings. It was as though all the curses they insisted didn't exist, all the jinxes and clouds and ill omens, came to haunt them in the end. How do you deal with that?

"You get ready to work hard all winter and do better next summer," said Marty Barrett, the sprightly second baseman who had 13 hits for the Series and five walks, but scored only once. For all the opportunites these Red Sox had to kill the ghosts, to rid themselves of the label as "Boston Stranglers" for parched throats in tight situations, these Red Sox were right back where they started. New England's reason to worry, to fret, to be eternally disappointed. Hard truths, but truths nevertheless.

Strange, too, because here was a team that had endured so many parades rained on because of extenuating circumstances. And then, the rains came Sunday, and the Red Sox had a few extra hours to ponder that brutal defeat in Game 6, to resuscitate, to change pitchers. And it was working, that reprieve of sorts, because Bruce Hurst, the Met-killer, had a 3–0 lead. If ever a Red Sox hurler could imagine himself on cruise control, he was it. He'd yielded one hit, retired 11 in a row, when it happened.

"I just got a little tired," said the Mormon left-hander. "I was losing it. I knew one guy I'd have to get out coming into this Series was Keith Hernandez. He's a great hitter. He's the one who got it going for them."

Hernandez, the Met leader, spanked a two-run single in the sixth, and soon, the feast was on. The Red Sox bullpen, vulnerable before and vulnerable to the end, was asked to stop the bleeding. The response was more bleeding. Calvin Schiraldi, the ex-Met, picked up the mess and made it messier. Then Joe Sambito. Then Al Nipper. Meanwhile, Jesse Orosco, the cool New York lefty, halted the season, in order, retiring Ed Romero, Boggs and Barrett before he threw his glove in the air, before the horses marched in from the bullpen.

"Great season," said Schiraldi, the loser. "But I find little consolation in that now."

His opinion, the Red Sox will soon discover, shall be shared by much of their constituency. Was this worse than 1946, when Johnny Pesky held the ball too long while the Cardinals' Enos

Slaughter barrelled home with the winning run in that Classic Fall? What of the lost playoff in 1948 to Cleveland, or the lost playoff to the Yankees in 1978, when Bucky Dent lifted the homer over The Wall? What about Jim Burton's serving up that bloop single to Joe Morgan in 1975, the night after Carlton Fisk beat The Big Red Machine? How many times can one franchise go to the 11th hour before turning into pumpkins?

"Game 6 . . . that was the one," said manager John McNamara. "We let them go . . . let them off the hook."

Saturday night, which became Sunday morning, the Red Sox were one out away, one strike away, from the World Series title. Then they lost the possible dream in near impossible fashion. Dwight Evans, who homered on the first pitch of the season at Detroit last April, homered Monday night off Ron Darling. And then Gedman followed with another shot into the foggy night in the second inning. This would have been the most improbable climax of all, to have the Red Sox arise from the big hurt to win the World Series, their first since 1918, their first in 68 years.

"How bad we wanted this," said Hurst, who was the Most Valuable Player-in-waiting Sunday morning until the Mets did the unbelievable. "I'd trade that award I didn't get, I'd trade anything right now for the World Series."

But the probable happened. The Boston Red Sox did not win. Those balloons on the floor of their clubhouse told the story, again.

BRETT SHOULDERS HEARTFELT PAIN

MARCH 21, 1987

FORT MYERS, FLORIDA—It is not George Brett's nature to be wistful, and we picture him as forever blowing bubbles, but this spring training has been less than shiny for the Kansas City Royals' popular third baseman. His shoulder is still tender after off-season surgery, though that's not really the problem.

If it hurt that badly, Brett wouldn't be seen sneaking up on the other team's batboy before a game and playfully wrestling him to the ground. Nor would Brett voluntarily wrap his throwing arm around an admiring fan when it's time to pose for a picture. That's the bubbly Brett everybody knows and enjoys.

But away from the public and the ballfield, George Brett—a star, a millionaire, a bachelor with no apparent worries—frets for a friend who is not doing well. Dick Howser, his manager for many years, is fighting for his life.

"He just had another operation," Brett was saying Sunday. "His third. In California. I don't know what his chances are, but I do know if anybody can lick it, it's Dick."

Howser, of course, can enlist all of baseball in his rooting section. If prayers and sentiment were all it took for a 50-year-old man to beat brain cancer, Howser would be back filling out lineup cards and arguing with umpires and chirping in the dugout tomorrow. But it's not that easy, which doesn't make it fair, and Brett still remembers Howser's courageous attempt to carry on with a body that didn't equal his spirit.

"When did we first come down here, the 19th of February?" Brett said. "Well, until then, I didn't know too much more than what I'd heard or read about Dick. That he'd been to the hospital again in December, and that he wanted like hell to manage again. But when I saw him the first time down here, he didn't look like himself. He didn't look well. You know those warm-up jerseys we all wear? Well, we went to a different company this year, and they were cut a little bigger to start with. But Dick. Dick's jersey, the V-neck came down to here."

Brett pulled his undershirt below the middle of his chest and remained silent for a moment. Then, as if to relieve his agony, Brett changed subjects. He, too, had gone under the knife of Dr. Frank Jobe in Los Angeles.

"Same doctor who did Jim McMahon of the Bears," Brett said. "In fact, we sort of crossed in the hospital. I was getting done when he was just about getting started. My operation was a lot different than his. Went up to his room to say hello. He's a little different, too, huh?"

Brett laughed, then turned quiet again. Then he asked about the White Sox and about their pitching and about the teams in Arizona and whether you'd heard that his brother Ken is a broadcaster for the California Angels now. And then, enough of that.

"Never realized Dick had so many friends," Brett said. "Wherever we go, people ask about him. You know, as a manager, Dick wasn't really close with a lot of players. He kept his distance. The office was always open, but he was also in it. Whitey Herzog, hell, he lived in the clubhouse with us.

"But Dick and I got friendly when he was third-base coach with New York for so long. We'd always kibitz when I was playing defense, and the Yankees were at bat. Same with Whitey when he was a third-base coach. That's how we got friendly. I know all the third-base coaches.

"Anyway, when Dick finally got the managing job in New York, I sent him over a bottle of champagne. And then when he came to manage at Kansas City in '81, well, we were already pretty close. I like Dick. I respect him. You remember when we finally beat Toronto for our first playoff win in '85? I made the last out, and made sure he got the ball.

"He had lost 11 straight post-season games until then, and I had lost eight. He never lost his cool, never got uptight, no matter what, however many times we were down that season. That was a great thing about Dick. This thing, though. This thing was too much for him."

Dick Howser had to quit, two days after his comeback began.

"At 10:27 in the morning on a Monday, the last Monday in February," said Brett. "He was on the field a long time Saturday, then went in after only about an hour on Sunday. Nobody thought much about it. But on Monday, he came out at 10, and never made it past the left-field bullpen. We were all playing catch at the time, and then he went back into his office. At 10:27, and never came out. That was it: 10:27. I went into the locker room to change shirts about 11:15, and the door was closed. I went in to talk to him. He said he was giving it up. He had no energy. He didn't look good. I told him we were all pulling for him, and we all are. We're thinking about him. I think you might see us all playing a little extra hard this season whatever happens, if you know what I mean."

And you knew what George Brett meant, because Dick Howser is not doing well.

"This shoulder of mine, some days it's okay, some days it's not," Brett went on. "But, what the hell, I'm not going to worry. It'll be okay. It's nothing when you think about it. This is my second time around with something like this. Charley Lau, who meant so much to me, he's gone now. You know, you always get wrapped up in little stupid things in this stupid game. You go 0-for-4 and you make an error to lose the game, and you think it's the end of the world. And you complain about having to take three-hour bus trips in spring training. Well, I know Dick wishes he could take a three-hour bus trip with us right about now. And there'll be a day when I'll be wishing I could, too."

What George Brett was saying, as he darted off to oblige more autograph-seekers, was that we'll all look at the clock one day and it will be 10:27.

Football

'WE'RE NO. 28!'

DECEMBER 21, 1981

BALTIMORE—It was everything you ever wanted in a bier, and less. The Baltimore Colts beat the New England Patriots 23–21 in Sunday's Stupor Bowl. Tapes of the game belong beneath the right foot of Rosemary Woods, Secretary of Erasers for former President Nixon.

As expected, this was a see-saw contest. That is, some of the things you really did see, you really didn't believe you saw. But then, both these teams were facing a must-lose situation, and they gave it all they had. In the end, they made the league look good. The Ivy League.

Mind you, there was no lack of intrigue surrounding this spectacle, also known as the Untidy Bowl. You could cut the suspense with a feather. Tickets didn't move too well in Baltimore this week, but there was a run on grocery bags. Not to carry Christmas presents, but to cover heads of many of the 17,073 customers who appeared to cheer their beloved Colts, also known as the Dolts.

Back in September, the Colts began their season by slaughtering the Patriots 29–28 in Foxboro, Massachusetts. Neither squad quite recovered. Baltimore lost its next 14 encounters, most of which were not of a close kind. Owner Robert Irsay talked of firing everybody but himself, and even resorted to calling plays from his private box. Nothing worked, except his tongue.

However, the Pats, also known as the Patsies, pretty much kept pace, losing 13 times. They managed to have the best pass defense in the NFL, but only because they're easier to run against than Harold Stassen. Fans in Boston promised them a parade at season's end. In the Charles River.

So the stage was set for Sunday's game, also known as the Roll Over Bowl. The prize for losing would be the No. 1 pick in the college draft next April, and—get this for drama—both teams want the same guy. He's Ken Sims, a defensive tackle for the

University of Texas. He'd be perfect for the Colts or the Patriots because he's got a broken leg.

Don't go away. There's more. Both these teams are interested in the same coach: Frank Kush, who taught character at Arizona State between scandals and before moving to Hamilton of the Canadian Football League. It is said that the Bears also covet him. Light a candle for Frank Kush. How much punishment can a man take?

Given this backdrop, speculation was rife that the Colts and Patriots naturally would like most naturally to do this Sunday what they most naturally do any Sunday: lose. Another defeat, and the Colts could claim, without a jury trial, "We're No. 28." Another setback would drop New England into an eminently flatfooted tie with Baltimore at 2–14, but because the Patriots' schedule of opponents was deemed slightly more underwhelming than the Colts, the Patriots would be awarded a broken leg up on picking Sims.

When New England selected Tom Owen to make his first start at quarterback, you could smell more than crabcakes around Memorial Stadium. But he was the picture of innocence. Somebody asked him if he was embarrassed about such an assignment. He said no. He said he only felt sorry for Jimmy the Greek, because he had to handicap this thing. When Owen trotted into the field for a series of downs, having forgotten to remove his parka, you knew he would have no part of any chicanery this frostbitten afternoon. He would be loyal to the occasion and the moment. Pete Rozelle's Twilight Zone.

Besides, if either side wanted to dump, they couldn't possibly rehearse some of their pratfalls. By the first minute, you knew that both teams would dance with who brung them here. On fourth down, while the 11th Colt was dashing in from the sidelines, the Patriots punted. Ray Butler of Baltimore fumbled, but New England had an illegal man downfield, so they did it all over again.

This time, deep in his end zone, Rich Camarillo dropped back to kick. He took the snap, took one step forward, then dropped the ball. You simply can't plan something like that. When umpire Art Demmas threw the next flag directly through Colt Randy McMillan's face mask, you knew the officials had caught the spirit, too.

Upstairs, Jim West giggled. After broadcasting the Cubs for

several years, he returned here to handle the Washington Capitals on television and public address for the Colts.

"Naturally," said West, "I don't take my job home with me."

Baltimore, which established NFL records for most points and touchdowns allowed, fell behind 7–3, but roared to a 17–14 halftime lead, their first of the season. It was a giddy experience. Until now, they thought spiking the football meant filling it with vodka instead of air.

Several Colts appeared disinterested in achieving bookend victories. The big attraction for them was a heating unit behind the bench. Derrick Hatchett, upbraided for not trying last week, spent the better part of three hours warming his toes with his back to the field. He had plenty of company. At one juncture, there were nine Colts gathered around. Was it really a heater, or a showing of *Debbie Does Dallas*?

But Bert Jones seemed involved. In what might have been his Colt swan song, he completed 17 of 28 passes for 267 yards and three touchdowns. Afterward, all he would say was, "Goodbye, it's been fun . . . I enjoyed it." He exited, pointing toward Los Angeles.

"We had a great start and a great finish this season," noticed Baltimore coach Mike McCormack. "But we weren't so good in between." Give that man good marks for sense of humor. Next week, give him a job.

The Patriots, unbeaten in their preseason, did not expire quietly. A week ago, they called a timeout on their third play of the game to talk things over. Sunday, they really put it all together, and under the fourth-quarter guidance of Matt Cavanaugh, almost won. But after they had driven to the Baltimore 15, the gun sounded. The Pats had run out of timeouts.

"Going into today, we wanted to win," admitted safety Tim Fox. "But now that we haven't, it's just as well that we lost. Not only because of the draft choice, but because we can be called the worst team in pro football. We've been called one of the best because of all the talent we're supposed to have. Now, being the worst, maybe it'll help motivate us. May sound funny, but I'm really looking forward to next season. I hope our fans feel the same way. I wish them all a Merry Christmas." Film at 11.

PURE HALAS— PERFECTLY UNCLEAR

JANUARY 8, 1982

President, Chairman of the Bored, Chief Executive Officer, General Manager, Special Events Coordinator, Speaker of the House, Commander-in-Chief, Ayatollah, Premier, Assistant to the President, Assistant to Himself, Himself and Assistant, Oldest Living Majority Stockholder, and Youngest Living Majority Stockholder in the Bears, Ticketron's George S. Halas staged a press conference Thursday to help us understand what's happening with his football team.

Wearing a blue suit and matching bedroom slippers, Papa Bear, who has been overthrowing more Bears lately than Vince Evans, saved his opening contradictory remarks for Buddy Ryan. Mr. Halas said he called this thing to reveal that Ryan just moments before had autographed a new contract to remain as the old defensive coordinator. Ryan—aware that with the Motleys of the Midway, re-signing and resigning are never more than a hyphen apart—looked puzzled.

"Actually," said Ryan, "I signed New Year's Eve."

"What I really want you all to do," continued Mr. Halas, "is *meet* Buddy Ryan."

Ryan looked perplexed again. He came to Chicago in 1978, and since then, he recalls leaving his house to appear in public at least three or four thousand times.

"You're talking to a heck of a man," said Halas, meaning Ryan, but still doing most of the talking himself. Finally, someone asked Ryan, who admitted speaking with Halas only four times in the last four years, how he felt being hired before he knew who his boss was. Halas, really feisty now, took umbrage at that suggestion.

"I am the boss," he said, adding that he was "pretty close" to being head coach, too. "I am the boss."

That much was made perfectly clear Thursday afternoon. George S. Halas is the boss. He said he was disgusted that the Bears were so bad last year. He said the Bears were no 6–10 team. He sounded mad. He also sounded like Leo Durocher sounded when he said the Cubs were no eighth-place team, later to be proven correct when they finished 10th.

"You bet I'm a mean s.o.b.," confirmed Halas, who has been a practicing deleted expletive for only 86 years. "I'm not gonna let this happen again, and I want the people to know that."

Moving right along, Halas expressed displeasure with the Bears' offense, which finished 28th in efficiency and 26th in total yards in the NFL last year, and close to the bottom of the Chicago Catholic League in both categories. But that doesn't mean Halas doesn't expect all his offensive coordinators back, because he does.

Now, if you don't understand that, then you might as well have been at the press conference gasping for air with the rest of us. The way Halas has been categorizing his athletes until now, you half expect his defensive platoon to wear halos and his offensive platoon pink jerseys next season.

But, no. Halas says "there is good talent here." Presumably, Jim Finks has helped put it here. Then, someone asked, why isn't Jim Finks here? Halas explained that Finks had planned to attend, but had cancelled 20 minutes ago. Someone called the Bears' Lake Forest office looking for Finks and was told he was at the Bears' downtown office. Someone checked the downtown office, where the press conference was, and Finks still wasn't.

"Nice fella. I'm not trying to get him to quit," said Halas, his stream of unconsciousness unremitting. "He's done a good job here, and, yes, Jim Finks has a future with the Bears." Then again, so does the last gallon of gas in your car's tank.

All right, but what about hiring all the Indians before the chief, George? What if the head coach you haven't obtained doesn't like all the assistant brains? Doesn't that make the assistant coaches more important than the head coach? And if you're so interested in offense, why don't you just make Jim Dooley, whom you describe as "brilliant," your coach rather than the head of your CIA?

"Because he was head coach here before and apparently

doesn't have the ability . . . look at his record," said Halas. "I don't think it's unusual to do what I'm doing, or in the order I'm doing it. I have a game plan."

Halas, who said Wednesday he had four possibilities for head coach, Thursday said he now has three. All three have coached somewhere, presumably football. One suspect is still in college, presumably graduated. Another really ornery candidate is still employed by Dallas: presumably it's not Larry Hagman. The *Tribune* did learn that Michigan State's Muddy Waters was dropped from consideration because his name resembles the job description, but extensive efforts to ascertain who Larry, Moe and Curly really are failed.

In due time, Halas promised, everything we didn't want to know about the Bears but were afraid to imagine will be revealed. He sees nothing odd about holding a press conference to introduce people who need no introduction. If the NFL is in a pinch for a Super Bowl halftime show, Papa Bear doing a soft shoe routine behind his desk would be magnificent.

"I don't know who the new head coach will be," fibbed Ryan. "But, while I don't wish them any bad luck, I sure wish the Cowboys would get their season over with. That would solve it."

Obviously, then, Halas has only one man on his list. Mike Ditka. He possesses all the qualifications. He's a former Bear, he wrote Halas a lovely letter, he paid for the stamp, and he's contracted water on the knees begging for the job. He's the last piece to this puzzle, sure as Papa Bear is intent on getting his dentures into the operation as firmly as he ever has. Is the old man shooting for all the marbles one last time, or has he merely lost a few?

Well, one of Thursday's guests did ask Halas about speculation that senility has gotten the best of his virility.

"Nuts to you," replied Halas. "There's no goddamn senility in this carcass."

Thank you, Mr. President. Can we do this again sometime soon?

49ERS DISCOVER GOLD MINE

JANUARY 25, 1982

PONTIAC, MICHIGAN—They used to say Joe Montana looks like Barry Manilow. Now, they'll say Barry Manilow looks like Joe Montana. The kid's a winner at 25. What's he do for an encore when he grows up?

"Maybe," he said, "they'll name a state after me."

It was just beginning to sink in now. The boy they had wondered about, the scatter-armed pitcher from Notre Dame, the blond enigma whose history didn't impress the National Football League draft board three years ago, was standing there admitting Sunday afternoon that he too had been fooled.

"They said we were 50–1 to do this, or 60–1, or 70–1, and I guess you can't blame them," Montana allowed, fidgeting with the brim of his baseball cap. "We had three rookies starting in our defensive backfield, we had a lot of holes to fill from the year before, and we had myself starting at quarterback for the first time.

"It had always been one of my goals to do this, but, no, I didn't think it would be this quickly. A lot of other people felt that way, too. People believed in Dallas, people believed in Cincinnati, people believed in the Giants. As late as this morning, nobody believed in us. Picked up the paper here and all the other coaches in the NFL were picking Cincinnati. Nobody."

When Montana was asked, will they start?

"Maybe they started," he replied, "about 20 minutes ago."

The San Francisco 49ers, destiny's doormats in July, won Super Bowl XVI Sunday by downing the Cincinnati Bengals 26–21. Truly, this one was over before it was over. Under Montana's calm leadership, the 49ers vaulted to a 20–0 lead at halftime. Cincinnati came back too late to make it a game, with too little to make Montana anything but the most valuable player.

He threw 22 times, completing 14, for 157 yards and one touchdown. Better yet, when the Bengals were trying to emasculate him in the second half, Montana never lost what got him here. Cool.

"It was getting a little testy there," Montana said. "But there's no sense in worrying while you're on the field. I do my worrying on the sidelines. My mom says I gain more yardage when I'm out of the game than when I'm in the game."

This is the same softspoken, slope-shouldered, mild-mannered Joe Montana who would kill himself to help his team win, and once, almost did. He authored several certified miracles at Notre Dame, but none better than his last—the 35–34 Irish victory over Houston in the 1979 Cotton Bowl. It was Montana's final college game, and it was cold in Dallas that night, and his temperature dipped to the danger level.

"They said hypothermia was setting in," he recalled Sunday. "They had to wrap me in blankets in the locker room at halftime, pour chicken soup down me, anything to keep me going."

It wasn't that Montana was worried about living as much as returning to the game. He did both, guiding Notre Dame from a 34–12 deficit. Moments like that convinced San Francisco coach Bill Walsh that Montana was no ordinary hunk of flesh.

"I am a little surprised that it all came together so quickly," Walsh said Sunday. "But I'm not surprised at who made it happen. Joe is the finest young quarterback I've ever seen. There's some John Brodie in him, some Roger Staubach, some Fran Tarkenton, and a lot of class."

You sort of expected Sunday would be a 49er day when they gained five yards without touching the ball on the opening kickoff. They fumbled it away when they did touch it, but got it back for Montana, and his first touchdown drive consumed almost 10 minutes. Montana capped it with a one-yard dive. Fitting, for Montana had stuck pins in the Bengal defense to get that far. He would orchestrate two other long marches before half's end—one of 92 yards in 12 plays en route to a second touchdown, another of 61 yards in 13 plays to arrange the first of Ray Wersching's four field goals.

"We moved well in the first half," Montana said. "But then in the second half, we went out and did exactly what Bill said not to do. We went out and got some quick penalties, and we didn't have the field position that we had in the first half. I didn't do much in the second half. Our defense won it for us. They deserve the award, not me."

But, no, Joe Montana has taken Walsh's nomination and made good on it for six months. It had not been easy, for Montana's early NFL experience consisted mostly of holding the ball on placekicks. Also, it had not been easy because Walsh's playbook is more encyclopedia than primer.

"It takes a lot of studying," said Montana, sipping a soft drink. "Maybe two hours a day. I don't know how far Bill is ahead of the other NFL coaches, but I know he's ahead. You look at some of the things he comes up with during the week, and you say they'll never work. Then you call them on Sunday, and they work. Different plays, different formations for every play, but they work. We had 10 or 12 new things we threw in there today. He's got the X's and O's."

But most of all, the 49ers have Joe Montana. Not brash like Joe Namath, not wild and crazy like Bobby Layne, just the story behind the season's most remarkable football story.

"Definitely, this is more important than being No. 1 at Notre Dame," said Montana. "This is the ultimate game. I don't know when it'll hit me. I'm going off to the Pro Bowl tomorrow, then a camera safari in Africa after that. That will help me relax, and maybe then I'll realize what's happened. I've reached one of my goals, but that doesn't mean it's over. You keep trying. You stay hungry. I hope to be back."

BUSINESS AS USUAL? BET ON IT

NOVEMBER 21, 1982

There will be no solidarity handshakes, because there is no solidarity, but no matter.

As proof that there is life after the strike—which wouldn't have lasted two months if Ed Garvey were alive—the games that National Football League people play shall resume Sunday.

Then, on Monday night, Howard Cosell will re-enter America's TV dens, consciousness and inner ears—even without showing us last week's highlights. Come Tuesday, 1,500 union members will vote on a contract which could bind them to their well-healed bosses' heels for five more years.

Unless ballot-counters are the same snails who tabulated Illinois' race for governor—the longest count since Dempsey-Tunney—we should have a decision before the five years are up. And unless the helmeted boys of winter decide that Abe Lincoln incorrectly assumed that slavery was dead, the games will continue.

You can bet that it will be business as usual, and you can bet just about anything else with your bookie, who is back in business, too. Now that the players have realized they can't beat the owners, everybody goes back to work only trying to beat the spread.

Football fans may feel betrayed, but really, they shouldn't. Their fare on the vidiot box has been reduced to Tasmanian taffy pulls and demolition derbies featuring unmanned kitchen appliances, but otherwise, the customers had little to do with the 57-day gabfest conducted by Garvey and guest host Jack Donlan.

The customers did part with some season ticket money on which owners accrued interest. But, consider it charity. After all, George Halas did say he and his lodge brothers, ho, ho, gave away the store last week. Mr. Halas should be careful, because laugh-induced hernias can be hazardous to the health of an 87-year-old man.

But the fans will come back, because the games always have been, and always will be, a release. If you're really disturbed by the strike, you should count your blessings, because obviously you've got life's worries whittled down to a precious few. Watch the scoreboard, and pox on the rhetoric.

A little empathy for the players might be forthcoming, because, at one time or another, we've all run flat-nosed into a monopoly. The NFL is a textbook example. Athletes are said to be adults playing a kid's game. But, when they sit down to talk finances with the boss, they tend to revert to kids playing an adult game.

What's remarkable about the strike scenario is that the football players are supposedly this conntry's best-educated group of sweat-setters. Or, maybe we should amend that to read, at least some of them are college graduates. Or, worse yet, perhaps the reason many of them aren't the former is because they are the latter.

Whatever, they have been thrown about like rag dolls by management, and not just during the 57-day war. For years, the players have ambled about, either disinterested in or oblivious to their situation. They didn't suddenly become underpaid or underprivileged last September 20. Their ditch wasn't dug in eight weeks.

If Garvey fooled the players into believing that he could deliver them to the Horn of Plenty, he was looking across the negotiating table with rose-colored spectacles. But, in the players, he also had a captive audience, vulnerable to being duped now as before.

At the beginning, Garvey made lavish promises. But at the bitter end, he delivered virtually nothing. The players didn't get the 55 percent of the gross that was "etched in stone," they didn't get half the TV bundle and they made no progress toward free agency. Fleeced again.

With minor alterations, the package being offered to labor now bears strong resemblance to the one management tendered three months ago. Call it compromise, if you will. Look closer, and it's surrender. Even the mechanics for its ratification are slanted toward the owners—players are to resume the games Sunday, then decide Tuesday whether they want to continue being paid.

But, more than likely, the players will settle for half a loaf, and realize if they dreamed of a better result, it was just that—a dream. Brian Baschnagel, the Bears' well-intentioned rep, probably is wrong when he credits Garvey for doing a decent job. But Baschnagel probably is correct in stating that the dissenters pack greater volume than numbers. Vocal? For sure. Minority? We'll see Tuesday.

Fallout from the strike might mean divisiveness on some teams, but that, too, shall pass. If it doesn't, the alternative isn't all that bad, either. Maybe if the Bears can arrive angry at the stadium every Sunday, they'll be a better team. In recent seasons, one must admit they haven't exactly approached the line of scrimmage in a state of ill-humor.

If the NFL kings and servants want to fret about something, they could ask themselves why so many people in so many regions didn't miss professional football. The baseball strike of last summer made a far greater dent. But then, baseball touches more citizens in more days and in more ways. Which is why, with apologies to Pete Rozelle, baseball is still The Game.

At any rate, football fans everywhere shouldn't report to their seats Sunday bearing imaginary scars. Anytime you spend $12 for the right to be aggravated, you've already paid a price. What you're watching can't be all that important. It's just business. As usual.

SUPER BEATING

JANUARY 23, 1984

TAMPA—It wasn't so much the animal in the Los Angeles Raiders. It was the animation. Sunday, in Super Bowl XVIII, their emotions clearly got the best of the Washington Redskins.

There had been championship games, and there had been championship games. But this one was advertised as the closest call yet, a postseason colossus involving free spirits to be witnessed by an audience of millions awaiting results from a super storyline.

After days and nights of premises and promises, threats and throats, picking a winner through the cloud of world-class hype would be difficult. Getting a handle on the teams' heartbeats would be nigh impossible, a task reserved for Sunday.

Surely enough and convincingly enough, the riddle was solved shortly after tee-it-up time at Tampa Stadium. The Redskins had more nicknames, but the Raiders had more gumption. Los Angeles romped 38–9 in the most lopsided of the 18 Super Bowls.

Tom Flores, who has the distinction of being the only mortal to earn Super Bowl rings for playing and coaching, credited his Raiders for approaching Sunday's assignment "the only way we know how ... all out." Credit him now, too, with the week's greatest understatement.

The Raiders were everything they said they'd be. Deep, resolved, aggressive, balanced, hungry. They weren't ill-mannered because they didn't really have to be.

Marcus Allen, the sprightly Los Angeles running back, gained a Super Bowl-record 191 yards on 20 carries and scored two touchdowns, including the final one on a dash of 74 yards, also a record. He was the game's most valuable player. Quarterback Jim Plunkett, as usual, wasn't flashy but was functional.

Those all-world cornerbacks, Lester Hayes and Mike Haynes, gave Redskin wide receivers Art Monk and Charlie Brown a severe case of static cling. Meanwhile, the Raiders up front—

on defense and on offense—used industrial-strength efforts to rule the trenches. No particular upsets there, either.

"Reality is upon you, gentlemen," Raider defensive end Howie Long told the press. "We handled the Hogs. Our defensive front seven came up with our name this week—The Slaughterhouse Seven. We never had a hog before that tasted so good."

But, for all the wagering conducted on this event, you couldn't have bet that a kid from Waukegan and a former Fighting Illini linebacker would turn in plays that would bring the Raiders their third NFL title. Sunday, Derrick Jensen and Jack Squirek had the honors, thank you.

Jensen "was thinking block" early in the first quarter as the Redskins' Jeff Hayes dropped back to punt on fourth down from the Washington 30. Jensen barrelled through the middle, stuffed the ball as it came off Hayes' foot, then pursued it to the end zone. Jensen recovered, but Washington never did. It was 7–0.

Squirek, drafted from Illinois in 1982, also spoke of a sixth sense he experienced late in the half. With 12 seconds remaining and the Redskins deep in their territory, quarterback Joe Theismann could have eaten it, handed off, thrown deep or headed for the locker room.

Instead, Captain America attempted to dump a screen pass off to Joe Washington on the left. A curious decision it was—and maybe the fatal one for Theismann. Squirek followed Washington to the ball, intervened and took the interception five yards for a touchdown that made it 21–3.

Theismann had done something akin to this during the Redskins' regular-season victory over Los Angeles, and it worked. But, from now on, he'll be asked to explain how he passed the wrong team to a title Sunday.

In defense of Theismann, he had little. He was harried and hurried into throwing wild high or not at all. Six times he was sacked by six different people. Neither Monk nor Brown was available for a completion in the first half. When somebody was open, it was usually tight end Clint Didier, hardly a game-breaker.

With Hayes and Haynes manning the flanks so brilliantly, bulldozer John Riggins was subjected to a fate worse than the flu that bugged him. He was straightened up, struck down and confined to 64 yards in 26 carries. As the rout grew, Riggins became less and less a factor.

The Redskins were thinking that they'd prevail with the better quarterback, but Theismann, helpless, couldn't have picked a worse time to be at his worst. The Redskins also figured their special teams would be just that, but such was not the case. They disintegrated in full view of 72,920 customers.

Turnovers? The Redskins, who flew to Florida with an 11-game winning streak, had been feasting on them. Not so, Sunday. The Raiders made mistakes, but they didn't make the mistake of letting their mistakes hurt. Meanwhile, when the Redskins weren't bobbling, they were bumbling.

They were caught with their thigh pads down when Cliff Branch snared Plunkett's 12-yard pass for Los Angeles' second touchdown. They were distracted by sideline confusion before their only point-after attempt was blocked. And, they merely blushed at the sight of Allen weaving through traffic on his sensational sprint to close the third quarter.

That comeuppance came just after Riggins had failed to gain a first down on fourth-and-1 at the Los Angeles 26. It was over then, for sure.

Plunkett, who doesn't enjoy particular fame, threw as well as necessary to satisfy a magnificent supporting cast. He can fire deep, and did, to Branch and between two Redskins on the setup for Los Angeles' second touchdown.

Plunkett threw short in quest of Los Angeles' fourth touchdown, but, typically, the Redskins interfered. Allen soon got it, wiggling in from the 5.

"The Redskins are good, but this is a new year," said Raider linebacker Rod Martin, who had his nose in Washington's business all day. "And we're the champions. I'm not surprised."

Sunday's surprise was that only one team showed why Super Bowl XVIII was showing us the two best teams in football. The hype was half right, anyway.

NOTHING SACRED TO 'KREMLIN'S TEAM'

NOVEMBER 18, 1985

IRVING, TEXAS—Never mind what happened to America's Team Sunday. What happens next to America, what does this mean for one nation, under God, indivisible? Now that the carnivorous Bears have run up numbers like 44–0 and 11–0, and clearly established themselves as role models for our youth, is Santa Claus safe? Does he slide down the chimney on Christmas morning and get sacked?

Might Mr. Rogers have to trade in his cardigan sweater for a holster? Will *Sesame Street* be taken over by motorcycle gangs? Do the neighborhood kids ditch Mickey Mouse for Mongo McMichael? Instead of a Cabbage Patch doll for her birthday, will your daughter want a tattoo?

"I don't know," pondered Dan Hampton, who was merely unstoppable Sunday.

"I think everybody's safe. I don't think we'll ever be America's Team. I don't think we want to be America's Team. But, if we keep playing like this, the other 27 teams in the league might start calling us the Kremlin's Team. They might want to have us banned."

It was the worst thing to hit Dallas since *Dynasty*, what unfolded in Texas Stadium Sunday. It was four quarters of manslaughter. It was such carnage that Mike Ditka, the pupil turned genius, had to apologize. Out of mercy, he cleared the bench and still his Bears couldn't avoid scoring.

Is nothing sacred anymore? If Refrigerator Perry, who should know the rules by now, can pick up Walter Payton like a picnic basket and try to carry him toward the end zone in broad daylight, do law and order have a chance? Can you, in good conscience, tell your son that the cop on the corner is a friend? Is graffiti in? Are arts and crafts out? Can we survive this changing of the guard in the National Football League?

"Oh, I suppose it's best if the Cowboys remain America's Team, anyway," allowed Mike Singletary, who was merely sensational. "It's best for the image of America if America's Team is clean, if they're nice guys. I mean, we're nice guys, too. Not all the time, though. So, it's better that way. It's better if they stay America's Team."

Yes, but what about fair play? After all, here were the Bears, trying to survive before a no no-show crowd of 63,855 without Jim McMahon, the straw that stirs the drink, the sore-shouldered quarterback who might miss one more week, one more month, maybe the entire season. Is it reasonable, then, that they would hog the ball for almost 36 minutes, out-gain Dallas by 207 yards and treat Cowboy prevent mechanisms like the Alamo? Can a visitor wreak such havoc in one afternoon without wresting the crown?

"We don't want it," insisted Keith Van Horne, who was merely immovable. "America's Degenerate Team, that's different."

It was different, all right. Cowboy passers usually figure on a pound of respect, or at least an ounce of protection. But, what was a game for a little while turned late in the first quarter when Danny White met Hampton, who needs no introduction. White, setting up from his own end zone on first down, suddenly encountered a raging sequoia tree in his midst. Hampton first swatted Jim Cooper away, not unlike a mosquito, then went for the ball.

"They're notorious for doing that in that situation," Hampton said. "It was just a routine pass rush. It was lucky that I tipped it. I was afraid for a moment that I deflected it out of the end zone, but then I saw two of our guys getting under it like they were fielding a punt. Mongo didn't catch it, because he's too short."

But Richard Dent did, for a touchdown, to move up on the Refrigerator, America's Appliance, in the scoring derby. In time, Leslie Frazier and Mike Richardson would supply silencer interceptions, and even though Hampton suspected the

Cowboys might have liked to crawl through the hole in the roof, sometimes enough is never enough.

"They had a lot of rhetoric all week," he explained. "We come here 10–0 and they're 7–3, and still they're talking like they're favorites. That's good. That just motivates us more. We might not have the most athletic ability, but we play together. We took it to them early, and this wasn't our toughest game of the season. We arrived here c.o.d., Chicago on Dallas. I said last night we'd shut them out. Today, you saw the piranha effect. We smell blood, we go into a frenzy."

Piranhas? Does that mean an end to computers, the flex defense, Tom Landry's fur fedora? Can we anticipate that those luscious Dallas Cowboy cheerleaders show up next week with acne? What about tradition, Texas and Roger Staubach? Can't he sell us Rolaids anymore? Do we tell our offspring about Mother Goose before bed, or Dracula? Is it all over?

"No, they're still a good football team," concluded Hampton. "It's just that, growing up around here, all you hear is Cowboys this, Cowboys that. The Cowboys do it this way, the Cowboys have the best practice facility, the Cowboys, the Cowboys. You know what I mean."

And now, Danny White knows. To him, the Bears were the ultimate pain in the neck. It was 10–0 when Otis Wilson smothered him once. Gary Hogeboom replaced White, found Wilson in his face, fired a scoring spiral to Richardson, got booed, got replaced by White, who got smothered by Wilson again. Now, White lay horizontal on the turf, and they brought a golf cart in to haul the vanquished quarterback away. White arose by himself, and the Bears let the ersatz ambulance escape without stripping it. After all, there's a limit. Isn't there?

"I wasn't trying to hurt him," said Wilson, who was merely possessed. "I just saw a pile, and I thought I'd help me to some of the pile. America's Team? Yeah, we could be America's Team. We're tough. America's tough. If President Reagan can't agree with the Russians in Geneva, maybe they'll send us over there."

So, then, it's not a closed case. This melting pot of a juggernaut is sure it wants to go to the Super Bowl, it's just not quite sure what it wants to be called when it gets there. This fun-loving aggregation that Payton says belongs in *One Flew over the Cuckoo's Nest* is having second thoughts about its identity, its place in society.

"What's wrong with the way we do it?" reconsidered Hampton. "What's wrong with busting your tails and enjoying winning?"

Absolutely nothing, of course. Just don't try to get your kids to scrub their elbows anymore. After what happened to America's Team Sunday, that might not wash.

MCMAHON ENJOYS HEAD-CASE IMAGE

JANUARY 13, 1986

When Jim McMahon debuted at Bears' headquarters in the spring of 1982, when he emerged from that limo wearing shades so as not to be affected by any sunlight reflecting off his close friend, the beer can, immediately those great NFL thinkers wondered what went on inside this man's head.

Now, what goes around it is their latest problem.

"ROZELLE."

So screamed the sweatband that Jim McMahon wore Sunday, the day the Bears squashed Los Angeles' Rams 24–0 at Soldier Field, the day this precocious draftee by way of Brigham Young University led the Chicago Grabowskis to Super Bowl XX in New Orleans against the New England O'Reillys.

"I'm ready for Bourbon Street," warned McMahon, "but I'm not sure Bourbon Street is ready for me."

Of course, we have come to be ready for most anything from the quarterback who always operates off an unbalanced formation. So, you knew he would not take it with hands folded, this $5,000 fine invoked by league enforcers, this ivory-tower reprimand for his supplying some free advertising to one of his many accounts last week, when the Bears were doing a number on the New York Giants.

"I've been with Adidas for years," McMahon said. "And I'd worn their headband all season. I'd been warned about it, but what the heck. We gotta worry about nitpicking stuff like labels? I guess the networks don't like us giving publicity to these companies. So, the league hits me for five grand, and I figure, I'll give Pete some pub. Maybe he needs it."

Give a felt tip marker to a Jim McMahon with a few idle

moments before game time and what have you? "ROZELLE."
A jab at NFL commissioner Pete Rozelle is what. McMahon,
who also dresses to his own drummer, thought such a touché
toward the Establishment might be fitting and proper. McMahon couldn't wait to unveil his creation, which is why he doffed
helmet with glee after all three scoring drives he choreo-
graphed.

"As soon as I saw him pulling out the crayons in the locker
room, I knew Jim was ready for this one," said Keith Van
Horne. "It's a good thing the commissioner doesn't have a
shorter name, because there might have been room for another
word up there, maybe a verb. And it's also good that Jim didn't
find the picture of Rozelle he was looking for. He had some
plans for that, too."

Rozelle, a press box observer, accepted the tweak like a good
sport, which you would be, too, if TV ratings were up 22 percent. "A great gag," said Rozelle, who regretted only that he
couldn't get a shoe line out in time to coincide with McMahon's
improvisation. Michael McCaskey, another figure of authority,
was a study in controlled amusement.

"Why didn't he have the McCaskeys written out?" asked the
Bears' president. "Or Halas. That would have been a nice
touch. What will Jim think of now? With his fertile imagination,
there's no telling what he could come up with in the next couple
weeks. 'This Space For Rent'?"

McMahon, an unselfish sort, shared his genius with a play-
mate, Walter Payton.

"Soon as he saw me making up one for myself, he asked me
to make him one, too, so we both wore them," McMahon said.
"What's the big deal? We all wear different shoes, different
gloves. Why do they worry about this chicken stuff? They're
trying to take all the fun out of the game."

And, leadership qualities aside for a moment, that is what
Jim McMahon has meant to the Bears. From that first day in
1982, when he emerged from the limo.

"I like to think I helped bring their personalities out," he
said, shaving now, away from the chaos. "When I first came
here, I could see maybe that some of the guys were a little tight,
a little afraid to let themselves go. But, there's no reason why
you can't be a little crazy, be yourself, and still play good football."

On a brutal afternoon for quarterbacks, what with gusts giving way to swirls bowing to occasional periods of stillness, McMahon was the difference. His fellow Bears thought so, and Rams' coach John Robinson seconded the notion. Meanwhile, Jerry Vainisi, the Bears' general manager who handles labor negotiations, was beaming over in a corner of the clubhouse.

"We redid Jim's contract a couple years ago. He was an exception," Vainisi said. "We looked at him as the first real quarterback this team has had since Sid Luckman. Jim McMahon, we could build around. He's the future."

The future was now when McMahon came out firing spiral darts on Sunday, to Emery Moorehead, to Willie Gault, before the Rams had their horns on straight. When coverage dictated, when an alley opened, McMahon rambled, as he did for a 16-yard touchdown, the Bears' first. When he was delivered a play he didn't like, McMahon changed up in the huddle, as he did on a bullet while sprinting left to Gault for a 22-yard touchdown, the Bears' second.

No automaton he, McMahon found causes to celebrate, such as when he jumped in place, whipping the 63,522 customers to a standing ovation. No shrinking violet he, McMahon threw the football at Doug Reed, one of a few overzealous Rams, after a late hit.

"Dude kneed me in the back," McMahon said. "That's why I've got the ice pack. They tell you if you slide feet first instead of head first that doesn't happen. So, I change and start sliding feet first, and I still get nailed. Why don't they worry about that instead of having some guy from the NFL up there checking for logos?

"My [left] wrist, I don't know where I hurt that. Smithsonian. This body's going right to the Smithsonian. I need rest, because I probably wouldn't be able to practice this week, and that means he [coach Mike Ditka] wouldn't let me play the next game. But, if you think I look bad now, wait'll you see me on *Good Morning America* tomorrow morning. There'll be no sleep tonight. I'll be wearing the ice pack tomorrow, but not on my back. It's party time, Chicago style."

McMahon, of course, is less a nightcrawler in real life than he is general of a splendid football team. He gets knocked for being himself, for sometimes brushing aside folk with notebooks and TV tapes to fill. But, the challenge and the joy of his existence are to play and to succeed. The rest can wait. The rest can wait forever, in fact.

While the Rams can finish the first half of an NFL championship like headless horsemen, in a slapstick drill that left them with one timeout but no points, the Bears rely on an impregnable defense that can catch a breath without fearing that the offense will fail to complement. McMahon, in charge, does more than draw funny signs.

"I'm happy for the guys who've been around here for years, going through the tough times," he said. "What I had today that the other guy (Dieter Brock) didn't have was protection. I wouldn't have wanted to be in his shoes. Our guys were all over him. They're great. This is why we've worked our butts off. To get this far. And 17–2 won't make it for us. Definitely. We got to win the big one before we're finished. Been a long time for this team."

Where, McMahon was asked, was he in 1963, when the Bears last won an NFL title?

"I don't know," he said. "Probably throwing rocks at somebody."

Would he relax for a couple of days?

"After tonight," he said, "I'll have to."

Would he relax after the Super Bowl?

"They tell me I've got to go to the Pro Bowl in Hawaii because (Joe) Montana's hurt," he said. "Maybe I can sneak in a round of golf out there. I wonder if the NFL will mind if I have a logo on my shirt. Shower. I got to have a shower."

And with that, McMahon was gone. But, some distance away, Vainisi was observing the scene.

"He is a card, Jimmy," he said. "I'll tell you what else he is, too. A winner."

PATRIOTS ARE CRAZY, TOO!

JANUARY 21, 1986

NEW ORLEANS—Billy Sullivan, team president, used to be a sportswriter. We mention that at the top of the show so you might understand better why these New England Patriots don't think of anything as very strange anymore, not even Jim McMahon.

"I wasn't there long, but I was there long enough to know they were, uh, different," Steve McMichael was saying Monday night as the Bears arrived, unsure now of their status as the only supernatural team in Super Bowl XX. The Pats are closing fast, by way of the Twilight Zone.

Really now, does Dick Butkus biting an opponent's ear hold a candle to the tale of Bob Gladieux, a Notre Dame grad who was cut by New England, then repaired to a stadium lounge before the game for a cocktail or three? And then he was paged on the loudspeaker system? And then he was put back on the active roster, because of an emergency, to return the opening kickoff? And the Bears think they own football history?

Have the Bears ever had a home game postponed by a hurricane, or a home game almost burned out? Have the Bears ever scheduled a home game in Alabama? Have the Bears ever won a game because of a snowplow? Fired a winning coach at midseason? A winning coach before the playoffs? And the Bears have the gall to call William Perry a phenomenon?

The folks in Beantown thought they'd seen it all back in the early '70s, when Steve Kiner showed up for practice driving a bus, trailed by a squadron of police cars. He had blown through every toll booth on the Massachusetts Turnpike. But then the folks in Beantown saw what happened early this month at Los Angeles, when the Patriots' general manager slugged it out with Howie Long and Matt Millen, a pair of rather estimable Raiders.

It didn't make sense, until you realized that the Patriots' GM is Pat Sullivan, son of sportswriter. Then, you could put the pieces together. What did it matter that Kathleen, daughter of sportswriter and sister of Pat, is married to Joseph Alioto, the lawyer for Al Davis, who owns the Raiders, whom the Sullivans detest? Well, most of the Sullivans, anyway. Family squabble? These things happen, especially to this franchise.

This franchise was hatched in 1960, the eighth and last in the original American Football League. Billy Sullivan wanted an NFL team but couldn't get one, and New England wasn't sure about the alternative. Thanks to years of television exposure, the region was loyal to the New York Giants. Sullivan never gave up. For his No. 1 draft choice, he went right to a college football factory. Ron Burton, running back, Northwestern.

The rest, as they say, is pretty hilarious history. Homes for the Patriots have been Boston University Field, Harvard Stadium, Boston College's Alumni Stadium, and Fenway Park, until Schaefer Stadium was built in Foxboro, Massachusetts. Later, it was rededicated as Sullivan Stadium. Before all of this happened, the Red Sox kicked the Patriots out of Fenway all the way to Birmingham, Alabama, where Joe Namath starred in college. He starred again in a Patriots' home game, beating them 47–31 with the New York Jets, much to the delight of the crowd.

The Patriots who lost the 1963 AFL title game 51–10 at San Diego were from Boston. The Patriots who transferred to Schaefer-Sullivan Stadium were from New England. Somewhere in between there, somebody decided they should be the Bay State Patriots. But that movement lasted only for hours, until somebody else figured out how newspaper headline writers might react when forced to abbreviate. Whereupon it was concluded that "NE Patriots" provided a better solution.

The Patriots were almost abbreviated by natural disaster one day when they were still playing at Boston College. A customer dropped a cigarette butt on a pole vaulting pit beneath the stands, and the foam landing pads raged rapidly into a furnace. While the fire was extinguished, fans were asked to move toward the field. It was not considered a mass evacuation job.

Don Shula, Miami coach, felt the effect of Yankee ingenuity in 1982 when his Dolphins were struggling through a scoreless game, conducted under blizzard conditions. The Pats lined up for a field goal, but not before a maintenance worker cleared the loveliest dry spot for John Smith. The kick was good. New England 3, Miami 0, final. Shula went bananas.

Before the Patriots were swallowed in a merger by the NFL, they were somewhat cost-conscious. They once had this pre-game agreement with a hotel in Buffalo. If players could lie down for a while in rooms without disrupting the beds, there would be no charge. Whereupon the coach, Mike Holovak, instituted one of pro football's rarest fines ever: $15 for messing up the sheets.

In time, Chuck Fairbanks was hired to fix a different type of mess, but being a slippery sort, he created his own chaos. Before the last game of a successful regular season, he announced he was leaving to take a job at the University of Colorado. Billy Sullivan dismissed him forthwith, the Dolphins whipped the Patriots, Fairbanks was reinstated for a playoff game, the Oilers whipped the Patriots, and Fairbanks bolted. That was 1978.

After the Patriots had spent three years under the aegis of Ron Erhardt, Ron Meyer took over, only to be canned in 1984 despite a 5–3 record. Reason: He tried to can defensive coordinator Rod Rust. Raymond Berry became head coach, which was predictable because he was making hats for a living when he got the call. In his first full season as head coach, Berry has the Patriots in the Super Bowl.

Doesn't figure? Try this. The Patriots, $10\frac{1}{2}$-point underdogs for Super Bowl XX, have covered the spread for 14 straight weeks. If you had bet $100 on them beating Buffalo October 13 and let it ride, you'd be closing in on $4 million. That's even more than Chuck Sullivan is said to have lost while promoting Michael Jackson's 1984 Victory Tour, which isn't easy to do.

Chuck Sullivan is another son of Billy, team president, former sportswriter. Are we starting to make some sense?

THEY COME TO PRAISE SIMMS

JANUARY 11, 1987

EAST RUTHERFORD, NEW JERSEY—Even on a team so basic and unaffected as the New York Giants, a quarterback cannot hide, although Phil Simms might have thought about giving it a try.

"A few years ago, when the rest of the league was laughing at us," recalled Harry Carson, the veteran linebacker and defensive captain, "they'd introduce Phil and he'd be booed. By the time we all took the field, the fans would be throwing eggs, golf balls, and oranges."

Should the Giants reward their legions of opinionated and long-deprived followers with a victory over the Washington Redskins in Sunday's NFC championship game, a change in attitude is likely. Eggs, golf balls, and oranges still might be hurled from the stands, because litterbugs in these parts don't necessarily watch the scoreboard. Besides, there is no real grass to destroy, or second base to steal, and the gendarmes undoubtedly will surround the goal posts. No more Shea Stadium at Giants Stadium.

But, should the Giants advance to Super Bowl XXI, which would be their first trip to an NFL title game since 1963, the brunt of new-found affection is likely to be felt primarily by Simms, a quarterback who has waited eight years for some polite applause. Since he was drafted out of Morehead State, of all places, the folks who still cling to the memory of Charlie Conerly handing the job off to Y.A. Tittle have been in Simms' face more regularly than those headhunters in foreign jerseys. When does a new attitude come with the new territory?

"As long as I'm playing quarterback for the Giants, I'll have critics," says Simms. "It makes good press, though, and I understand that. That's okay. If that's the price I have to pay to play here, that's okay too.

78

"When I'm playing, I don't hear the booing. Coming off the field, though, or in the parking lot before and after a game, maybe I hear what people say. They can be very mean. I've been called a lousy so-and-so. I've been called everything.

"I've heard it so many times here. What can I do? What do you want me to do? All fans are fickle. They're all coaches. I've sat in the stands at other pro games here. The Knicks, the Yankees. You hear the same thing. When I go, I go to enjoy. I play, so I think I have a different perspective. I just marvel at how good these athletes are at what they do."

Bill Parcells, the Giants' blue-collar coach, had bucked the trend of indicting Simms, although even he detected a tentative streak in his quarterback earlier this season. The wolves kept pointing to Simms' awkward record, statistics that showed more interceptions than touchdown throws, and it was as though the guy with the slight twang was calling signals with trepidation instead of confidence.

"I told Phil," recalled Parcells, " 'I think you're a great quarterback. It doesn't matter what anyone thinks of you except me and your teammates. You got to be what you are by being daring and fearless. So let's go. Be yourself.' "

Simms, in need of friendly advice from someone other than his wife, promptly guided his team through a siege of difficult games. At Minneapolis in mid-November came what is still referred to as "The Pass." New York seemed whipped when Simms connected with Bobby Johnson for a first down on fourth-and-17. Raul Allegre kicked a field goal with 12 seconds left for a 22–20 conquest of the Vikings, and the Giants will tell you that game was the one. After that Sunday, they had an inkling it was a Pasadena type of season.

Still, the Denver Broncos were next, and the Giants again were in danger. But, with a third-and-21 problem inside two minutes, Simms found Johnson for 24 yards, then Phil Mc-Conkey for 46. Allegre's field goal soon broke a tie, and New York prevailed 19–16.

At San Francisco Monday night, December 1, Simms was spectacular. The Giants were behind 17–0 at halftime, after which he completed eight of nine for 167 yards and two touchdowns toward a 21–17 triumph. Then, it was cross-country to Washington, six days later, and Simms threw three crucial third-down passes that led to three touchdowns, two on passes.

During that meat portion of the Giants' schedule—four games against foes with winning records—Simms was 78 of 125, a 62 percent clip, with six touchdowns and 1,111 yards.

"That's when it began for us, with the game in Minnesota," said Parcells. "And that's when Phil was at his best. One thing I really like about Phil is, the better he gets, the harder he works at it. Last week, we ended practice at 2:30 in the afternoon. I went into the weight room at 4:15 p.m. and he's still in there working out. He's tough, tough as they come. He took a couple of vicious shots Sunday, and still hung in there."

Sunday was last Sunday, when the Giants' defense swarmed the San Francisco 49ers. That's still the pride of this New York team, defense. But Simms was brilliant, though not untouched, in that 49–3 rout. As Parcells recounted, a couple of touchdowns occurred with Simms on horizontal hold, and one he had to be told about.

"Phil came to the sidelines and asked what happened," said nose tackle Jim Burt. "He was hit so hard, he didn't know where he was for a while. We got the smelling salts out."

Simms' grooming has been a gradual, uneven process. For four of his first five seasons, he started but did not finish. Two shoulder separations, a broken thumb, torn knee ligaments. In 1984, Simms had to wrest the job from Scott Brunner. Last year, he opened at quarterback for the NFC in the Pro Bowl and was the game's most valuable player, but the Giants didn't get past Chicago. This year, though Simms is 4–0 against Pro Bowl quarterbacks, he's not headed for Hawaii. Pasadena perhaps, and that will do.

"I'm not a great player," said Simms, who will make his 54th straight start Sunday, the longest string among current NFL quarterbacks. "There's not a lot of those in the league, but when you get a lot around you, it makes it easier to stay around. We've gotten better, and I've helped, and the important thing, as Bill keeps saying, is that we win. It doesn't matter how we win. We win.

"They say it's supposed to be windy Sunday. That doesn't worry me. It's for all the marbles. That doesn't worry me, either. I've been in big ballgames before. If we win, maybe people will be talking more about the Giants in a positive sense. Me, I don't worry about what they say. Look at Joe Namath. He caught all kinds of hell when he played. As much as you can catch. If that's all you have to put up with, that's not bad.

"We had some injuries to our receivers [notably Lionel Manuel] earlier this year. For two weeks, we didn't throw a lot, and people act like we didn't throw all season. They want to know what's happened to the passing game. Well, the first four games, we threw almost 160 passes and people griped. They wanted to know what happened to the running game. When we stopped throwing, they started complaining. When it goes the other way, they complained.

"I don't go out in practice and worry about my job. I'm loose. I've thrown so many interceptions [22 this season] that it's lost its luster. Now, aggressive. It's an up-and-down thing. If we get ahead, we're going to run more. If we get behind, we're going to throw more. It's not that complicated."

Neither is dissecting the Giants' climb. Joe Morris is a splendid running back, Mark Bavaro is the quintessential tight end, and linebacker Lawrence Taylor is the fulcrum of a punishing defense. Yet, as Bear loyalists discovered, a quarterback is necessary, whether he be outrageous or just plain old straight-laced Phil Simms.

"If Chicago had him," concludes Burt, "they'd be going to the Super Bowl."

A GIANT
CELEBRATION

JANUARY 12, 1987

EAST RUTHERFORD, NEW JERSEY—He showed up six years ago as a free agent nobody wanted and wound up Sunday in the stands, with family and friends. Jim Burt figured that was the only proper way to complete his joyride, though these New York Giants aren't done traveling just yet.

About a half-minute remained in their 17–0 conquest of the Washington Redskins when Burt realized he couldn't do the moment justice by just hanging around, hands on hips. The NFC championship was secure, and Super Bowl XXI was next, dreamy stuff for a nose tackle who almost cashed it in a few years ago because of a herniated disc.

"That was '83, the same season we were 3–12–1," recalled Burt. "On a day like today, you think of those things."

So he watched the customary ritual, Harry Carson dumping a vat of Gatorade over coach Bill Parcells, but Burt wanted more. So he latched onto a tub of water and spilled it on Carson, but that wasn't enough, either. So Burt ambled toward the 12-foot wall behind the Giants' bench and sprinkled a few fans, who hadn't felt this good in a long time, either. It might have ended there, this bit of spontaneous combustion, except that Burt now let his eyes wander.

"I saw my wife, Colleen," he said. "She sits right behind us, up a few rows, and she had left her seat and come on down to get closer. I don't mind telling you, I'm a miserable guy to live with during the season, especially the day of a game. She puts up with a lot. Too much. I looked at her, and how happy she was, and, what the heck. I just wanted to be with her and give her a big hug."

So Jim Burt, all 260 pounds of him, pads and helmet in tow, scaled that barrier and joined the fun. It's been a sporting custom in this region for fans to invite themselves onto playing fields whenever a big game is won, but Giants' rooters, like the Giants themselves, are a mite more conservative. Besides, Burt had a better idea. He'd just go right up there among them and check the pulse rates himself.

"They've been through a lot, these fans, just like my wife," said Burt. "I wanted them to know how I felt, because I'm like a fan too. I grew up in Buffalo, watching the Bills suffer, just like these fans have suffered with us. I just wanted to say thanks to these fans, and, as it turned out, they wanted to say thanks to me. They were great. We exchanged high-fives, and they were yelling, and then I said to my wife, 'Take care, because I gotta go. I'll see you later.' "

And then Burt came back down to earth, for a while, anyway. All by himself, he danced and whirled toward the locker room, a tough hombre overcome by exhilaration. For three hours, gusts had straightened out flags, knocked down punts and caused awkward gyrations in forward passes. Now it seemed that the wind also had swept up Burt, like a piece of confetti. Yet, 10 minutes after he spun out of control, Burt was back at his stall and back at work.

"It's pretty subdued in here," he said. "But that's just the way we are. There are no selfish guys on this club, no jerks, just players who put the team first. It starts with Bill. You have no idea what the coach has going with us, the way we respect him, the way we still regard him as a friend. We aren't interested in a lot of media attention, a lot of publicity, we're just interested in winning.

"No videos here. No videos for us. We must have had a dozen offers to do a video, and we'd have each been guaranteed $10,000. But we turned 'em all down, and if we win the Super Bowl, we'll probably still turn them down. We aren't arrogant, we don't like to rub anything in anybody's face. I'm not saying what the Bears did last year was wrong. I'm not saying the way we do it is right. I'm just saying that's them, and this is us, and we aren't going to change."

Certainly, there weren't many alterations in the Giants' manner or manners Sunday. They destroyed, then praised. They won the toss, took the wind and took their chances.

"Critical," said Burt. "A critical decision, and a great coaching decision by Bill. Our defense, I don't know whether it's as good as the Bears' was last year, or this year, but it's good. It had to be good. Washington is a great football team. Even in the fourth quarter, I was telling guys on our sideline that the Redskins weren't going to give up. They never do."

But the Redskins couldn't cope. They couldn't run on New York, even with an extra blocker, guard Raleigh McKenzie, in their backfield. They couldn't get there through the air, either, though quarterback Jay Schroeder tried 50 times. They couldn't wait for critical turnovers, because Doug Flutie was last week. They couldn't make it on third down, when they were 0-for-14. They couldn't hold onto the ball, they couldn't move the ball, they exited stage left quietly, with their quarterback dazed.

"Schroeder hit his head on the turf near the end, I think," said Burt. "He was hurting, but there's no way he was going to come out of there. He's a great one. So's Joe Montana, and we roughed him up last week. We're tough on quarterbacks, because we're aggressive. And we've got another great one in two weeks. John Elway. We played Denver before this year and beat them, but he can tire you out. I just hope we can finish this job off. If we do, I'd like to fly all the way back here from Pasadena to be in the parade. Even though I have to go on to Hawaii."

Burt has to go to Hawaii because he was voted to the NFC Pro Bowl team, a first for this free agent nobody wanted. Well, almost nobody. As Burt spoke, Parcells burrowed through the masses, and they hugged.

"My man," said Burt.

"My man," said the coach.

A shirt arrived.

"NFC Champs," related Burt. "It says 'NFC Champs.' I'm going to put this sucker on right now."

It will wear well.

'OTHER' QB OUTGUNS ELWAY

JANUARY 27, 1987

PASADENA, CALIFORNIA—Phil Simms had to travel almost 3,000 miles to hear a nice round of applause from Giants' fans, a relatively painless experience considering those eight grim years that came before.

Why, even during this week of calculated hype preparatory to Super Bowl XXI, it was as though there were only one quarterback in town, one guy who could throw a spiral, one blond who might drop a bombshell in the Rose Bowl. John Elway got everybody's vote, including his counterpart's.

"It's understandable," Simms was saying. "When you think of the Denver Broncos, you think of Elway. When you think of the New York Giants, you don't think of me."

But after Sunday's wondrous effort by the man with the pasty complexion and the buttoned-down verse, there shall be a total rethinking around the NFL on what it takes to dethrone the Giants, who became world champions on more than defense alone. Their 39–20 conquest of the AFC's emissary to Pete Rozelle's annual picnic disproved that sickly chant about how the Giants had to win despite Phil Simms, instead of behind him.

Boo this, New Jersey. Simms completed 22 of 25 passes for 268 yards and three touchdowns, thereby annexing most valuable player honors for this rout, case closed. Like the band, the Broncos did not appear after halftime, but much of the vanishing act was caused by Simms, who put in a third quarter that cast a hush throughout Colorado's ski slopes.

"I felt we could move the ball on them, but not in my wildest dreams did I expect this," said Simms. "I just felt so confident, so good today. The guys will tell you. I told them before, during the warm-up, 'I got it going today.' It was like when you're playing golf and you know every putt's going in. Even the three incompletions, I felt good. I wouldn't even want to take those back."

And his tenure as a Giant—drafted from Morehead State in 1979, benched on occasion, injured frequently, criticized incessantly—what of that? Did this one afternoon justify all the scars, all the scowls, all the evenings driving home listening to talk shows talking bad about you?

"Makes it all worthwhile," said Simms, sipping from a can of diet soda, his sweatshirt drenched. "Makes it all worthwhile."

"Are you underrated?" someone asked.

"What do you think?" replied Simms, smiling.

"Yeah," said the interrogator.

"Well, I do, too," Simms concluded. "Heck, I'm a hell of a quarterback. Even I can't deny that now."

That's about as far Simms would go in taunting his doubters. Truth is, to all but a few of the Giants' inner sanctum, Simms didn't rate, period. He was forever living down his reputation as a rally-killer, the bloke who threw the wrong ball at the wrong time.

Even this year, the absolute best in Giants' history, Simms posted curious numbers: 22 interceptions and 21 touchdowns. He was, then, no match for Elway, the charismatic sort who could pull off an upset.

But New York coach Bill Parcells, who never left Simms' side, gave the back of his hand to the myth early in the third quarter. Denver was still up by 10–9, though it should have been more, when the Giants found themselves in an uncomfortable spot, fourth and 1 at their 46. With that defense, the best at least this side of Chicago, the situation screamed for a punt. But New York shifted from convention, and Jeff Rutledge, Simms' understudy, plunged for two yards and the first down.

What better way for Bill Parcells to tell a nation how he felt about Phil Simms?

"I thank the coaches for having the guts to call that," said Simms, who finished the 63-yard drive on the ninth play, a scoring bullet to Mark Bavaro, who only catches everything. The Giants led 16–10, and Simms was feeling rather feisty. In his own gritty manner, he had taken it upon himself to squash this ugly rumor that the Giants' best offense was a handoff.

"I watched the films of our first game against them," said Simms, alluding to New York's regular-season 19–16 triumph over Denver. "I don't want to knock them, I'm not taking away anything from the Broncos, but they just acted as though they could bump us on the line, then play us one-on-one."

The Giants thoroughly scrambled that equation Sunday, even when they got away from basics. It was 19–10 when Simms worked a flea-flicker with Phil McConkey for 44 yards to the Denver 1.

"When we pulled that off," said Simms, "I thought we had it won. I don't know what it was this week. I was so relaxed. I don't know whether I talked myself into it or not, but I felt great. I thought people thought our receivers couldn't be part of this game, and we had something to prove. We talked about it all week. We were going to come out running, and we were going to see if they could cover us. The receivers, everything, the game plan, was just terrific.

"In the first half, we moved it well most of the time, but we had a couple of breakdowns. Nothing was said at halftime except stay with the same stuff. And we just got it going. When you get it going, it's just hard to stop. It was a lot like that third quarter in San Francisco, when we came back from 17–0 to win. You go into the huddle, you know you're going to make the right call. You throw a ball, you know it's going to be there."

"How would you describe your performance today?" someone asked. "Perfect?"

"As close to it as you can get, I guess," said Simms.

"What does it all mean?" requested another truth-seeker.

"Means I won't have to hear about them '63 Giants anymore," said Simms, who paused for a moment. From outside the Rose Bowl, he could detect New York fans yelling for him at last, instead of at him.

DADDY, WHY DON'T THEY PLAY?

SEPTEMBER 21, 1987

"Daddy, who are these guys playing football on TV? Where's Walter Payton and Wilber Marshall and Steve McMichael and Dan Hampton?"

"They're on strike, son. The real Bears are on strike. Those players on TV took the place of the real Bears until the strike is over."

"What's a strike, Daddy?"

"That's when people who work for somebody stop working because they're unhappy with the people they're working for."

"But Daddy, I watched TV last night and the real Bears and a lot of other real football players said they were unhappy about not playing. None of them said they were unhappy about playing. So why are they not playing if they say they all want to play?"

"Well, that's a good question. You see, the players have a leader, Gene Upshaw, and the owners have a leader, Jack Donlan, and they sort of run the strike because the players and owners are too busy with other things."

"Did the strike happen all of a sudden, Daddy? I saw Upshaw on TV Monday night from one city and Donlan from another city. Did the strike happen after they went on TV?"

"Well, not really. The strike has been a possibility for a long time. Actually, since the last strike in 1982."

"Gee, you mean they did a strike then, too? How come if both the players and the owners say it was so dumb then, they're doing it again? Are they still dumb, or are they just too busy with other things to get smart?"

"Son, you ask some very good questions, and I don't have the answers for all of them, except that there's a lot of money at stake here. That's why they're having these games, like the one you're watching there."

"But it's not a real game if it doesn't have real players, is it? And if the players and owners are too busy with other things, what could be more important than having real games? Daddy, who are these players if they aren't real players?"

"Well, some of them are players who couldn't make the Bears and some are players who played in other leagues, like the United States Football League and the Arena Football League."

"But didn't the people from the National Football League once say they had the best league in the world? How can the NFL say that one day and then use players from a league it said was a joke and expect fans to come and watch? If our doctor goes on strike, do we go see a fake doctor?"

"No, not a chance, son. But these are only games."

"Well, if they're only games, why don't they just play them?"

"Because the real players want to make more money and things like that, even though they make about $230,000 a year."

"How much do you make, Daddy? Did you ever go on strike?"

"No, I have to work because I only make about a fifth of that. I can't afford to strike. Sometimes, the more you make, the more you can afford to be unhappy about not making more. But the real players are unhappy about other things, like free agency."

"What's that?"

"That gives the real player a right to move from Chicago to another city to play if he's unhappy playing here."

"So, now the real Bears go on strike so they can play some-where else, and meanwhile they stay here and don't play at all? That doesn't make much sense. I watched the baseball players on TV the other day and they were all unhappy because of a collusion. What's a collusion?"

"Well, son, that's when owners try to fight free agency by doing something they aren't supposed to do. The baseball play-ers have free agency and are trying to use it to their benefit and the football players are trying to get free agency in the first place. The baseball players have had free agency since 1976."

"Gee, Daddy, that means the real football players are 11

years behind the baseball players. I don't blame them for being unhappy now. But if the baseball players have free agency, why do the football players have to ask Mr. Upshaw to get it for them? And why do they have to strike to get something that they deserve anyway?"

"Son, I can't answer all your questions because you make too much sense."

"Daddy, I don't like this game on TV. Can we go see a college game next Saturday?"

"Well, we can't, son. Your favorite college used to play football, but they got caught doing things like cheating, so they won't be playing games this year. Some of the players there took money for playing football."

"Isn't that why they go to college, to get ready to play pro football? Why shouldn't the college players be paid? And if they aren't being paid to get ready to play pro football, why can't the pro football owners use some of the money they're saving there to pay some of the real football players who are out on strike?"

"Well, that's not the way it works, son. You see, you're supposed to play college football for fun."

"But if they aren't playing games, how can they have any fun? And if the pro football players aren't playing games, how can they make any money? Are the owners having fun or are they making any money?"

"Probably doing both."

"Daddy, is the pro football strike a tragedy? I heard the man on the TV say it's a tragedy."

"I can answer that one, son. No. It's just a small fight between two parts of the entertainment industry. That's all. A tragedy is when someone dies too young or when a child like you goes to bed hungry at night. In fact, just this past week, the president of our country and the president of the Soviet Union, which is our enemy, agreed to decrease the number of missiles in the world. That's a lot more important than football games. That might mean we don't blow each other to bits."

"Daddy, if we can't go watch football, can we go to watch Michael Jordan play?"

"Well, the basketball players are going out on strike, too."

"They're unhappy, too, huh? Well, maybe if none of the players are having any more fun playing, we should forget them like they're forgetting us. Maybe we should go out in the yard and just throw the football around and have some fun ourselves."

"Son, you're wise beyond your years. Turn off that TV, and let's go."

Golf

GRAHAM'S PERFECT ROUND

JUNE 22, 1981

ARDMORE, PENNSYLVANIA—Growing up in Australia, David Graham endured frequent career directives from his demanding father. Knocking a little white ball around the countryside was not included in the list of chosen occupations.

"He wanted me to do something decent and respectable, like being a doctor," Graham recalled. "When I told him I wanted to be a golfer, he said he would never talk to me again. That was 21 years ago. And he hasn't talked to me since. If he walked through the door right now, I probably wouldn't recognize him."

And so it was that on Sunday, Father's Day, David Graham enjoyed the finest day of his golfing life. He not only shot a 3-under-par 67 to win the 81st U.S. Open by three strokes, he did it while being what he always is—decent and respectable. As he patrols the fairways, Graham is dignity in spikes. He congratulates fellow pros on good efforts, acknowledges well-wishers with a gentlemanly wave, and even refuses to smoke, lest it tarnish the image of his sport.

And when his victory over Merion Golf Club's East Course had been completed, Graham could have talked about a lot of things. He could have talked about how he had punished third-round leader George Burns by playing a perfect fourth round. Or about how he had taken his second major championship, the first being the 1979 PGA. Or about how he had added another $55,000 to his near-million-dollar bank account. But he didn't. He was too busy expressing decent and respectable emotions.

"I am not yet a citizen of America, but I can tell you I will never leave here," said the first Australian to win an Open and the first foreigner since England's Tony Jacklin in 1970. "I will be forever grateful for what golf in this country has done for

94

me. Americans have been wonderful to me. The other players on this tour are all class. I come from the other side of the world, but I live the life of an urban cowboy now in Dallas. Boots, cowboy hat, the whole bit. I love every minute of it. I have America to thank for today."

Graham, with two previous 68s and a 70, began Sunday's round three strokes back of Burns. But on the first hole, the 35-year-old Aussie started sending smoke signals. Graham missed his only fairway, but canned a 20-foot birdie putt.

Another birdie on No. 2 brought Graham to within a stroke. The heat was on, and Burns in time would be burned.

Not that he lost the tournament. Graham won it with a 7-under-par 273 by never making a bad shot Sunday. He tied Burns at No. 4, fell one behind again a hole later, then caught his scrambling partner at No. 10. Always, Graham was the picture of discipline, deliberation, and good shotmaking.

"I've never been in better command of myself mentally," said Graham.

Graham seized the lead at No. 14 when he knocked a 7-iron stiff to the pin and went 7-under with a 6-foot birdie putt. He added a 10-foot birdie putt at No. 15, by which time Burns was struggling for second place. A 73 let him tie Bill Rogers at 276. The rest of the field couldn't cope with Graham's precision.

"I'm very happy for David," Jack Nicklaus said after his 72–280 finish. "He is getting better and better at the majors. He's learning how to shut out all the distractions. He's the type now who will get in a position to win and won't blow it. A true champion."

In all respects. When Graham came to the United States a decade ago, he was properly scared. But fellow Australian Bruce Devlin took him in and showed him the way. Graham's first tour triumph was in 1972 at Cleveland. He beat Devlin in a playoff.

"I owe a lot to that man (Devlin), too," said Graham. "He showed me the way. In Australia, you couldn't make a living unless you won tournaments, and even then, you didn't make much of a living. My first win was the Tasmanian Open over there. I won $1,100.

"Bruce encouraged me to come over here. This was where the best golf was played. If it hadn't have been for him, I don't think I would have lasted. That's why I feel I now owe it to a young Australian like Greg Norman to help him in any way I possibly can. It is only right."

Burns, playing the Open with a new putter, new driver, and new confidence, didn't collapse so much as he wavered. Nerves bothered him; so did an incident at the third hole. His first of two putts there was weak, and he heard United States Golf Association official Harry Easterly say as much.

Burns called Easterly an appropriate unprintable. Later, USGA officials issued an apology as flimsy as Burns' putt. They said it was a misunderstanding. Often it is easy to misunderstand the USGA, some of whose ruling blowhards were born with starch in their shirts.

"It was lousy sportsmanship on Easterly's part," fumed Burns. "I hate to tell you this, but this is just another tour event. The ones the PGA sponsor are run just as well, or better. I don't want to take anything away from David, though. He played brilliantly."

Graham thought the turning point was No. 10, when Burns perspired out of a poorly raked trap to par a hole that might have been birdied. But, really, the Open turned on Graham's consistency.

"You can't expect to win any tournament, because you're not going to win as often as you lose," said Graham. "For me, the important thing is being in contention in any tournament. Here, I was right there for all four rounds. That's exciting. The PGA I won in a playoff; I was conscious of being a gracious loser if I lost. Today, same thing.

"Where's all that champagne?"

Someone brought David Graham a glass, and he raised it.

"I toast to my.... everybody's father on Father's Day," he said.

TIGHT-FITTING HERO

APRIL 12, 1982

AUGUSTA, GEORGIA—Craig Stadler won the 46th Masters Golf Tournament Sunday. Make it a green jacket, extra large. It was almost a straitjacket, extra tight.

In the exalted history of Aprils along Magnolia Lane, it has happened too often to call it coincidence. Some of the best players who ever put on spikes have had their swings on cruise control only to have this Godzilla of a course named Augusta National chew them up and spit them out.

But this Easter, which had to be the prettiest afternoon in creation, Craig Stadler almost took the prevailing gag rule a bit too seriously. Much of the day, he had his first major professional title tucked in his hip pocket, which sags somewhere below his third stomach.

He led the Masters by six strokes with seven holes to go, and nobody was going to catch him.

Except Augusta National, and it did. Stadler, "The Walrus," bogeyed four of those last seven holes. The man who looked like a champion from tee to green, and in between, suddenly looked like your neighbor from South Succotash trying to break 100 on the Fourth of July.

What's worse, Stadler looked like the exploding scoreboard whose temper had bested him before. Like three years ago here, when he tied for the lead on the final round, only to unravel with bogeys on the 7th and 9th holes, a double bogey on the 10th, and bogeys again on the 11th and 12th. Before his drive at No. 13, Stadler ducked behind the azaleas and wept.

Sunday, it was wife Sue doing the crying on what was shaping up as the all-time Masters' death watch. She hid behind trees along the fairway, whispering "Oh, God," and removing herself totally from the premises whenever her hubby challenged Augusta National's porcelain greens.

Stadler had been fortunate when his approach on No. 15 careened out of a gully, unlucky when a sand shot on No. 16 stretched out farther than the dollar, and downright star-crossed when a splendid drive on No. 17 nestled in a divot that had not been replaced.

Still, after making par-bogey-par on those three, all Stadler needed was par on No. 18 for $64,000, a green jacket and immortality.

He landed 24 feet from the pin, and two putts would do it. But on the first, Stadler stiffly tapped the ball, which came up eight feet shy. The second he also missed. Shades of 1979, when, after he had drained his eyes on those azaleas, Stadler witnessed partner Ed Sneed's egregious fluff under similar circumstances.

"Now," Stadler said, "I know how Ed felt."

But Ed Sneed never really will know, because Craig Stadler beat Dan Pohl on the first playoff hole Sunday. For Stadler, it was a triumph over himself, and Godzilla. For all us bindlestiffs from South Succotash, it was a triumph, too, because Craig Stadler is not your basic matinee idol. Bless him.

Stadler, you see, has succeeded by being all substance, not style. Too many of today's athletes are pretty. The only thing pretty about Stadler is that he's pretty fat.

The joke on the tour is that Stadler adheres to a light diet. That is, whenever it's light out, he eats. You won't find him at the Nautilus center, but you might try 31 Flavors.

"I lost 40 pounds a few years ago and got down to 190," he says. "But I just wasn't comfortable. So I put some of it back on. In fact, I put a lot of it back on."

It is said that because he selects his wardrobe from the Yellow Pages instead of *Gentlemen's Quarterly*, he was not selected for the Walker Cup team several years ago. Naturally, Stadler can't prove it. But he can't deny that in the 1975 British Amateur, his caddy quit in mid-round, complaining that it wasn't his bloody job to pick up the bloody clubs that this bloody American butterball was throwing all over the bloody course.

"There are times when I'm not much fun to be around," admits Stadler.

Most of all, the business firms that shower tour players with everything from free head covers to free shower heads, haven't called him. The blond bombshells in beltless pants have famous names on their golfbags: Spalding, Ram, Wilson, MacGregor.

Until recently, the inscription on Stadler's bag was that of a bar and grill he used to patronize back home in San Diego. He hasn't even been asked to endorse Almond Joy. Alligators have pictures of Craig Stadler on their shirts.

"I prefer to do my own thing," says Stadler. He attended USC, but the Statue of Liberty had more of a California image than Stadler does.

"You don't like reading all the time that your husband is a fat slob," says Sue. "But he handles it pretty well. He still gets mad on the course, but he doesn't get mad at home anymore."

Now, Craig Stadler doesn't have to be mad again. After four years as a vagabond, he won four tournaments starting with the 1980 Bob Hope. Then came the Greater Greensboro Open, Kemper and Tucson last January.

But nothing will match what happened to him this week at Augusta National. He's not just the tour's leading money winner. At least until the next major—the U.S. Open in June— he's golf's leading man, even if he does look like a blowfish after he flubs a putt.

For four days, while everybody was carping about unfair greens and unclear skies, The Walrus was best in class. He started with a first round 75, but at dusk Sunday, he was one of only six players to break par.

They said he didn't have the hook to fit the course, or the putting savvy, or the self-control. Most of all, they said he didn't look the part. Does a Craig Stadler win the noble Masters? Do they serve ham sandwiches at 10 Downing Street?

But Stadler won, and was reminiscent of Jack Nicklaus' first Masters in 1960. The Golden Bear was no oil painting in those days, as Sam Snead noticed.

"Jack Nicklaus?" remarked Snead. "He looks like a couple of pretty good golfers."

Sunday, Craig Stadler, who's still fighting the battle of the bulge, won the war. And the win was as elegant as the winner.

LIVING A FANTASY

JUNE 21, 1982

PEBBLE BEACH, CALIFORNIA—At the time, dusk was approaching, seals were barking, the Pacific waters were buffeting the rocks behind him and Jack Nicklaus was in the scoring tent ahead of him, smiling.

It was not shaping up as a very pleasant Sunday afternoon for Tom Watson, particularly after he had yanked his 2-iron tee shot to the left of the green on the par-3 17th hole that juts out into Carmel Bay.

The ball rested atop deep grass, above the cup, and there wasn't much room to play with. Watson had to be as delicate as a surgeon, and for his scalpel, he chose a sand wedge. He needed to get down in two to save par.

But Tom Watson, denied this prize for 10 years, got down in one, and the reward was justly his. The 1982 U.S. Open champion chipped in for a birdie, then did a victory lap near the dunes of Pebble Beach. Back in the scoring tent, Jack Nicklaus wasn't smiling anymore.

"It was the greatest shot of my life," said Watson. "Certainly the most meaningful. When I was a student at Stanford, Jack was already the best golfer in the world.

"I used to come down here on Saturday and Sunday mornings, fantasizing about playing him. I couldn't ask for a better scenario than this. Playing against Jack Nicklaus, the greatest of all time, on one of the five best courses in the world."

Watson, though playing cautiously, birdied the 18th hole, too, with a 20-foot putt for a final-round 70. So his aggregate of 282, six better than par, was two better than Nicklaus, who closed with a 69—good enough for his fourth second-place finish in the Open, but not quite good enough for a record fifth championship.

But when they talk about the 1982 Open in years to come—

and surely they will, for it was a classic shootout between two masters three groups apart—they will go back to No. 17, where Nicklaus' third Open title was decided a decade ago.

"When I first hit the tee shot, I thought I was in trouble," recalled Watson. "But then, when I got to the ball, I felt better about it. The ball was in heavy grass, but it was sitting up. If it had been buried, I couldn't have gone for the hole.

"As it was, I could get the leading edge of the club under it. I was 16 feet from the cup, with about 10 feet of green to work with, and it broke about a foot and a half to the left. I practice it all the time. For hours and hours.

"My caddie, Bruce Edwards, said to me, 'Now just get it close.' I looked at him and said: 'I'm going for the hole.' As soon as I hit the ball, I said to myself, 'That ball is in.' I looked back at Bruce, and he was choking. The shot of my life."

After one hop, the ball softly glided toward the pin, banking in. It had been struck with such a marvelous touch that had the ball not dropped in the cup, it wouldn't have slid dangerously past. In this case, if it were luck, luck was the residue of design.

For Watson, Sunday meant he could travel a little lighter the rest of his life. He had won 27 tournaments, including the Masters and British Open for majors, and more than $2.8 million, second only to Nicklaus on the career money list. But at 32, with a lot of golf still left in him, the gap-toothed, red-haired, Kansas City, Missouri, native was making like Sam Snead. Great, but no U.S. Open.

Watson had led entering the final round in 1974 at Winged Foot, but shot 79 and came in fifth, five shots behind Hale Irwin. The next year, Watson carded an Open-record 135 for 36 holes at Medinah, but faded to ninth. Two years ago, he tied for third. Last year, he tied for 23rd.

"I wanted this one very badly, almost as badly as my family and friends," Watson said. "I woke up nervous this morning, too, but I read two newspapers—front to back. About the earthquake in El Salvador, about the budget problems. That helped relax me."

At round's start, Watson was tied with playing partner Bill Rogers, but a battery of smoothies also were hunting on this relatively calm, cloudy afternoon. Eleven players were within four shots, Nicklaus was within three, and last year's Open champion, David Graham, was only two swings back.

Gradually, they all fell like autumn leaves. George Burns double-bogeyed No. 1 on his way to an 80. Bruce Devlin double-bogeyed No. 9 on his way to a 74. Bobby Clampett double-bogeyed No. 12 on his way to a 70. And Rogers, after gaining the lead at 5-under on No. 8, skidded to bogeys on three of the next four holes for a 74—286, or a third-place tie with Clampett and Dan Pohl.

Then there were two. Nicklaus, after starting with a bogey, birdied Nos. 3 through 7 to go 5 under and tie Rogers. But Watson, never more than a stroke shy, drained a 22-foot birdie putt on No. 11 and a 35-foot birdie putt from the fringe on No. 14.

Nicklaus moved to 4 under at No. 15 with a 15-foot birdie putt. He parred in. Watson dropped into a deadlock with him at No. 16, when he missed his first fairway of the day, then had to blast out of a bunker. The bogey put him at the 17th tee tied with Nicklaus.

"I tried to put everything else out of my mind at that point," said Watson. "But on the tee shot, I came over top of it. I really think I might have won the tournament Friday. I played bad. I could have shot 76.

"But I did the things Tom Watson does best. I got up and down and shot 72. Still, the one I'll remember is the sand wedge. After that, I'm bound to have a letdown. I guess that's the one everyone will remember."

At the 18th green, Nicklaus approached Watson.

"You s.o.b., you are something," said the Golden Bear, smiling and extending his hand.

Rogers, who had been an eyewitness to The Shot, was still shaking his head.

"You could hit a hundred balls from where Tom hit his and not do what he did," Rogers said.

"Maybe a thousand," said Nicklaus.

WHITE FLAGS FLUTTER

APRIL 12, 1983

AUGUSTA, GEORGIA—If all worldly conflicts were as fierce as Monday's Spanish-American war at the Augusta National Golf Club, we'd have a globe covered by mistletoe instead of missiles.

With apologies to Yogi Berra, this one was over before it was over. All calm and no storm. All talk and no action. All Severiano Ballesteros and no supporting cast. The trouble wasn't finding a winner for the 47th Masters; the trouble was finding a runner-up.

"Us chasing him," mentioned Tom Kite, "was like a Chevrolet chasing a Ferrari."

All week long, the beltless brigade and their galleries had paused under their umbrellas, waiting for the Atlanta Ocean to retreat to its normal boundaries so that the first major tournament of the dimple season could proceed.

At dawn Monday, the leader board was bathed in sunshine, dollar signs, and sweet expectation. The first four players all had won this noble nature walk at least once. What's more, there were 14 men within five swings of the top, most of whom were long on success and short on anonymity.

Alas, it was not worth the wait. Jack Nicklaus, one would think, was not the only golfer in Georgia suffering spasms. Of all the luminaries in the last seven groups, only Ballesteros managed to shoot par or better in the final round.

It was so anticlimactic that the morning's co-leaders—Craig Stadler and Ray Floyd—were putting out on No. 18, a lonesome last twosome, while Ballesteros was being fitted for his second green jacket inside the clubhouse haberdashery. You'll get more tension at a bakery sale.

"The day had all the makings of a super final round," said Tom Watson. "But it just never materialized. You'd have thought it would be a chase. But there was no defense for his offense.

"I felt like I was a fighter who was knocked down twice early in a bout where they were using the three-knockdown rule. I got up, and at one point, I thought it was a two-man chase. Then one of the men tripped and fell."

The bereaved party of whom Watson spoke was none other than himself. He had been the unwilling tortoise to hare Ballesteros on the opening four holes, when the moody Spaniard jetted from five under par to nine under with a delirious assault on a course that was treating everybody else unkindly.

On No. 8, though, Watson halved his deficit to two strokes with an eagle putt of about 45 feet. It energized Watson into thinking he'd resurrected the anticipated shootout from the ashes of an apparent runaway. But Watson should have known better. If his putt hadn't hit the cup, it wasn't about to stop for a while.

The temporary magic in Watson's wand disappeared on No. 9, when he used it thrice toward a bogey, and on No. 11, when he three-putted again. Watson called his double bogey on No. 14 the "nail in the coffin," but sort of changed his mind afterward.

"I made too many mistakes today, most of them putting," said Watson. "Seve broke from the pack, and I just didn't putt well enough—I haven't been putting well at all lately—to catch him. Seve is a lot like Arnold Palmer. Makes enough great shots to make up for his mistakes. He's bold and aggressive."

Though Ballesteros is more conservative than when he won the 1980 Masters, Watson's point is well taken. Ballesteros showed his brass on No. 13, when he coolly bashed a 3-iron some 200 yards toward the green. His ball landed three feet shy of getting wet.

"Lucky," huffed Ballesteros. "Just keep saying I am lucky."

An hour listening to Ballesteros is like watching him play golf for five. He bares all, some of it good, some bad. He says he feels utterly at home in Augusta, then he turns around and says all he ever hears about are his bad shots. One minute, he's Seve with the quick wit; the next minute, he's Seve with the chip on his shoulder.

"Two Masters is like two marriages—the first is always the

best," he says. Then, boom: "Tom Watson says I have a bad back? My back is fine. How's yours?"

Thus, the diversity of his emotions. Part of the Ballesteros mystery is his schedule. Fans enjoy his daring style and engaging grin. But he is only an occasional visitor to America, the mecca of pro golf. Seve picks and chooses eight tournaments a year, preferring to beat up on lesser Europeans while collecting guaranteed appearance fees.

"Why don't I play over here more often?" he says, petulantly. "Ask the Americans how many weeks they play in Japan."

He boasts that he's the highest-paid player in the world, and sometimes acts the part as the best. But if Ballesteros is revered accordingly in his homeland, Yankee tour regulars refuse to pamper him. Lon Hinkle, for one, called him for cheating during a match overseas. At the 1980 U.S. Open, Seve was disqualified for missing his tee time. He can please crowds— and perplex contemporaries.

Still, no less an authority than Nicklaus predicted five years ago that "Ballesteros won't win one Masters jacket, he'll win many." Perhaps Nicklaus realized that Seve's game—distance over direction—is ideally suited for Augusta's expansive fairways and negligible rough. Or perhaps Nicklaus just saw raw talent awaiting a coat of varnish.

Monday, Ballesteros got a coat of green. Nobody questioned his ability. In fact, nobody raised an argument all afternoon.

'I'VE DIED 16 DEATHS IN GOLF'

JANUARY 13, 1984

PALM SPRINGS, CALIFORNIA—On a pro golf tour that sometimes can be too vanilla, the best story might be this guy who swings from the right side, putts from the left side, and knows what life is like on the flip side.

Meet Mac O'Grady, the fittest survivor.

"I am like a mosquito out here among dinosaurs," O'Grady said Thursday at the 25th Bob Hope Desert Classic. "But nobody could be happier than me. Happiness in life is measured by how deep sorrow has cut within you.

"That's why I'm not afraid to cry when I sashay down the 18th fairway. I feel like a Pilgrim walking toward Plymouth Rock. I feel like I've died and gone to heaven. Because, you see, I have. I've died 16 deaths in golf."

Starting in 1971, O'Grady tried 16 times to qualify for the PGA circuit. The previous record, he's been told, was seven. Sponsors bailed out on him, and one official at a qualifying school told him to get lost, to return to his odd jobs as a busboy, dishwasher or night manager of a funeral parlor back home in Los Angeles.

But, Mac O'Grady would hear none of it, partly because he's had seven ear operations, mostly because all he ever wanted to do was be a professional golfer. Finally, in 1982, he earned his card. At age 30, Mac O'Grady was the oldest rookie in the most cutthroat of sports.

"I was at the Florida PGA school in Jacksonville," O'Grady recalled. "The night I made it, I went out and bought 16 baseball bats. One for each time I'd missed. I went and started breaking the bats against a big tree. A psychologist I know says it's good to relieve your frustrations, your anger."

O'Grady has experienced too much of both. There were five brothers in his middle-class Irish family. The other four were handsome, athletic, intelligent. Until they turned to drugs. One died; three are alive but wasting away.

"I was crushed," O'Grady said. "They were my idols. I never took a drink or smoked after that. I've never talked to my father since, either. My mother died because of a brain hemorrhage when I was 15. He got married two weeks later. I couldn't believe it. I was crushed again."

So crushed that he changed his name, from Phil McGleno to Phillip McClelland O'Grady, the latter his mother's maiden name. But, a change in moniker didn't change Mac O'Grady's luck. When he failed his first qualifying test, one man who organized O'Grady's backers pulled the rug out. The money was gone.

"I was naive, I trusted everybody then," O'Grady said. "I wrote a 50-page letter to that guy who blackballed me, Walter Keller. Then I went down to the beach and burned it. I left my anger there, forever. I matured."

O'Grady made new and better friends here in Palm Springs. He also met Fumiko, his wife, a former flight attendant. At first sight on that plane ride in 1978, O'Grady told her he had dreamed he would someday marry a Japanese woman. At first, she thought he was crazy. But, then, she is not alone.

"Hey, I know I've got the reputation as a space cadet, a moon man, out here," O'Grady said. "But the real space cadets on the tour are the guys who have made millions, drink, fool around on their wives and have nothing left to shoot for. When they can't play golf anymore, they'll go off the deep end. They'll die.

"Like I said, I've already died and gone to heaven. Every day is a new day, a wonderful day. I don't take golf that seriously. Whether I ever win a tournament doesn't matter. What matters more is what I've gone through to get here. Adversity. No silver spoons for me."

True to his monologue, O'Grady was full of perspective after struggling to a 72 in Thursday's second round. He earned only $50,379 during 1983. Now, he's already nine strokes back of Jim Simons, whose 69–63–132 leads the five-round tournament. But Mac O'Grady, veteran that he is with depression, can deal with it.

"I'm not as bingo, bango, bongo in the head as you think," he said. "Someday, I want to switch around. I want to play left-handed and putt right-handed. I can play left-handed, as you know. It just means using a different hemisphere of your brain.

"It's simple, really. The right half of your brain controls your left side. The right side also governs your intuition, the left side is your analytical side. Putting left is better for a dominant right eye.

"Why? Because your right eye looks down the line at the hole. But if you putt right-handed with a dominant right eye, you'll line up three balls to the right of the hole."

Well, he told you it was simple. Don't doubt Mac O'Grady because he is a physical fitness, er, nut. He runs at least 35 miles a week, and when time permits, he will ride 100 miles a day on the exercise bike. Maybe it will pay off. Maybe it won't.

"If I win a tournament, it will be a classic underdog story," O'Grady said. "It will be for every guy who's had his nose pressed against the candy store without ever getting in, for every guy who's been pushed around all his life. It will be for every American.

"I've played golf in 45 countries, and that's made me realize there's really only one. We're the only country where you can have an impossible dream, persevere, die 16 times and still walk up a green fairway feeling like a Pilgrim. It is the American way. Freedom at last."

Mac O'Grady's golf bag is red, white, and blue.

THE MASTERS:
Still Graceful

APRIL 12, 1984

AUGUSTA, GEORGIA—Were this the 50th anniversary of any other sporting event, there would be brass bands, gaudy banners and testimonial logos stamped on everything from the portable toilets to cocktail napkins.

Dare we imagine, for example, what type of megahype the National Football League will pelt us with before Super Bowl L?

The Masters, bless it, will have none of this. No special flags or streamers along Magnolia Lane. No buntings or bedsheets hanging from the austere white clubhouse at Augusta National. No golden gobbledygook forced onto the branches of The Oak, that famous landmark with a wingspan of 80 feet.

In March, 1934, over what had been a 370-acre nursery, it began as the "First Annual Invitation Tournament" for Bobby Jones and friends. In that respect, nothing has changed. Thursday, the Masters will resume by acknowledging history according to custom. With classy elegance. To wit:

"Pairings and Starting Time. April 12, 1984. 8:30 a.m. No. 1 Tee—Gene Sarazen, Sam Snead." No more is said. No more needs to be said. The official Masters insignia still is a map of the United States with a flagstick stuck in Georgia. Further identification not required.

Hord Hardin, the grandfatherly Masters' chairman, points out that this spring's event actually is only the 48th, not the 50th. During three war years—1943, '44 and '45—there was no Masters. But, that doesn't explain why the anniversary is treated without pomp or pomposity.

"We're not much for show," he says. "Or publicity."

Despite that posture—maybe because of it—the Masters is unique. Tickets aren't purchased; they're willed. Gaining admittance to the Masters gallery is harder than getting a seat for any Super Bowl, World Series, Kentucky Derby or Final Four.

Princes from foreign lands and politicians in limos have been turned away at the gates, because here, clout doesn't count. Deane Beman, the PGA commissioner, admits having scaled the steep Augusta National fences with his University of Maryland golf teammates many moons ago. But crashers don't last long. Security personnel are forever checking.

And, green. Everything is green. The wrappers on sandwiches sold at the green concession stands are green, so as not to be so visible if some spectator dare drop one on the ground rather than in a green trash receptacle. Bleachers? Green. TV towers? Green. TV trucks? Draped in green. Eyesores, begone.

"Of all the events we do," says Brent Musburger of CBS, "this is the most special. Last year was my first Masters. And, I was a little uptight before it started."

With some reason. The Masters is the only major athletic spectacle that gives, instead of takes, instructions. Commercial time is half what it usually is, Ken Venturi does not provide golf tips during lulls in the action and you'll not hear that Fred Couples is the present money leader with $237,523.

The Masters' purse is not revealed until the final day, and even then, it is whispered instead of shouted. Crowd figures are nobody's business, and if you label the gallery "a mob" as Jack Whitaker did in 1966, you pay the consequences. He was banned from Masters' telecasts for eight years.

"For me, the Masters is the start of the golf season," says Jack Nicklaus, who is making his 26th appearance. "But, that's not why this place is so special. If I'm around 20 years from now, I'd still want to play here, even if I couldn't compete."

Tradition and taste don't work too well in professional sports these days. The alphabet of the '80s begins with 'A' for amphetamines and ends with 'Z' for zonked. Coke is available in too many locker rooms, but not as a thirst-quencher. Dignity means being able to declare free agency. And, wherever you look, 16 teams make the playoffs.

But the Masters, though contemporary, is a throwback. Though profitable, it is sport. Spectators can't take their shirts off, but they won't lose them, either. Programs are free. People are polite. Discipline dominates and, still, it is a joy. The Masters is a time warp, and a welcome one.

"Overwhelming is the only way to describe it," says Ray Floyd. "There is nothing like the Masters on God's earth. Most of what is good in any golf tournament was done here first."

Even Seve Ballesteros, the defending champion, seems to have caught on. When he won in 1980, he seemed a trifle cocky. Last year, a bit more tame. Now, he acts in awe, and speaks with respect. When asked what he did with last year's rewards, Ballesteros' cash doesn't register.

"I know I won," he says. "But I don't remember how much."

It was $90,000. But, at Augusta National this time every year, when golfers talk about that gorgeous green stuff, they aren't talking decimal points.

MR. MISCHIEF WINS THE OPEN

JUNE 19, 1984

MAMARONECK, NEW YORK—At the first tee of Monday's U.S. Open playoff, Fuzzy Zoeller went into his golf bag for a little mischief and whipped out a telephone.

"I wanted him to know this was last call," Zoeller later explained.

"It could have been worse," said Greg Norman. "I was expecting a snake."

Some three hours later, at the No. 18 tee, Norman was down by eight strokes and utterly helpless. But, the blond Australian had a plan to re-enter the fight.

"Fuzzy," he said. "Whatta you say we play this hole for double or nothing?"

"Okay," replied Zoeller, wearing that perpetually whimsical look. "If you promise to hit your second shot the same place you hit it yesterday."

Moments later, with Zoeller standing on the green waiting to clinch victory, Norman went to his golf bag and unfurled a white towel. He waved it at the 84th U.S. Open champion, just as Zoeller had surrendered Sunday after Norman's dramatic 40-foot putt saved par following his misdirected approach shot into the aforementioned bleachers.

"I just thought I might finish the tournament on a nice note," said Norman, who is as much a complete gentleman as Zoeller is a complete character. Together, this Monday, they made sure to remind everybody that the world would still turn Tuesday.

John McEnroe could play tennis against Ivan Lendl until the year 2001, and they wouldn't have had as much fun, or created as much enjoyment, as Fuzzy Zoeller and Greg Norman did at Winged Foot West this dank Monday afternoon. They worked overtime for golf's most honored title, but, in the end, it wasn't work at all.

The mirth began late Sunday night when the two opponents sat at adjoining dinner tables in their hotel. Zoeller, thinking ahead to Monday's playoff, kept telling the waiter to buy that big blond stud over there another bottle of wine. Norman declined, with a roar of laughter.

The grins, pranks, and jabs continued for 18 holes Monday. Unlike Sunday, when Zoeller wisely let partner Hale Irwin stew in his own grim juices, nobody needed to cut the tension in the playoff pairing, because there was none. How many times will two men vying for a U.S. Open crown sip Coca-Cola out of the same soft drink cup?

Of course, Fuzzy Zoeller would have it no other way. The galleries love him, because he loves them. And he is immensely popular with fellow golfers because they respect his ability not only to play the game, but to keep it a game. He's both a clown prince, and prince.

"Everybody's entirely different," Zoeller says. "Some people might not take me seriously. They might think, 'He can't concentrate, crazy as he is.' But, I know my outs, and my limitations, and I go with them. I'm just an ordinary golfer. I'm still an ordinary golfer.

"Today's special, but it doesn't change that. I'll never be thought of as a great player. I'd rather just keep sneaking in there. If it's between being remembered as a great golfer, or a good guy, I'll take the good guy.

"I'm fortunate that I don't have a real bad temper. If you dig down into my goody bag, you might find it, but you'd have to go deep. You've got to give the crowd what it wants. If it wasn't for the people, I'd be out here today playing in front of a bunch of trees for a couple hundred dollars."

The folks whose house flanks the No. 7 tee at Winged Foot West understand that. When Zoeller arrived there Monday, he cast covetous eyes at a beer cooler sitting in the back yard. Fuzzy exchanged greetings, then got to the point.

"I'd love one, but if I start now, I'll be playing this round from a porta-can," he said. "I'm still fighting last night's escargot. Keep a couple on ice for me."

Zoeller's golf coach at the University of Houston tried to fit a flippant Fuzzy into a serious hole, and it didn't work. That's one of few personality conflicts Zoeller ever had, though, or ever will. He doesn't inflict his carefree attitude on people, particularly others players. But, if you share his wavelength for eschewing sacred cows, well, he'll be just delighted to rub elbows.

Frank Urban Zoeller—take those initials, and you have the origin of his nickname—almost quit the game six years ago and went home to New Albany, Indiana. A high school basketball injury left him with a cranky back. In late May, he withdrew from the Memorial Tournament with his worst attack ever.

Now, he's got new hope with new therapy and he's also got a new recognition. Zoeller always has been a factor on the tour. He was second on last year's money list with $417,597. But he'd rather go to his golf bag and pull out a telephone than go to the bank.

"I don't thrive on winning, I thrive on fun and friends," Zoeller says. "This will sink in in a few weeks, but, there's no sense getting too serious, folks. My caddy hurts his hand at this year's Masters, so I ask my brother Ed to take over. They call him 'Pump' because he's always thirsty. He says he won't rake traps and won't go into woods. We had a few laughs."

People around Fuzzy Zoeller usually do. There isn't a better ambassador in golf. And, at Winged Foot West for this U.S. Open, there wasn't a better golfer, either.

THE MASTER AGAIN

APRIL 14, 1986

AUGUSTA, GEORGIA—In a stirring conclusion to one of golf's most memorable tournaments, 46-year-old Jack Nicklaus Sunday shot a final-round 7-under-par 65 to win the 50th Masters at Augusta National by one stroke over Greg Norman and Tom Kite.

Nicklaus, four swings behind leader Norman at afternoon's start, surged from a star-studded pack with five birdies plus an eagle on the back nine to close with 30—tying a course record—and acquire an unprecedented sixth green jacket. Arnold Palmer is closest to Nicklaus with four Masters triumphs.

The victory was Nicklaus' 20th in a major but first since his fifth PGA Championship at Oak Hill in Rochester, New York, in August, 1980. Two months earlier, at Baltusrol, New Jersey, Nicklaus captured his fourth U.S. Open. He also has won three British Opens and two U.S. Amateur Championships.

Nicklaus finished first at the 1982 Colonial and at his own Memorial tournament in 1984, but has not been a frequent threat or participant on the professional tour since. Before Sunday's charge, Nicklaus had missed the cut in three of only seven events this season and was 160th on the official money list.

"There are other things in life besides golf," said Nicklaus, referring to his family and extensive business interests. "I don't play the way I did 10 or 12 years ago, but at times I can. And I've always said I want to continue playing because I love it, and because I thought I could win again.

"People have said that 46 is too old to win a Masters. I'm not sure I didn't agree. But I felt good about my game coming in here, and I'm absolutely delighted with what happened today. I hadn't been playing this year, and I wasn't going to go out that way, even if people were telling me to retire, that I'd had it. I wanted to go out playing well."

In his 28th Masters, before an adoring throng, Nicklaus couldn't have played much better than he did Sunday. He began slowly, with a birdie on No. 2 cancelled out by a bogey on No. 4 through eight holes. He recalled remarking to his caddy, son Jackie, that "if we want to make any kind of a move, I've got to start sinking some putts right away."

Nicklaus did drop an 11-footer on No. 9 for a birdie, but he reached the turn at only 3-under par. Norman, the Australian who led the field by a stroke after three rounds, completed nine holes four twosomes behind Nicklaus in 7-under par. Seve Ballesteros, two pairings back, also was 7 under after the front side.

Clearly, Nicklaus required a spectacular rush, bordering on a miracle, for his 71th PGA Tour and 89th conquest worldwide since becoming a professional in 1961. And clearly, he needed cooperation from the putting stroke that had so often deserted him during his slump. For the last two months, he'd been using a putter—called a "spatula" by Jackie—with an extended blade, painted black.

"You think we sold a few of those today?" quipped Nicklaus, whose MacGregor sporting goods company is the manufacturer. "It's amazing. I hadn't been making a lot of makeable putts for the first three rounds. A little better each day, but still not enough. Then on the back nine, every time I held the thing, it seemed to go back in just the right place. I was a little nervous. Maybe I should be nervous more often. Everything went in."

With the guile of a Pete Rose or Muhammad Ali, the venerable Nicklaus then went on a binge to become the second oldest golfer to win a major (Julius Boros was 48 when he took the PGA Championship in 1968.) Nicklaus canned a 25-footer at No. 10 and a 20-footer at No. 11, both for birdies. He had moved to 5 under par.

"The next hole was one that helped get me going," said Nicklaus. "Which is strange. Because I bogeyed it. I hit a 7-iron in there and pulled it. I chipped to within six feet and two-putted. I knew I had to be aggressive the rest of the way, and I was so pumped up that I was taking one club less that I normally would."

At No.13, a scenic and winding par-5, Nicklaus clubbed a

3-wood off the tee, then a 3-iron to within 30 feet of the pin. He missed the eagle putt but got a birdie to repair his score to 5 under. He parred No. 14, then remembered glancing at the leader board. Only Ballesteros and Kite were to be caught at that juncture. Defending Masters champion Bernhard Langer was faltering; Norman had double-bogeyed No. 10.

At No. 15, Nicklaus nailed his drive and had only 202 yards left of 500. He drilled a 4-iron to within 12 feet and holed the eagle putt. Now the galleries were swarming for a peek. Now the Golden Bear was seven under par. Ballesteros would eagle No. 13 to go 9 under, but Nicklaus reasoned, "he's still got a lot of golf to play."

Nicklaus was correct. A brilliant 5-iron to the No. 16, a par 3, yielded a three-foot birdie putt. And an 11-footer at No. 17 brought Nicklaus to 9 under for the tournament. Meanwhile, he mulled a peculiar crowd reaction from behind. "It wasn't an eagle roar—it was something different," he recalled. Indeed, Ballesteros, after waiting several moments for Tom Watson to complete No. 15, yanked his approach into Rae's Creek. The Spaniard bogeyed there, and again at No. 17, removing himself from contention.

Nicklaus completed his round in strong fashion. A 3-wood and 5-iron at No. 18 left him 40 feet from the cup, but an excellent lag putt that fell just shy of dropping produced a tap-in par. The Golden Bear—a Masters champion in 1963, 1965, 1966, 1972 and 1975—now had to wait to see if either Kite or Norman could match his aggregate of 279.

They were the only candidates left. Kite, who birdied Nos. 13 and 15 to move into a temporary triple tie at 8 under, was the first to reach No. 18. He was putting for birdie from 10 feet but didn't stroke it quite boldly enough, and the ball slid left of the hole. He wound up with a 68 and 280.

"I was back at the cabin then, watching it on TV," said Nicklaus. "Someone mentioned that it was all over, that I'd won. I said no. Norman was still out there making a run."

Nicklaus had been down that disappointing route before. In the 1982 U.S. Open at Pebble Beach, California, he was in the scorers' tent, thinking victory, when Watson chipped in for birdie from the high rough beside No. 17. "I'd seen these things happen," Nicklaus said, ruefully.

Indeed, resilient competitor that he is, Norman birdied Nos.

14, 15, 16, and 17 in succession to reach 9 under in the last pairing with Nick Price. At No. 18, Norman scorched his drive but then failed to come through an uphill 4-iron toward the green. He pushed it deep into the gallery—reminiscent of his 72nd hole at the 1984 U.S. Open at Winged Foot, New York. Norman's second shot there landed in the bleachers, but he recovered splendidly for a par to force a playoff against Fuzzy Zoeller.

However, there was no playoff Sunday and no miracle, except perhaps, Nicklaus' back nine. Norman, not the surrendering type, pitched from traffic to within 15 feet but missed his par putt, winding up with a 70 and 280. The Golden Bear had gained $144,000 and, much more significantly, renewed praise and self-esteem.

"Somebody asked me earlier this week if I thought Jack was washed up," Norman said. "I replied, 'You'd be foolish to count him out.' The man can still play some golf."

"Jack is past his prime, yes," added Kite. "But it's not like you reach your prime, then fall off a ledge. If he played more often than he does, there's no telling what he could do. That's speculating. Nobody knows. But he sure put it together today."

Nicklaus, with previous rounds of 74–71–69, credited Jackie with encouraging words: "He told me to keep my head straight on a couple putts," said Jack. Also, the Golden Bear revealed that he'd borrowed from a lesson on pitching and chipping that Jackie had taken recently from Chi Chi Rodriguez.

"It all came together this week," Jack said. "It may be as fine a round as I've ever played, particularly the last 10 holes. I was hitting the ball longer—I don't know why—and the putts finally fell. Today, a couple guys were nice to me and allowed me to win. Maybe the smart thing to do would be to say goodbye, but I'm not that smart. I'm not retiring. I still enjoy playing too much. I still love the game."

HOW MANY MIRACLE SHOTS MUST ONE ENDURE?

APRIL 13, 1987

AUGUSTA, GEORGIA—When last seen with that Australian tan drained from his face and jawbone down around the shoe laces, Greg Norman was slumped in disbelief beside the 18th green at Inverness Country Club in Toledo one August ago. To his right Bob Tway danced alone, having kicked sand in Norman's face with a bunker shot for golf's libraries.

There is no way in fair play that such a thing should happen to a man once, let alone again, not to mention in a second consecutive major tournament. But Norman, the Great White Shark who thought he'd seen it all, experienced another nightmare that was another man's dream this special Sunday at Augusta National. To Norman's right this time, Larry Mize was airborne, a purple passion celebrating a miracle shot that clinched the 51st Masters.

"Nice to be a part of history," concluded Norman. He did not sound entirely convinced that he belongs in the same breath as Ralph Branca, who served up Bobby Thomson's home run for the century in 1951—or, for that matter, any of sport's other tragic figures compelled to stand there in public view while the rest of the world goes crazy at somebody else's magic.

And it required nothing less than that to deprive Norman of this event he so dearly wants. True, Tway's blast from a bunker to snare the PGA Championship was magnificent and improbable, but his ball was sitting up in greenside trap. And besides, sand to these pros is not what it is to us weekend whiffers. They get in and out of there like cabbies through rush hour traffic. These golfers don't leave anything in the sand except footprints and pleasant memories.

However, Mize's method of ending a stirring fourth round, which became a three-man playoff that came down to him against Norman, was holier than Toledo. Seve Ballesteros, a somber competitor if ever there was one, unaccountably three-putted the first extra hole and cried all the way back to the clubhouse. Then Mize had pushed his 5-iron approach to No. 11 well wide of the green—Norman estimated 140 feet. The best golfer on the globe, the Great White Shark, had teeth sharpened for an acceptance speech.

"There was no way I was going to take more than par there," recalled Norman. "And from where Mize was, I might have been happy to take a bogey, a five. I thought he might chip the thing into the pond behind the green. Difficult? He could stand out there for three days and not do what he did again. Difficult? I'm not a betting man, but it had to be 30 percent harder than Tway's shot. Not only because of the distance, but the firmness of the green."

So Mize steadied, with all of Augusta rooting for this hometown lad in psychedelic attire. He dug his sand wedge into the very turf he once stared at from the other side of the fence, and the ball went one hop, two hops to green's fringe before it flattened out like a putt. And the ball went, and it went, and it went, and then it kissed the pin and disappeared into the cup. Birdie. Delirium. Dogwoods shaking in the twilight.

"I couldn't believe it," Norman recalled. "I just couldn't believe it. I was glad when he tried a bump-and-run there, because I thought there'd be no way he could stop it. Like I said, I thought to get it to the hole, he might have to hit it so hard, it would go past and roll into the water. I would have tried to loft the ball more than Larry did, get it up high, let it land softly. What can I say? What can I say? Three days. Three days he could stand out there and not do it again. Tway's shot was like Tom Watson's shot that beat Jack (Nicklaus) in the U.S. Open at Pebble Beach a few years ago. This, this was unbelievable. What can I say? The better man won."

A lesser man than Greg Norman, however, would have cursed the fates and made off for the nearest cocoon. Champion that he is, though, even without a green jacket, Norman faced the media hordes, then signed his autographs, then had a beer with his caddie, Pete Bender, in the locker room. Somewhere, some silly will write or broadcast that Norman is destined to such observances because he cannot put the cap on the bottle, because he's a shark that's not a killer shark, because his throat under pressure becomes parched. There is only one polite word for this type of gibberish, and that word is "fiction."

"That's the only way you can beat this guy, he's so good . . . with miracles," said Bender, who is biased, but closer to the truth.

Fact is, Norman's tremendous talent allowed him to knife through a contentious and excellent leader board on a windy afternoon when his game was shy of faultless. He missed a couple of makeable putts on the front side, then bogeyed Nos. 10 and 11 to fall to even par for the tournament. But then, aggressor that he is, Norman went on a binge. He might have opted for a conservative posture and a comfortable paycheck. Instead, he swung from the heels and only at flagsticks. A guy who does that will know some disappointment as long as he plays, because the hunt rewards only one hunter.

The birdie at No. 12 was a springboard, because it was the toughest hole all week. The drives were akin to sonic booms. On No. 13, a 465-yard par-5 that Norman birdied, he was 175 yards from the green after his drive. On No. 14, a 405-yard par-4, he was 45 yards away—too close to birdie. He got that on No. 15, though No. 17, 400 yards, he lopped off all but 80 with his tee shot, and birdied. At No. 18, 405 yards mostly uphill, Norman hit driver then sand wedge from 96 yards out, then came this close to sinking a 20-foot putt that would have sent him directly to the clubhouse, to shake hand with Jack Nicklaus, for the fitting of the revered jacket.

"I thought it was in," said Norman. "I couldn't believe that, either."

Two groups before, Mize had birdied No. 18, which isn't supposed to happen. He had something in mind, too. He had something in mind when he showed up at Augusta shortly past noon. A guy asked him about his violet outfit. "Anything goes with green around here," said Mize, and it did. But first, he had to pull that 140-foot bump-and-run out of his closet.

"I knew it would be tough to top last year for an encore," said Norman, sipping on his consolation prize. "It would be nice to win here anytime, because I love this place so much, but it would have been special to get the jacket from Jack Nicklaus. But it wasn't to be. When Tway got me in the PGA, I didn't have any majors left. At least now, I've got three to go this year. I've got to play next week, so I won't be going home and throwing things around the house. This will just make me work harder, make me more determined than ever."

The world's best golfer doesn't deserve to be the world's unluckiest, too, but Greg Norman can handle it. When the chef at Augusta National asked him to pose for a picture, Norman was only too glad to oblige before departing. Golf is a gentleman's game, after all, even when it gives you a face full of slaps. Twice.

MYRA KEEPS SWINGING

MAY 5, 1987

Male chauvinist pigs and piglets are oinking in dismay about events of this past weekend, when our dwindling superiority complex suffered yet another wound.

Women are gaining better jobs and improved salaries all the time, which is only fair, but we of the alleged stronger sex always assumed the athletic field to be sacrosanct, our last bastion of exclusivity. Men are stronger, bigger, tougher, and so yawn.

This equation even extended to the pastoral game of golf, where macho outlets such as spitting and swearing aren't considered necessary. Or at least, spitting. The rotten ball still must be compressed to travel great distances, so brawn counts, even if it helps to have soft hands, too.

But the days when we bravely carry our own bag and think of ourselves as soldiers marching off to war are now history, because there's this athlete who just played a professional tournament carrying her own baby. Myra Blackwelder, 7½ months pregnant, should be remembered the next time we approach the first tee moaning about hangnails, hangovers or other minor annoyances. Ever tried to sink a five-footer with a child in the oven?

"That was maybe the main problem, putting," Blackwelder was saying Monday from her home in Oldsmar, Florida. "As you know, when you're putting, you want to have your eyes directly over the ball. But I've become very large—I've gained 24 pounds—and I found that I had to hold the putter out farther from my body than I should, because of my stomach. It was so extreme, the toe of the club was in the air. If I'd have putted better, I might have won."

Myra Blackwelder, of course, was a winner anyway, even though she finished nine strokes behind Cindy Hill Sunday in the S&H Classic at St. Petersburg, Florida, a regular stop for the Ladies Professional Golf Association. That Myra finished was a credit to her competitive fiber, though the fact she started a 72-hole grid in searing climes wasn't too shabby, either.

"I'd planned to stop playing after the Nabisco-Dinah Shore early last month," she said. "That's an event I really like, and it was getting close. Nancy Lopez also played the tour while she was pregnant, but she wasn't as far along as I was, and I also remember them having to carry her off the golf course one day in Canada, it was so hot.

"I'd talked it over with my husband, and we thought I'd take off until I gave birth. I was going to stay around the house, take it easy, and plant some begonias. But I became depressed and bored. You can only plant so many begonias. The tournament this past weekend is right in my back yard, so I asked my doctor if I could play, and he was all for it. In fact, he encouraged me. When you're an active person, it's best to keep active, even if you're pregnant. Especially if you're pregnant."

Blackwelder, 31, already mother of a 2-year-old son, shot 69 in Thursday's opening round and followed with a 66—at which point she was tied for the tournament lead with Jan Stephenson. Myra—who played under her maiden name, Van Hoose, until 1985—was astounded. She was merely hoping to make the cut, participating for the fun of it. Which is probably why she made birdies instead of bogeys. This is a weird game, she noted.

"I faltered in the last couple rounds a bit, with a 71 and a 74," Myra went on. "I suppose that's understandable. The more you walk, the more fatigued you get. The more you play in the afternoon hours instead of the morning, the more it takes out of you. It was very humid over the weekend and I did get a little tired and I did stub a couple of chip shots because of what I was wearing. Those maternity outfits are pretty blousey, you know, and if you choke up on the club at all, it can get caught up in that loosely fitted clothing. Plus, there were a few times walking those fairways when I felt the baby moving. You're getting ready to hit a shot, and you feel a foot in the ribs.

"It was a new experience, but one of the best I've ever had. The $2,800 I earned was just a bonus. The real thrill was the reaction from the galleries. People offering you water, people telling you to come on over here and stand in the shade. My husband said there were six pregnant women sitting by the 18th green with their fingers crossed while I was putting for birdie the other day. All sorts of mothers pushing strollers following me. Jan said she wasn't used to playing in a tournament where she wasn't the crowd favorite."

Myra's situation necessitated certain swing adjustments, and she did just that, opening her stance slightly to help the shoulder turn and the weight shift. More importantly, though, she played and played well while awaiting either Mallory Christine if it's a girl or Matthew Ryan if it's a boy.

"This is my eighth year on the pro tour," said Myra, "but this last tournament is one for the scrapbooks. I played golf, and my blood pressure actually went down."

Few of us hacking hunks can say that about golf, a blasted game designed to make the plasma boil. But, then, maybe we aren't as tough as we think.

Can't you wait until the next flat-bellied surfer on the men's tour gripes about greens being too fast? About the rough being too thick? About a helicopter flying overhead when it's time to putt? About a caddy who recommends the wrong club? About a spectator snapping that camera during the backswing?

We're in trouble, fellas, after what Myra Blackwelder did last weekend. For us, from now on, it's either be quiet or begonias.

Basketball

IT'S MAGIC!

MAY 18, 1980

PHILADELPHIA—Magic Johnson played guard, forward, high post, low post, and 47 minutes. He blocked shots, dunked shots, airmailed shots, and invented shots. He hounded, rebounded, confounded and dumbfounded. He did everything but polish the Liberty Bell. Hard to believe the man's mind was 3,000 miles away.

"But it was," said Magic. "I was thinking of the big guy back home. We won it here, but he got us here. I know his left leg hurts, but I hope he can do a little dance for us tonight. I know we did one for him."

Strange but true. Minus ailing Kareem Abdul-Jabbar, the Los Angeles Lakers Friday night shocked Philadelphia's perplexed 76ers 123–107 to claim the National Basketball Association championship 4 games to 2. See? Hollywood endings even happen in Philadelphia.

With rookie Johnson scoring 42 points to annex the series' most valuable player honors, and Jamaal Wilkes pumping in 37 more, the Lakers completely negated the ghost that was sure—well, almost sure—to haunt them: Jabbar, the game's most dominant player, out with an ankle injury until Game 7 in Los Angeles Sunday. Contact the Forum for ticket refunds.

"This is just amazing," said Wilkes. "With Kareem here, I would have said that our chances of winning on this court tonight would have been just 50–50. Without him, I thought maybe we had only a 10 or 15 percent chance. But we did it."

The Lakers did it by running, by refusing to panic, by leaving the defensive breakdowns to the Sixers, who were supposed to exploit the middle, with Jabbar lame, but wound up being exploited everywhere themselves.

"I think it was Walt Whitman who said that the ultimate goal of a teacher is to teach so well that his students eventually outdo him," rasped Paul Westhead, the Lakers' coach. "Well, Kareem is our teacher. He's synonymous with this basketball team, and I know he is proud of us."

All of Tinseltown should be proud of the Lakers. Not once did they waver in their mission this night. They vaulted to a sudden 7–0 lead, then after trailing by as much as 21–46 in the second quarter, they gained a 60–60 standoff at halftime.

"Obviously," said the Sixers' Dr. J, "they did something during the intermission that we didn't."

In a coup de grace, the Lakers scored the first 14 points of the third quarter for a 74–60 margin. It was later shaved to two, but never fewer. The Lakers ran the table the way they ran the game. By taking it to Philadelphia. To lay back without The Franchise, Jabbar, would have been to surrender.

"Without Kareem," said Magic, "we couldn't play half the court and think defensively. We had to play full-court and take our chances."

Johnson's 12-footer from the baseline stung Philadelphia first during the fatal siege, and it was 62–60. Then Mike Cooper took a lay-in off Magic's assist, 64–60. Johnson stole Lionel Hollins' in-bound pass and fed Wilkes for a fastbreak layup, 66–60. Then Cooper canned a 20-footer and Wilkes converted after Norm Nixon blew a layup. Lakers by 10, 70–60.

Johnson sank a 21-footer from the top of the circle to make it a dozen, and Magic fed Wilkes for another layup. Philadelphia, which had missed all eight of its shots during the Laker blitz, called timeout. It was 74–60 with 8:28 remaining in the third quarter.

"We just couldn't put together a whole game against them this series, and that was an example," said Dr. J. "Those three minutes ended the season for us. We weren't overconfident, but we were flat."

And the Sixers sure were dumb. They had opportunity after opportunity for high-percentage 12- or 15-footers, but they repeatedly tried to penetrate the middle. Los Angeles' collapsing defense was a perfect foil, for the Sixers forced things, turned the ball over, gave the game away. When the Lakers didn't get it on the floor, they got it on the boards—they outrebounded Philadelphia 52–36.

"They were out to prove that they weren't Jabbar's team only," said Philadelphia Coach Billy Cunningham, "and they did. That was the best basketball that's been played against us all year. They just outplayed us. We got close, but Johnson and Wilkes killed us."

The Sixers did, in fact, nip at the Laker heels four different times in the final quarter. But after unheralded Steve Mix added his 18th point on a bucket to draw Philadelphia to within 101–99, and after Bobby Jones answered a Laker score to keep the Sixers two back at 103–101, the hometown heroics ceased and desisted until at least next October.

Johnson tapped in a rebound—he had 15, plus 7 assists and 6 steals—for a 105–101 lead. Then Wilkes, shackled with his fourth foul late in the third quarter, drove the lane for a three-point play.

Maurice Cheeks cut it to 108–103. But, with only 2:26 left, Norm Nixon purloined an outlet pass by Bobby Jones and found Johnson for another layup, another three-point play.

The Lakers were champions for the second time since moving to Los Angeles. And 20-year-old Magic was a champion for the second time in as many years.

"You can't compare this one with winning the NCAA at Michigan State," he said. "That was great, but this is the one. This is the professionals. This is better. A lot of people expected us to fold tonight, but that's not what we were all about. It hasn't been that way all season.

"We started here with a bunch of new faces. Then we lost our coach in the first month of the season. Tonight, we didn't have the big guy. But we did it as a team, which is what we are. Jim Chones played great. Jamaal Wilkes played great. We all played great."

CELTS SIMPLY GREAT

JUNE 13, 1984

BOSTON—In a series that could have used the 10-point must system as well as a 24-second clock, the Boston Celtics Tuesday night annexed their 15th National Basketball Association championship.

To place such magnificence into some sort of perspective, try this: If the silly, comatose and utterly confused Bulls won every NBA crown from now through the turn of the century, and then the Celtics returned to glory in 2001, the teams would be tied for titles. Stranger things haven't happened, but you get the idea.

The 14,890 customers who paid heavily to attend Game 7 in this musty abatoir carrying the misnomer of Boston Garden might ascribe the clinching 111–102 victory over the Los Angeles Lakers to parquet power or all those banners hanging from above.

But the Celtics' latest parade didn't have everything to do with floors or flags. On the contrary, it had much to do with character. The Celtics might have had the biggest mouths these last two weeks; they also had the biggest hearts. Celtic pride is no cliché. It's a game plan.

If Tuesday night's tiff wasn't over when James Worthy heaved an early free throw that became an air ball, or when Kareem Abdul-Jabbar found nothing with his sky hook, or when Magic Johnson double-dribbled with nobody near him, surely it ended when Boston turned a four-point lead late in the third quarter into a 13-point cushion with Larry Bird on the bench, cheering his estimable guts out.

After this 1,965th contest of an NBA season that really is finished, the Lakers can rest uneasily in the knowledge that the series they allowed to last too long ended sooner than it should have. Without a will, there was no way. They possessed neither Tuesday night. So long, fast break.

Conventional wisdom had it that the more talented Lakers would breeze through the finals as they did through a bland schedule in the not-so-wild West. But the Lakers were so unaccustomed to adversity that they couldn't handle it when it slapped them in the face, or ribs, or solar plexus.

"Is there anybody tougher? Is there anybody better?" asked Bird, who was named most valuable player of the tournament. He spoke of his team, but he was in essence describing himself. Bird was sealed off in Game 6 by Jamaal Wilkes and didn't become totally involved in the Celtic offense Tuesday evening. So all the sport's finest individual did was dig trenches so his mates could dance.

Rebounds are largely the residue of desire, and Celtic fingerprints were all over the glass backboards Tuesday. It wasn't all that warm in the Garden, but it was still too hot for the Lakers. They had three offensive boards in the first half. They were out-rebounded by an unholy total of 52–33.

Meanwhile, Magic was almost tragic, hobbling along on a gimpy left knee. Worthy wasn't worthless, as the sign from the second balcony indicated, but he was no bargain. And Jabbar, forced to run, had little stamina and less help. The Lakers went a long way in finesse, but perished quickly when they couldn't execute it. They'll be seeing Boston elbows for months.

Meanwhile, with Bird fairly neutralized, the Celtics adjusted. This was a club with a supposedly mediocre backcourt, and depth that bordered on shallow. Explain that to Danny Ainge. Or tell Cedric Maxwell that big games are only for big names. Dennis Johnson? 22 points. Robert Parish? All arms.

It was a strange series, to be sure, involving blowouts, overtimes and players from Los Angeles begging to return home in quest of fresh air, would you believe. It was also a highly visceral series, underscoring again that pro basketball players can be the best athletes of all, when they want to play. Or have to. The ludicrous NBA schedule and playoff system preclude total effort.

The series could have done without the flaming rhetoric and the crackback blocks. To borrow from Rodney Dangerfield, the good folks of L.A. and Boston too often went to a basketball game and a hockey game broke out. Nobody needed clothes-line shots, or warnings of war or a call to hardhats.

Referees Earl Strom and Darrel Garretson, impervious to shenanigans or hometown fervor, put the clamps on Tuesday night's affair with their whistles, but early. With Kareem busting for the hoop on a three-on-one in the first quarter, Ainge made real sure the fatigued Laker legend wouldn't get a shot off. But that was a smart foul. Too many other moments in this series simply smarted.

But it's over, and even though the Garden was a cauldron Tuesday night, it was no sweat for the Celtics. The customers who bought up all the seats, but often didn't bother using them, feed the Celtics. But, they feed off the Celtics, too. Foreign emotions for Chicago, where the season ended 57 days ago. Or was it 57 years?

"We worked hard for this," said Bird, showing a rare smile after Boston's 113th game of the campaign. "Anybody gonna say we didn't earn it?"

Is there anybody tougher? Is there anybody better? No, and double no.

LITTLE NOURISHMENT IN THIS FEAST

JULY 30, 1984

LOS ANGELES—There's only one problem with meeting the Chinese in basketball: A half hour after playing them, you want to play them again.

You've been hearing for years how we in the United States stage all these silly games that a billion Chinese don't care about.

Well, Sunday night, all of that changed. The Chinese cared. Let's hope only that the Chinese didn't care too much, because a totally hilarious thing happened at the Forum.

In the opening cartoon of the basketball tournament at the 23rd Summer Olympics, the United States thrashed China 97–49 before 13,248. It was like the Harlem Globetrotters all over again, toying with their erstwhile foils, the Washington Generals.

Bobby Knight, the U.S. drill sergeant by way of Indiana, has said no fewer than a dozen times since arriving in Hollywood that the international hoop revival is absolutely marvelous. For depth, there is no country to match America. But on any given night, any given national team can give the Americans a run for all that money they're making in college.

Sunday was not that given night. In fact, a day-long orgy of basketball at the Forum seemed to prove what everybody's been thinking all along. The Americans have too many skills, too much instinct and too much reserve strength to worry about anything in this two-week carnival. The gold medal is theirs, as long as they stay awake.

The Chinese, like the Yugoslavians who played before them, appear to have all the book learning they need about the sport.

Which is to say, they know that on a jump shot, the jump comes before the shot. But the ability to adjust and improvise simply isn't there.

All these other teams look like they've spent a few Julys and Augusts in basketball camp, which is nice. But it's no preparation for spending this July and August trying to upend a brilliant U.S. crew, masterminded by Knight, a genius in wolf's clothing.

In Sunday's rout, the Chinese never led, never hoped to lead, never dreamed of keeping matters close. You got that idea when, after numerous theatrical maneuvers that set up U.S. baskets, China's coach Qian Chenghai was caught laughing and shaking his head. On international courts, that's the signal for distress and surrender.

Knight, meanwhile, was kicking ballbags by his bench and screaming at his athletes after every little blunder. Bobby, no doubt, is doing all within his power to convince his stars that this will be no easy task. Apparently, by maintaining a scowl on his face, Knight is succeeding at creative tension.

"There's no way, even after a game like this, that we can afford to get over-confident," said Arkansas' Alvin Robertson, who paced the Americans with 18 points. "The game we do that, that's the game we're gonna blow."

Knight preached that his athletes be anxious to play—but not play with anxiety. He chided Robertson for taking three fouls in the first half but congratulated the gyrating guard on committing none in the second half. That's what Bobby means by discipline and controlled aggression.

"I thought we started out playing fairly well, as well as I might have expected early," Knight said. "We had a little down-spell, came back and played fairly well at the end of the half. In the second half, I was very disappointed at the way we played in the first seven minutes. We were very careless offensively.

"But then we settled down. I think we're all relieved that this thing has started. I mentioned the other day, there is a great deal of apprehension at the beginning of a college season and even more at the beginning of something as significant as this."

Knight's starting lineup, which he had clutched secretly to his bosom, turned out to be Robertson, Wayman Tisdale of Oklahoma, Sam Perkins and Michael Jordan of North Carolina, and Vern Fleming of Georgia.

Knight had been carrying on that the starting five didn't matter, and, against China, it certainly didn't. Everybody played no fewer than 11 minutes and no more than 24.

Georgetown's Patrick Ewing, hampered by an injury, was colossal at times and dominant always. Jordan scored 14 points in 16 minutes, and, of all the Americans, he should savor these moments before the Bulls conspire to ruin his basketball life.

The Americans have four more first-round games, with Canada next. Then comes the medal round, with a possibility of three more games. If the United States doesn't win all seven—in a romp—Knight will be kicking more than ballbags.

The Forum crowd, bless it, was sympathetic toward the Chinese. When their huge but uncoordinated 7-foot-1-inch center, Hu Zhangbao, found himself all alone beneath the basket with the ball, the customers roared as he deposited it home, looking not unlike an octopus trying to set up a beach chair.

There were other awkward moments on this glorious opening day of worldly athletics. In an earlier basketball tilt between Uruguay and France, there was a bench-emptying brawl. But referees called nothing. International rules: no homicide, no foul. Peace through sport they call it.

IN A CLASS
BY HIMSELF

AUGUST 12, 1984

LOS ANGELES—Whatever the going rate is for rookies in the National Basketball Association, Michael Jordan's is going higher with each moment under the gold standard. The man, like his price, has no apparent ceiling.

"He's like an airplane," marveled Antonio Diaz-Miguel, coach of Spain's Olympic basketball team. "Everybody else is on the ground, he hangs up there when he should come down. In the air, he runs. Most valuable player for them. Michael Jordan."

This was Friday night at the Forum, where the United States crushed Spain 96–65 for the "championship" of international hoops at the XXIII Summer Games. It was not as close as the score of the Americans' eighth straight rout indicated.

The Spaniards were willing subjects, committing 27 turnovers—enough to qualify this team as the official Olympic dessert. But don't blame Spain, Uruguay, China or any of the minor annoyances. The average U.S. victory margin was 33 points. Bobby Knight, the volcanic coach, had one technical foul in two weeks, and he didn't have laryngitis. Only the Olympic boxing judges could have made the basketball tournament close.

"The Americans," concluded Diaz-Miguel, "are 50 years ahead of the world in basketball."

There was, in the end, only one shred of drama. And that occurred early Friday evening when Jordan arrived at the Forum. He realized he had packed the wrong uniform, white instead of blue, when he left the Olympic Village. A police squad car, weaving through miles of traffic, retrieved it. A flat tire stood between Spain and the inevitable.

"I never did that before," said Jordan, laughing sheepishly.

There were a couple of high-wire routines Jordan performed during his 20-point evening that he probably did before, and probably will do again, until he invents something better. That is why he became to this basketball charade what Edwin Moses became to his event. He saved it from being utterly tedious and predictable.

There was that one glorious gesture—Jordan driving toward the basket, with ball tucked beltside. Laws of gravity dictated that Jordan land sooner or later. It was later, much later. He took a flying 8-count, above glazed Spanish eyes, then bore in on the basket and stuffed it. Chicago will love him.

"That was Michael's 'rockabye moonwalk' maneuver," explained teammate Leon Wood. "Not bad. I saw him do a better one in practice the other day. But don't forget, Michael's been bothered by a toothache."

Then, later on, there was that snapshot of Jordan near the top of the circle, looking, looking, for either two points or one teammate. He could have chosen either, but he had to do so quickly. Except the great ones tend to reduce fast action into slow motion, so as to dissect what is before them. Jordan found Pat Ewing, who scored. Chicago must have him.

"I think, the last two weeks, I showed the world a little of what Michael Jordan can do," said the Bulls' No. 1 draft choice, No. 1 hope and No. 1 priority. "People will say we didn't have anything to motivate us. But we did. Ourselves. If the Russians were here, we would have whipped them, too. We'll play them anytime, anywhere. This is the best Olympic basketball team, ever."

Ralph Sampson, an esteemed freshman, is said to have banked $1 million—give or take a few farthings—last season. If Jordan isn't worth that—and nobody who watched him here is prepared to make that statement—this genius of a young man from North Carolina is worth some of that. A huge sum of that.

"From a strictly business sense, let's hope the price went up off what happened here," Jordan said. "I haven't really thought about it. I want to relax a couple of weeks. I've heard the Bulls don't pay. I don't know. I haven't talked to them. I don't know if my man has."

Jordan's man, representative Donald Dell of Washington, is already dropping hints. Jordan merits "one of the best, if not the best" windfalls ever for an NBA rookie. Jordan wasn't drafted first only because he's got 6 inches to go to make 7 feet. Jordan is the most dramatic all-purpose player to come out of the college ranks in eons.

One would not want to be a member of the Bulls' front office when time comes to dispute any of those hosannas. Jordan is a jewel who strives to polish himself. Only effort explains how he went from the worst defensive player on the Tar Heels to the best.

"I was watching," Bulls general manager Rod Thorn said Saturday from his home in Northbrook. "Michael's got a chance to be a great player in our league. He's not only got tremendous talent, he's got great basketball instincts. He's in line for a heck of a contract. I don't foresee any troubles signing him."

Neither side has any reasonable alternative. Jordan could balk and play in Europe, but if the Bulls let him slip away, they might as well go there, too. For Olympic basketball fans at the Forum, night after night, blowout upon blowout, Jordan's histrionics turned a dead issue into live entertainment.

With Michael Jordan, that scenario could be reenacted in Chicago, the Uruguay of pro basketball. The question is not whether the Bulls can afford to pay him. The question is, can they afford not to? If they make him happy, he just might make them respectable. At least, interesting.

A TRAGEDY
FOR ALL

FEBRUARY 27, 1986

What has happened to Micheal Ray Richardson—or, rather, what this athlete dying young has done to himself—is a tragedy. Too often, we misuse that term on sports pages to describe inconsequential events, such as an error with the bases loaded, a flubbed putt that costs a tournament, a missed field goal with one second left in the fourth quarter.

But Micheal Ray Richardson is a person, and though his time is also just about up, he won't get another chance next week, or next year. He's already over the limit, as they say in the NBA, where Richardson was a star with the New Jersey Nets until he destroyed himself, his career and perhaps his life. For Richardson, there are no more games scheduled to make amends.

This would be a tragedy even if Richardson weren't just 30, even if he were earning a normal salary instead of $750,000 for six months' work. He has taken talent, one of the greatest gifts besides existence itself, and wasted it. He has squandered what's left of his youth, his prime production years, and he has shattered what remains of his self-esteem. He stopped short only of the ultimate tragedy, killing himself.

Consider what befell the man. He is a four-time All-Star, the comeback player of last year, his best season. He couldn't have asked for more positive reinforcement: a new contract from a franchise willing to believe that he'd beaten his drug problem, teammates willing to listen, doctors willing to help, a league willing to let bygones be gone, a public willing to accord him a fresh start. Even a new wife, willing to build his future beyond basketball.

Micheal Ray Richardson had to balance all of these reasons to go straight with the alternatives of one more wrong turn. He knew every day would be a cross-examination, because those were the rules. He knew he was threatened with loss of job, identity, purpose, and still he couldn't cope. And still, when he was apprehended for testing positive, his situation was beyond his grasp. "It's not so," said Richardson. It was that pervasive, this addiction of his.

"What this shows is that there is no such thing as recreational use of cocaine," Larry Fleisher, general counsel for the NBA Players Association, was saying Wednesday from his New York office. "We knew somebody was going to get hurt sometime, and it's Micheal Ray Richardson. It's sad, but you can only hope that this sets an example and sends a signal."

Indeed, one can only hope. NBA players provided more than a blessing for the current drug plan; they provided the impetus. The program, announced in September, 1983, stipulates that a first-time offender undergo treatment with pay, a second-time offender be suspended without pay but be treated again at his club's expense. A third-time loser, such as Richardson, is banished, though application for reinstatement can be entertained after two years.

"Richardson is the first active player to suffer the most severe consequences," Fleisher said. "I suppose there's a slight chance he could return, but only if all parties are absolutely sure he's absolutely clean."

Fleisher has huddled with representatives of other professional sports about this insidious locker-room drug culture, but he declines to talk at length about why inertia is the code word outside the NBA. Hockey doesn't feel it has a problem, he says, and maybe it doesn't. Football seems "sort of ambivalent," and baseball's stance is affected by its players' union, what with its strong views on individual rights, invasion of privacy and confidentiality.

Perhaps it is time to shelve all the rhetoric and committees for the only pertinent criteria, the laws of the land. Drugs are illegal. Period. Case closed. If the other sports can't act from within, or won't, then perhaps a higher authority must step in, such as government. Professional leagues invariably look to the courts for solutions to stirring issues such as whether the Colts should be blocked from moving from Baltimore to Indianapolis. Maybe, for lack of a better idea, other sports should go to Washington for help on antidrug, instead of antitrust, matters.

Peter Ueberroth, the baseball commissioner who volunteered a notion that drugs threaten the very fiber of our national pastime, has been conspicuously quiet concerning immunity-seekers who testified at last autumn's drug trial in Pittsburgh. A high NFL official, Don Weiss, claimed the league knew about the New England Patriots' habits before the *Boston Globe* made headlines of them. He was later overruled by another high official, at which point commissioner Pete Rozelle authorized an inquiry by other high officials. Gentlemen, results, please.

Some deluded observers suggest it doesn't matter anyway, that the public doesn't really care. They point to increased attendance and booming TV ratings as proof that the fans, who have their own problems, just want the games to continue, even if the games are being played by junkies. But here is one area where the customers don't get a vote. They can elect their preferred forms of entertainment; they cannot legislate what is legal and what is not.

Meanwhile, Micheal Ray Richardson languishes, a tragedy worthy of pity but not a pardon, a lesson waiting to be learned by all players, all leagues.

WALTON'S
COMEBACK

JUNE 10,1986

BOSTON—In Sunday's afterbath of a sweet 16th pro basketball championship, with wives hugging trainers and assistant coaches toasting superstars, it was not difficult to ascertain
who among the Boston Celtics' family had contracted the most
pronounced case of ecstasy. Choices were two.

"This is unbelievable," Bill Walton, the 33-year-old redhead,
was saying over and over again, his left arm extended toward
the inner wall of his locker. Beneath him, oblivious to the
droplets of perspiration from above, was Nathan Walton, age
seven. He never spoke, and only occasionally perked his nose in
search of a breath. Mostly, Nathan repeatedly tapped his fist on
his father's fanny, an affirmation that daddy hadn't been quite
this happy in too long.

"This is everything I had ever hoped for, and more," Bill
Walton said. "It's more fulfilling, more rewarding, more fun.
To have a dream and then to go out and live it. It's just unbe-
lievable."

On the best team in sports, where whites and blacks and
rookies and retreads play for one common banner, Bill Walton's saga was special for its means, if not its end. If one is lucky
enough to become a Celtic, then the real flush comes when one
feels like a Celtic, fits like a Celtic, stays a Celtic. Sunday, Bill
Walton comprehended that for a basketball lifer, you haven't
reached the other side of the fence until you finally wear green.

"Hey, I gotta get on your team," he said, shaking his head,
savoring every sweaty minute as Nathan took the shower
below without blinking. Bill Walton was recalling a conversation he'd had last summer with Red Auerbach, the baron of
Boston basketball. Walton had failed a physical with the Los

Angeles Lakers, but Auerbach figured it might work anyway. When Auerbach thinks that, he's seldom wrong.

So Walton, a preeminent performer with the world champion Portland Trial Blazers in 1977, came aboard. A stress fracture restricted him to 14 games in four years, but Walton had a notion that he hadn't passed the prime of his career, only delayed it. The Portland franchise, which he sued, had retired four numbers from the title team, but not his. San Diego was the next stop, and then he moved with the Clippers to Los Angeles. But the foot wouldn't seem quite right, quite without pain, until it could land a home on the parquet floor.

Was Robert Parish, the regular center, offended?

"I visited his home to make sure he'd accept me," said Walton, who took a pay cut in exchange for a spot on the most honored bench this side of the Supreme Court. "I wanted him to feel comfortable with me around."

"I played better this year," admitted Parish, 32, "because I played fewer minutes."

Was Larry Bird, the heart of the Celtics, cautious?

"Every American kid in my generation had heard about Bill Walton," said the basic Hoosier hick from French Lick. "Hiding Patty Hearst in the closet, wearing a ponytail and smoking that bang-bang. None of it's true. What's true is that he's the best rebounder in basketball, and a winner. Even if he failed a physical and even if I did carry him on my shoulders all year."

Does Larry Bird love Bill Walton? Does every Celtic love every other Celtic? After Bird drilled an unconscious three-pointer from the Houston Rockets' bench Sunday, did not the champions-to-be adjourn during a timeout to clutch the first teammate in sight? When the Celtics were in Atlanta, coinciding with the selection of the Hawks' Mike Fratello as NBA Coach of the Year, wasn't that Bird lifting the hand of his coach, his black coach, K.C. Jones, into the air as a touché?

"This is really very unique here," Walton went on, his huge bandaged body treating a humid afternoon like Nathan might react to a crisp Christmas morning. "I mean, we were all dead tired out there today. Dead tired. Larry had nothing left. Nothing! And then he goes and sinks those three-pointers, and, man, we all know we gotta keep going.

"I was reluctant to leave California because I loved it there, and my family loved it there. But basketball is the most important thing in my life. My wife and kids don't like that, but that's the way it is. And I had to get on a great team one more time for one more chance at something like this. When you're 23, you think you'll always win. But when you're 33, you wonder if you'll ever win again.

"Boston. That's why it had to be Boston. All my family has seen the last two years has been the negatives of professional sports. Now my kids can see the positive side. A team like this, it makes all the sacrifices, all the hard work, all the sleepless nights worthwhile. All the mornings you wake up and you feel like you can't go on because you're so beat up."

Beer. Bill Walton wanted a beer. A bunch of the Celtics had sworn off it in April, just in case they'd need an extra ounce of bounce for an extra loose ball in June. Even Bird surrendered, the same Bird about whom Kevin McHale once said, "His idea of heaven would be a garage filled with Budweiser and every time he drank one, it would be replaced."

Bill Walton got his beer Sunday, and so did Larry Bird, and so did they all. The Celtics, a team that money can't buy, had opened up their quarters to the world. It was too busy for them to hug each other now, but as Nathan love-tapped daddy on the behind, and as Dennis Johnson screamed in glee at Jerry Sichting, who was yukking it up with Parish, who was putting on his championship cap, Bill Walton stood there as though he never wanted to leave.

"I knew we had it when we walked into this room this morning," he said. "I knew it as soon as we all showed up. I knew it when I looked in Larry's eyes. When did it all begin for this team? Probably the day Larry Bird was born."

Of course, it began long before that. The Boston Garden ceiling that is lost behind all the banners tells you that the Celtics have only one prejudice, a prejudice against losing. That's why Bill Walton picked up the phone last summer. In this crusty old building, pride lives.

FOOT-IN-MOUTH DISEASE

JUNE 14, 1987

Larry Bird has been white and slow for something like 31 years, so he chose not to make a scene. For that, clear thinkers should give thanks, because the playpen has had its fill of incessant babbling lately.

Isiah Thomas and Dennis Rodman, vanquished warriors from the Detroit Pistons, started it all with childish remarks. Even after they excused themselves, make-believe editorialists droned on, spreading hate while writing from the I-formation. Then along came that noted seer, Lefty Driesell, informing the free world that cocaine, used in proper doses, can be a useful substitute for aspirin.

To what do we attribute this epidemic of foot-in-mouth disease? Is it the heat, earth tremors, overlapping seasons, or simply the Curse of Campanis? Or has the PTL funneled a portion of that missing $92 million toward the sports industry, so as to take Ferdinand and Imelda Bakker off the hook? And you thought Casey Stengel made absolutely no sense.

Bird, with more important things to worry about than post-game petulance by losers, employed his overrated self in a peaceful and forgiving manner. He absolved Thomas of all blame, claiming that if Isiah said he was joking, then Isiah was joking. Period. Bird was not so kind to Rodman, who initiated this mindless discussion of Bird's being viewed as a great basketball player on account of pigment, not talent. But Thomas, a star himself, was the focal point of this mess and Bird did a handsome job of trying to extricate him.

It was an act of friendship beyond the call of duty, and if Thomas doesn't comprehend as much, he's got more problems than a bad head. You had to wonder about Thomas' character since he participated in—some would say, invented—the alleged freeze-out of Michael Jordan at the NBA All-Star Game a couple years ago. Jordan was black then, and still is, but more significantly, Jordan was on his way to becoming a spectacular and popular player. That's what mattered then, not Jordan's ancestry.

Thomas, who insists that his Bird platform was built on sarcasm, doesn't fess up to the Jordan episode, either. Apparently, that also was just a ha-ha, a little fun to dilute the tedium of just another ballgame. Apparently, too, Thomas is an excellent athlete who cannot tolerate other athletes' being more excellent.

Thomas was no bargain in Detroit's series against Boston, and he evidently forgot his coloring book when he flung an inbounds pass to Bird's waiting arms during the closing seconds of Game 5. That monumental gaffe kept the Celtics in the tournament. A basket followed, and soon, the Pistons were eliminated. Had Thomas thrown the ball to, say, one of his teammates, he would be too busy participating in the NBA finals now to issue any foolish proclamations. Unless, of course, envy of Magic Johnson overwhelmed Isiah.

Thomas isn't the first player to pout after a difficult defeat, and he won't be the last. Isiah is no angel, but whether he giggled or not to take the edge off his statement regarding Bird, Isiah shouldn't be condemned forever, either. He said what he thought, or didn't say what everybody else thought he said, but he apologized, and Bird accepted. It's over, or it should be.

Unfortunately, there are those fire-breathing sociologists who had days to think the issue through and still threw the ball in the wrong direction, anyway. It is one thing to raise a point— that there are dangerous stereotypes of blacks in sports, as in life—but it is quite another thing to run off at the typewriter and destroy any semblance of constructive criticism that might emerge. What impact is there if lack-of-responsibility charges are brought by the blatantly irresponsible?

Thomas is chastized for playing "kissy-kissy" with Bird at a press conference. What was a better alternative, the basic fist fight? Is this the solution? And a professor puts this lunacy on paper, for public consumption? Ah, but we must consider the source. The same truth-seeker who might pick Larry Bird for his team "after about eight or nine other players" is the same pundit who accused Bears quarterback Jim McMahon of being a racist from way back. This, the same Jim McMahon who had a black man as best man at his wedding.

Another gift from another institute of higher learning, Driesell, shared his genius the other day. The longtime head basketball coach at the University of Maryland explained, "I'm a firm believer that, if you know how to use cocaine and use it properly, it can make you play better." Driesell was trying as best he could to shed light on the subject of drug testing, but the old left-hander is infinitely better at cover-ups. Len Bias killed himself with cocaine just after being drafted by the Celtics a year ago, and Driesell was front and center, telling how he saw nothing, heard nothing, knew nothing.

Now, Driesell knows everything. He's the former Maryland coach—the entire Maryland basketball program ought to be former—but Lefty has found work as a commentator, of all things, and he might yet show up as coach someplace. Perhaps even with an expansion team in the pros, where he can say more dumb things. And where he will not be alone, as we have seen lately. He will have to fight to get a stupid word in edge-wise, and, a week later, some seer will author a column about how Lefty is right on the money. Cocaine does indeed cure headaches.

Larry Bird might have flat feet, but at least he needn't stick out his tongue to get at them.

Boxing

DURAN EATS AWAY AT MENTORS' FAITH

NOVEMBER 27, 1980

NEW ORLEANS—Just before noon Wednesday, Roberto Duran, surrounded by his people, bounced into the hotel coffee shop and ordered a substantial lunch. Some 14 hours earlier, across the street at the Louisana Superdome, with a cavalier wave in no particular direction, the same man had surrendered his World Boxing Council welterweight crown to Sugar Ray Leonard.

Roberto Duran later explained that he had a stomach ache. But now his appetite for food—which always had been deemed the equal of his appetite to be a champion—had returned. Now it was time for corn flakes, steak and eggs, biscuits and juice. He didn't merely eat his meal, he wolfed it down, inhaled it as though there were no tomorrow.

Of course, there is no tomorrow for Duran. For after he abandoned Tuesday night's fight, he revealed that he is abandoning fighting, period. He would retire, if not in disgrace, in mystery. "No questions," said Luis Henriquez, Duran's interpreter, shooing away uninvited guests from the fighter's alcove. "No questions."

But there must be questions about what transpired Tuesday night. And boxing does not need more questions; it needs more answers. Six weeks ago, Muhammad Ali, a legend, dishonored himself and his sport with a futile tap-dance atop a Las Vegas parking lot. And now this—Roberto Duran, a legend who everybody thought would rather die in the ring than embarrass himself or his beloved country of Panama, running up a white flag before the world.

"A man calls me in the middle of the night and says to me, 'After all these years in boxing, how could you be part of a fix?'" said 81-year-old Ray Arcel, Duran's brutally candid trainer. "Imagine that. I been in this sport since I was a kid, and now they tell me I'm involved in a fix. I suppose, though, the people have their suspicions, and you can't blame them. They're bewildered. I'm bewildered. It was the last thing I ever thought Roberto would do. Just quit in the middle of the ring.

"It's like you live next door to your neighbor for years and you think he's a perfect human being. You think you know him well. Then, the next morning you get up and read in the paper that he went out and killed somebody. I don't understand this any more than you do. They have performed all the physical examinations on him (Duran). Maybe, in the end, what they ought to do is have a mental examination.

"I haven't been able to really talk to Roberto yet. There are too many people around him. I know he is embarrassed. And I don't know if I will be able to talk to him. This is it for me. Finished with boxing. I've had enough."

Gnarled Freddie Brown, 73, Duran's other trainer, also packed his bags forevermore Wednesday. He, too, was still perplexed at what he had seen the night before. "Unbelievable," said Brown. "I mean this man was an animal in the ring. A savage. That's why you couldn't imagine what happened. When you consider the character of the fighter, it's unbelievable."

Both trainers fully considered Duran's pleas of illness sincere. As early as the fifth round, he had come to the corner complaining of nausea and stomach cramps that extended to his arms, then his shoulders. Arcel and Brown had encouraged Duran to keep fighting, hoping the problem might vanish. Instead, 2:44 into the eighth round, Duran vanished. Even if he had lasted the round and relinquished the title from his stool, it would have appeared more authentic.

Carlos Eleta, the millionaire Panamanian sportsman who bought Duran's contract for a mere $300 in 1971, sat at ringside and was shocked at his warrior's concession.

"He was not himself," Eleta said Wednesday. "Something was wrong. It was my decision that he retire. He did not show the

Roberto desire. He was very ashamed. He cried with me. There is a pitcher in your country (J.R. Richard) who was doubted when he said he was sick. But it turned out he was sick. That was a mystery, and so is this a mystery, what has happened to as great an athlete as Roberto."

After the fight, and after submitting to a press conference, Duran went to a nearby hospital for examinations. Spokesmen for the hospital said tests "were still being evaluated" by Wednesday nightfall. Dr. Orlando Nunez, Duran's personal physician, said the 29-year-old veteran of 74 pro fights had suffered "an acute abdominal pain . . . and indigestion."

That prompted speculation that Duran's ravenous hunger, which caused him to balloon to 172 pounds shortly after he wrested the title from Leonard in June, had, alas, done him in. He was slightly over the 147 limit at midday Monday, so he fasted until after the noon Tuesday weigh-in, when he came in at 146. Thereafter, Duran put away two steaks and four glasses of orange juice. Perhaps he overate, Arcel admitted, but Duran had been that route before and won.

Then, at 4 p.m. Tuesday, Duran nibbled again—a small steak and one cup of tea.

"Maybe that could have caused it," said Arcel. "I don't know. I just don't know."

But would a stomach ache, no matter how pronounced, cause a champion of Duran's ilk and reputation to quit a fight in which he had not been cut, or knocked down? Against an opponent he detested?

Before his Montreal fight, Duran had been checked for supposed heart irregularities, and cleared. Had danger signs reappeared? Had Eleta or Duran or both hidden the problem from Brown and Arcel to reap that one, final, grand paycheck?

"No way," said Arcel. "We do everything but watch Roberto go to the bathroom during training. We would know if anything was wrong. And if there was, there is no way I would send a man into the ring in that condition. There was nothing wrong with him physically before the fight. And, mentally, I felt he was as committed as ever to win."

And surely, just before noon Wednesday as he bounced toward the coffee shop, Roberto Duran looked in fine fettle.

"He is okay now," said Henriquez. "He was sick last night,

though. The water is very bad here. All over the city, the water is bad. And the food at this hotel, he did not like it at all.

"I admit it will be hard for Roberto to go back home. I have had hundreds of phone calls from Panama. We have lots of heroes there but Roberto is *the* hero. The people do not like what happened. We have only two million people there. There is no place to hide."

But, after lunch Wednesday, Duran hid in Eleta's 18th-floor suite. Reporters were told to stay outside. "There has to be something we don't know," said Arcel.

Only one interloper was welcomed after announcing his purpose. "Room service," the waiter bellowed. "Room service."

'AIN'T NOBODY DONE WHAT I DID'

DECEMBER 13, 1981

NASSAU, THE BAHAMAS—It was the morning after the sham the night before, and Muhammad Ali was beautiful. Not so much the body, but the soul. He took a potentially maudlin situation—another pitiable performance in the ring, followed by his long overdue promise never to re-enter it—and left 'em laughing. Till the end, he was The Greatest.

"I'm not depressed, because I'm still nice looking," he grinned. "But this ain't gonna be no Watergate. No mystery. It's not that the reflexes may be gone. They have gone. I shall return . . . to Los Angeles."

At midnight Friday, the world's most famous athlete had completed his 61st and worst professional bout—a 10-round unanimous-decision loss to Trevor Berbick, a pillow fight beneath a full moon in a decaying ballpark buffeted by cold, haunting island winds. Ali had acted all of 39, going on 49, and afterward—in a trailer that served as his dressing room—he cut the laces forevermore.

He had quit before, of course, and one and all expected a different melody after he had slept on it. True enough, Saturday morning, he rolled out of bed in a blue suit, talking like Tom Landry. He would have to look at the films to see if it was that bad, because those who loved him had told him it wasn't. He even jested that he might think otherwise in a month or so, but it was just that. Jest. This was taps. Ali, who had stolen many a decision on reputation alone, couldn't even come close to winning this one against an eminently average fighter fighting an average fight.

"If Berbick could have done any better and didn't, then I say thank you," purred Ali. "After the Holmes fight last year, I had excuses. But I have no excuses now. It's all over. I knew the things I had to do, but I just couldn't do them anymore. I'm not hestitating. I'm not crazy. There are other things for me to do.

"This was just a means to an end for me. Boxing was like the bait. Now, I can hook people to listen to me because of boxing. I will become an Islamic evangelist preaching around the world. I won't be part of boxing. Too boring. Broadcasting? No. You think I want to go around gyms the day before a fight, building it up like Cosell?"

There was a finality to his voice, but the glibness which made sports' most charismatic figure lived on. Beside Ali sat Berbick, bashful and quiet in the presence of his idol. When someone asked Berbick what *his* plans were now, The Greatest interrupted, his eyes big as tennis balls.

"You talk to me," Muhammad joked to the questioner. "I'm Berbick's manager now."

This had been some ride. Ali took boxing out of Madison Square Garden to Manila, Kuala Lumpur, Jakarta, and Zaire, always spending wildly en route on his wives, his malingerers, his favorite charities. He shuffled, danced, jabbed, jived, rope-a-doped, blustered, filibustered, spoke out on Vietnam, spoke down to Howard Cosell, spoke warmly with the little people, and spoke calmly with the big people.

"I've played on Brezhnev's living-room rug with his grandchildren," Ali said. "And every time Indira Gandhi saw me, she kissed me. I've been a hero to the rich and to the poor, the one man in a white world who questioned why we never see a picture of a black Jesus or a black angel. Ain't nobody done what I did."

He's right. Ain't nobody who did. He carried boxing for two decades. Unfortunately, he carried it too far. Boxing was as much to blame as Ali, though. If ever a sport begged for a ruling body or a czar to straighten out all the crookedness, it is boxing. But the fight game remains a disparate, desperate pastime that invites sleaze, dirt and knaves.

There is no one commissioner, no one commission to determine what is and isn't in boxing's best interests. If there were, there would be no Joe Frazier trying to belie his birth certificate 10 days ago in Chicago; no Ali trying to win the battle of the bulge here.

And there would be no promoters like James Cornelius, the airhead who mismanaged the "Drama in Bahama." Don't blame the Bahamas for him; he's American. And don't blame Bahamians for Friday night's traumas. They waited patiently for two hours while the fools-in-charge scurried about looking for gloves, water, a pail, a bell. The last match on the card was timed by a wristwatch borrowed from a spectator. The Ali bout was judged by Alonzo Butler, an assistant police commissioner "investigating" Cornelius' alleged mugging of promoter Don King. There was even a fire outside the Queen Elizabeth Sports Centre to complement the fire drill inside.

In New York or Chicago, the crowd might have rioted. Here, they just waited to witness The Greatest while Cornelius and his hired scalawags tripped over their thumbs. But don't blame Cornelius on Ali. Ali never could say no. His heart is as big as his mouth. Another hood ornament, a character in Los Angeles, recently embezzled $21 million using his name.

But Ali's last hurrah was a fetid whisper. He didn't punch Berbick, he slapped at him. On this card, Ali won the second, fifth, and sixth rounds. Other observers were not so benign.

"I gave Ali the fifth only, and that was charitable," said judge Jay Edson. "He was pathetic. He was hitting Berbick like a girl. A shame. But it could have been worse. What if Ali had been killed? Then what?"

Better we remember Ali as the brash ebony whirlwind who won all those electric fights in the '60s, or as the exiled king who returned from a 3½-year layoff after his draft protest to become three-time champion. The Thrilla in Manila with Frazier. The brawls with Ken Norton. The Rumble in the Jungle, when he regained his title by stopping George Foreman in 1974.

"My favorite fight," Ali said of the rope-a-dope victory over Foreman. "My best fight. The Thrilla? I felt like I was 39 that night, too. It'll be a long time until the world wakes up at 4 in the morning to watch two boys beat up on each other, won't it?"

Indeed, the sun never set on Ali's fandom. Most of the $60 million he earned is gone, and now, so is the foolish dream. But, for all his pretense, he was among the least phony of them all. And, like the judge said, the man could have quit from the back of an ambulance instead of a hotel suite on Paradise Island.

"I was standing at the end." Ali reminded. "Just think how

you white folk would have loved to be leaning over me with those cameras while I was lying on the canvas. I fooled you. Till the very end. I didn't give you that satisfaction."

But Muhammad Ali, his career punctuated by the seedy sound of a borrowed cowbell clanging in the dark, didn't leave us empty or sad. Berbick, who said he didn't have the heart to demolish a monument, claims he learned much from the master Friday night.

"Yeah," said Ali, laughing and interrupting again. "I taught him to retire before 40. Arteries get hard, just like the head."

The Greatest got up to sign autographs. First in line was Trevor Berbick. It was a long line. It always will be.

'LARRY WHO?'

JUNE 13, 1982

LAS VEGAS—Four years and four days ago, in this haven of hedonism, Larry Holmes defeated Ken Norton to capture the World Boxing Council heavyweight championship.

Friday night, Holmes successfully defended his title for the 12th time by stopping Gerry Cooney. Fittingly, at the fight's merciful end 2:52 into the 13th round, it wasn't Cooney who was left standing in the ring but trainer Victor Valle, who had climbed through the ropes to surrender.

If Holmes' luck continues according to Hoyle, it won't be long before we start to hear that, well, Cooney isn't all that much of a boxer, anyway. He's a lumbering bloke, a creation of the New York media, a one-dimensional green pea with thunder in his left hand, sawdust in his right, and more heart than savvy.

He may be all of the above, of course. And if and when Cooney acquires the varnish to call himself a complete fighter, Holmes might well be punching coupons instead of real or imagined threats to his well-earned gold belt.

But it has happened before, this *ex post facto* rape of Holmes' résumé. When he politely dismissed Muhammad Ali from the competitive scene two Octobers ago, Holmes thought—by eliminating this legend whose shadow he had chased—he wouldn't have to defend himself anymore, only his title. But Holmes was wrong, because Ali wasn't Ali anymore, they said.

"We come into his fight, I pick up *Time* magazine and Cooney's on the cover with Sylvester Stallone," said Holmes. "I pick up *Sports Illustrated*, and Cooney's on the cover, and I'm folded underneath. That doesn't bother me, though. Not anymore.

"I wasn't born to be Muhammad Ali or Joe Louis. I was born to be Larry Holmes. You can take my money and my cars, but not my pride. I'm not Larry Who anymore. I'm Larry Holmes. The other stuff don't matter."

Naturally, it does matter. But Holmes needn't worry about his niche in boxing after Friday night. He shouldn't have had to worry before Friday night, but such is his position in the sport. Because the heavyweight division has been as bland as a crash diet during his reign, Holmes has been blamed.

As though it were his fault. He has been ready, willing and one of the most available champions of our time, if not one of the most charismatic. Maybe he is right when he says he should move to Manhattan and run a few red lights. Then he'll be a hot item.

Strange, isn't it, that in a money-grubbing, underachieving athletic community, we have a heavyweight champion who works against the grain, and he gets a cold handshake for a 40–0 record? What is it? Is it the lisp?

"I've had 20 champions," says Ray Arcel, Holmes' 82-year-old consultant. "And I find it unbelievable that he isn't treated the way he should be. On record alone, he should rank with the best of them. Maybe it'll be one of those cases that, in 10 years from now, everybody will look back and say the man was a hell of a fighter, after all."

This peculiar attitude toward Holmes apparently has infiltrated even the heads of the judges. Maybe his consistency has left them jaded, too. A look at their cards after Friday night's memorable rumble suggests they are not men of great vision, or objectivity.

Two judges, Duane Ford and Dave Moretti, had Holmes ahead only 113–111 after 12 rounds. In other words, had it not been for the three points Cooney was penalized for delivering grossly low blows, he would have been ahead in the fight. Bleeding, outclassed, frustrated and fatigued, Cooney would have been ahead?

It cannot be. On this card, Cooney won two rounds, the fourth and 10th. All three judges, including Jerry Roth, determined that Cooney would have won the ninth, when his best shot landed in Holmes' protective cup. Valle saved boxing another blemish by recognizing the inevitable, because the judges weren't. Their addition simply didn't add. And to think it was the Cooney camp that bellyached about fair treatment.

"The scoring was hideous subterfuge," said promoter Don King, whose hairdo Saturday morning made him look like a porcupine in heat. "Cooney hit Holmes 10 times in the definitely delicate groinal region. If Holmes did that to Cooney, Larry would have been disqualified."

In the sixth round, a cut opened near Cooney's left eye. In the seventh, his nose started to bleed. Later on, a strawberry was growing over his right eye. At the end, when Holmes calmly removed his mouthpiece as Valle removed his fighter from the twine, the champion was unscathed.

One couldn't look inside Holmes' rib cage to check for damage left by Cooney's body blows. But many of those punches were deflected by Holmes, who absorbed the expected lefts and the unusually frequent rights that Cooney used as decoys. They are too harmless to be described as anything but.

At Saturday's perfunctory post-mortem, both gladiators doused the flames. Holmes admitted that all the talk about racial stigma was balderdash designed to sell the show. He cited how many white employees he has hired, how his black brothers have married white women.

"How," wondered Holmes, "could you call me racist?"

Cooney, whose manners should not be questioned, was crestfallen after his performance. But he cracked a smile between funks and had the dignity to reflect kindly on Holmes. Gentlemen Gerry knew what hit him.

"He's a champion," Cooney said. "Last night, I learned such a lesson. I wanted so much to go the distance, I held myself back. I was trying to show I could take it. It wasn't smart. I apologize to those who put their hopes in me. I have no excuses, but I shall return."

What's done is done, and now if Holmes only could do the impossible by muzzling Dennis Rappaport, the incorrigible blabbermouth who co-manages Cooney.

"C'mon Gerry," Rappaport yelled from ringside Friday night. "For America! Win it for your dead father. Boxing needs you."

We know one dunderhead boxing doesn't need.

MARVELOUS CHAMP

APRIL 17, 1987

LAS VEGAS—You knew Marvelous Marvin Hagler would be trouble when he selected Palm Springs, a slice of heaven in southern California, as a training site. "I'm going to jail for a month," promised Hagler. Anybody who goes to Palm Springs for the expressed purpose of being miserable, of leading a Spartan life, means business.

Tuesday morning, out of jail, his business finished, the Marvelous One wore a grin that might have circled his shaved head. Only a red baseball cap interrupted his blissful morning-after countenance; a red baseball cap with large white capital letters on the front. "WAR," the crown cried, and what a war it had been.

Monday evening, in back of Caesars Palace, where many a gambler has lost his toga, Hagler experienced what he so aptly described now as "the pinnacle of my career." With a brutal eight-minute clinic on how to take a lot of punishment while dispensing a lot more, Hagler defended his world middleweight title by stopping a bewildered Thomas Hearns at 2:01 of the third round.

Rarely had a bout in any division during any era contained such fury—339 punches thrown in 541 seconds, according to one computer—and if any scalped customer who paid $1,500 for a $600 ringside seat felt cheated, the complaints were lost amid roars of approval. You didn't just walk away from this fight; you sat in your chair for a while.

Besides the perfunctory hate-for-hype exchanges, this was a fight without many of the usual onerous overtones dealing with race, color, creed, whatever. Hearns came off as somewhat starstruck and cocky, and his brother, Billy, made a rube of himself by taunting Hagler's corner with thumbs-down hand signals during the national anthem. Hagler, as always, was himself. Pounding leather in purposeful seclusion, an athlete doing painful time in Palm Springs, passed by Rolls Royce after Jaguar through-out his early morning laps.

Beyond that, though, it was only a fight, not a social statement. And from it all came the inescapable conclusion that Hagler is thoroughly accomplished at these search-and-destroy missions, a veteran of 65 bouts who gained his crown in 1979 and still deserves recognition as the planet's best fistfighter 11 title defenses later.

"I just wanted to show Hearns who was boss, and I think I did," said Hagler, who grabbed his 3-year-old daughter, Cherelle, after the resounding TKO, at which point she mentioned that Daddy had a"boo-boo." The Marvelous One had indeed prevailed through two gushers—one on the forehead, another below the right eye—and the morning after, he admitted what everybody had suspected.

"I was a little scared about the cuts, I didn't want it to end because of that. So I had to speed things up. Blood turns me on. Gets me motivated. It brought out the monster in me. I said I would cut him down like a tree. I said I would be like Pac-Man with his punches," said Hagler, doing an eat-'em-up pantomime. "Sensational fight. But I hit him with that last right, and it closed the show."

Hagler related how Hearns showed a "lot of class" by coming to the winner's locker room after the fray. What Hearns never exhibited was smarts. After the Motor City Hit Man unloaded every bit of his arsenal to no avail during a visceral first round—"my guy fought 15 rounds in three minutes," said trainer Emanuel Steward—the wise move would have been to reconsider strategy. Instead, Hearns made the macho move.

Sugar Ray Leonard, broadcasting ringside, chided the tactic, though his similar toe-to-toe posture might have cost him his first assignment against Roberto Duran. Steward and company were imploring Hearns to box, to use his reach and quickness, to exploit Hagler's scarlet predicament.

But Marvelous was relentless, heaping leaping rights on his challenger and muscling away any efforts by Hearns to tie up his monster of a foe. "My offense was my best defense," assured Hagler, rubbing the bill of that red baseball cap, revealing plans to fight one more year, then abandon this ruthless occupation.

"I was shocked," said Pat Petronelli, half the brother combination that brought Hagler from a New Jersey ghetto to their Brockton, Massachusetts, gym two decades ago. "We knew Hearns would come out storming. But after he shot his wad in the first round, and Marvin took it like we knew he could, we thought Hearns would back off a little, move around. 'Course, the way Marvin was going after him, maybe Hearns couldn't. He had nowhere to go but down."

Hagler had planned to attack Hearns' body, figuring the leaner they are, the easier to double them up. It worked, everything worked, and Hagler said he was never hurt. Those old wounds that broke open, he said, will heal in time for him to pursue Carlos Monzon's record of 14 title defenses. That's what Hagler wants now, now that he has gotten his proper salutes.

"I said last night I was the greatest," Hagler went on, mellowing. "But I want the public to decide that. I'd rather have them say that than me."

And then he went to the bill of his cap until it was backwards on his head. "I turn it around because the war is over," he said. It was, and there's no guarantee that a rematch ever could match the original. Marvelous Marvin Hagler, though bald, still has too much hair for Thomas Hearns.

THE RIPPLE EFFECT

NOVEMBER 24, 1986

LAS VEGAS—Exhibiting a rare sense of order, the insubordinate sport that is boxing has blessed us with a series of bouts designed to produce one, and only one, heavyweight champion. Demolition in the name of unification, and all the alphabet soups agree it's the best thing, especially HBO.

However, there's a real possibility that Mike Tyson will organize the division by himself, with his own two sledgehammers, without smoke-filled meeting rooms peopled by crooked commissioners with crooked teeth and double dandruff. At age 20, his neck as expansive as his future, Tyson could just shake some cold logic out of the sweet science.

"At his stage, I've never seen anyone like him," said Angelo Dundee. "How do you fight him? With a gun."

Dundee has spent the better part of his life whispering tactics in crowded corners. He has trained Muhammad Ali, among too many others to count, but after Saturday night's exhibition of purposeful violence, Dundee was left to conclude that, true, Tyson is young, the youngest ever to wear a heavyweight crown. But given the proper direction for his aggression, this onetime delinquent can be a marquee man-child as long as he chooses.

"In boxing, there's always somebody out there who can lick you," said Dundee, allowing for the possibility that Tyson's conqueror still might be in a crib. "But I don't know who it is. I'd like to look at the films of this."

It's not often that Dundee talks like a football coach, but he was somewhat confounded. After the first round of Saturday's World Boxing Council rout, he barked at his man, Trevor Berbick, for risking his title by attempting to prove he could absorb punishment instead of dance. However, after Berbick was mesmerized by a left hook to the temple—and rescued by benign referee Mills Lane at 2:35 of the second round—Dundee comprehended that perhaps the only strategy against Tyson is to seek a desk job until the lad from Brooklyn gets fat, lazy or old.

"The kid puts so much pressure on you that he doesn't let you do what you want to do," Dundee said after the resounding TKO, the 26th in 28 professional matches for the undefeated Tyson. All of Berbick's perceived advantages in his otherwise distinct underdog's role—reach, experience, mobility—were rendered null and void by Tyson's venom. It was brutally succinct. Even the veteran Lane seemed dazed as he scooped up Berbick from a neutral corner where only the ropes restricted him from collapsing into press row. At the end, Berbick floundered about the canvas like a goldfish taken out of water and forced to fend for itself on a kitchen table.

"I am the youngest champion and I'll be the oldest, too," claimed Tyson, an ominous presence in black trunks, no socks, no robe. "I refuse to get hurt. I refuse to get knocked down. I refuse to lose. I want to keep this title as long as I can. It's what I've wanted for years. Hydrogen bombs. I threw hydrogen bombs out there, every punch with murderous intention."

Tyson, mind you, is not so much an animal that he forgot for a split second Cus D'Amato, his savior who died a year ago, the same guru who honed Floyd Patterson into the previous youngest heavyweight champ, in 1956. Tyson, declared a wimp by fellow hooligans for his short stature and his lisp, was relieving New York City subway passengers of their jewelry when he was shipped to an upstate reform school at age 13. D'Amato—"this crazy white dude," as Tyson referred to him—took the ghetto out of the kid and put the kid in gloves.

"He said I'd be champion if I wanted it," Tyson recalled. "Without Cus, this never would have happened. He's probably up there, real proud right now. Also, he's probably up there saying, 'You made a lot of mistakes tonight.' "

Jimmy Jacobs, Tyson's latter-day saint, felt a disquieting calm before the bout. Would Tyson be sufficiently motivated for this $1.5 million moment? Not to worry. Tyson, in "my best fight yet," packed too much speed, which from bodies like his invariably means too much power. Jacobs, a boxing historian, also detected the "Joe Louis Syndrome." That is, Louis' opponents developed stage fright on cue, utterly intimidated by that appearance of invincibility. The flat-footed Berbick, Jacobs suggested, was a slow-motion version of the usual Berbick.

"He fought no more like Berbick than I did," Jacobs said. And Berbick had to consult replays to determine what exactly hit him—another common post-Tyson symptom.

According to the elaborate plans, Tyson in March will meet the winner of December's elimination tiff between World Boxing Association champion Tim Witherspoon and Tony Tubbs. Whoever survives March will confront International Boxing Federation champion Michael Spinks in the unification ceremony. Spinks, at ringside Saturday, mentioned, "I ain't afraid of nobody." Neither was Berbick, who lasted eight months as the WBC's ruling heavyweight body. Then, within six minutes against Tyson, he was looking at the ceiling through foggy lenses.

"Can I save the heavyweight division?" Tyson wondered. "I just want to be as good as I can be. People say I'm the greatest. I feel like I'm just learning."

Such is the conundrum for outsiders like Dundee, films or no films.

"How do you slow him down?" he said. "I don't know. He's young. Maybe he'll find himself a girlfriend."

YOU CAN GO HOME

APRIL 7, 1987

LAS VEGAS—Whether the judges rendered the correct decision is to be argued later, as it surely will be, because the fight was too close and too visceral to inspire anything but volumes of conversation and debate.

What cannot be disputed, however, is that Sugar Ray Leonard made the right call. He said he needed to put away the cummerbund and put on the gloves again, and the minute he danced into the ring Monday night behind Caesars Palace, you knew he was home again.

Sugar Ray had retired twice, to various endeavors, because of different reasons. Once he quit because doctors warned that his eyesight might not take another hit; once he quit because he felt embarrassed at barely beating a brash tomato can by the name of Kevin Howard. But the fire never went out in Leonard, who figured that being 30 years old was too young to die.

So Leonard picked his spot, and his opponent, and Monday night in an upset that defied all odds in this city of oddsmakers, the special guy with the pearly smile and the will of granite beat Marvelous Marvin Hagler to claim the World Boxing Council's middleweight championship. Only when it was all over and a split decision went his way did Sugar Ray concur with what a majority of experts had been saying for months. He said it was indeed impossible. But he did find a way.

Strange verdicts have emanated from this cement and neon slab that passes for a city, and the Hagler camp was roaring about the injustice of it all well into the night. How could one judge, JoJo Guerra, award but two of twelve rounds—the fifth and last—to the Marvelous One, and a 118–110 plurality in points to Leonard? How could another judge, Dave Moretti, imagine that Hagler won only five rounds toward a 115–113 defeat? Our card had it as judge Lou Filippo's had it, 115–113 for Hagler, but for the moment, we should cast aside statistics for aesthetics.

Sugar Ray Leonard, you see, would have won even had he lost. He emerged from a five-year sabbatical, added pounds that might have bogged down a lesser man and, above all, appeared as though he had never left us. The thinking man's boxer thought his way out of inactivity when almost everybody thought he should do otherwise, and then one of the most splendid former champions of this or any time became a champion again. Alas, Leonard took more that a hard head into the ring, and he took more than an oversize ego. He took with him a heart too immense for common folk to measure.

There was that ninth round, for instance, when Leonard's early quickness and deft footwork seemed to have vanished. Hagler, who had missed too often and had given away too much during the opening four rounds, was now taking it back. He had Leonard trapped in the latter's corner, working Sugar Ray over, the legs wobbly, the end in sight, perhaps. But then, on blind courage, Leonard burst from the cocoon with his own fury, like nothing had happened, like he'd never been away from his element. He lost the round, did Leonard, but when he gazed into the crowd at the bell, he found wife Juanita and gave her a wink. It had been worth the wait, he seemed to be saying.

Leonard had the world at his grasp, with all that money and all that fame these past few years, but the only thing he craved was this. He was the consummate showman as always, frowning at Hagler and giving him the bug-eyed try-to-hurt-me-if-you-can looks. Leonard mixed in a few bolo punches for good measure, too, blended with a dart here and an Ali shuffle there. You can't do that sort of a thing in your back yard, no matter how many acres, at least to the applause of a worldwide audience. And that's what Leonard required, more than food, more than breath. Boxing. And he did a fair bit of that, too.

Hagler mentioned after the shock of the judges' wisdom that he had not sought a knockout in the late going because "I thought I was way ahead." Truth is, in a match that will be remembered more for its tactics than its ferocity, the Marvelous One never could pull the trigger—whether he fought from the right, via the southpaw route, chased or patiently waited for the opening. In combat with a superior angle player such as Leonard, Hagler missed often and loudly. He has slipped, as we all do, but his greatest miscalculation was underestimating Leonard's determination. In that, Hagler was not alone.

"My greatest accomplishment," said Leonard, who had to be carried to his corner at fight's end. The droplets of perspiration on his closely cropped hair made him look gray in the bright lights, but he was smiling and winking again at Juanita, who was crying all over her blue dress. The comeback attempt had worked so smashingly well that a victory now would be a bonus, not unlike the evening itself. The fight had justified its billing, and Sugar Ray Leonard had justified his presence. He said that he had nothing to prove, and then he went out to prove everything.

Many of his friends and admirers imposed their advice on Sugar Ray Leonard, but special guy that he is, he said enough. He had fulfilled all requests during his career, from being a decent guy to a splendid fighter to a fighter in absentia. Now, Leonard would do someting he wanted to do, something for himself, to clear the itch. He would shed the tuxedo and start up training again, because there was the Monday night in April of 1987 that would be his moment. You watch, he said, and we all watched.

And, as it turns out, we forgot more about Sugar Ray Leonard the last five years than he forgot.

Hockey

'SHORT-PANTS BOYS' SAVING GAMES

FEBRUARY 17, 1980

LAKE PLACID, NEW YORK—The boys in short pants are saving the Olympics. The United States hockey team.

It's still a cartoon up here, folks, and there's absolutely no chance that the people running this thing ever will lose their amateur standing. But the boys in short pants indeed are threatening to make it all worthwhile.

Saturday, the Americans beat Norway 5–1 to remain undefeated—two wins, one tie—in the Blue Division. The victory was achieved in virtual secrecy because Olympic disorganizers scheduled the game in the tattered 1,500-seat "Old Arena" here rather than the spanking new Fieldhouse. Please, please don't ask why.

Neither was the victory very pretty. The Americans were bland at the start, better at the end, but never did they dance as they had against two previous and superior foes—Sweden and Czechoslovakia. Just as coach Herb Brooks, who says you can never trust a bunch of young hockey players as far as you can throw them, had forecasted.

"He told us not to take the game lightly, our friends told us not to take the game lightly, our families told us not to take the game lightly, and we told each other not to take the game lightly," said Capt. Mike Eruzione. "So what happened? We took the game lightly. That's all right, though."

It's all right because, after Norway scored first to lead 1–0, and after a game goalie, Jim Martinsen, had made it stand up for a period, the Americans beat him five straight times over the next 40 minutes.

After an eminently arguable tripping call, Eruzione tied it

172

1–1 on a powerplay 41 seconds into the second period. Then Mark Johnson, wounded but willing, won it with a 20-foot bullet four minutes later. Then Dave Silk, Mark Wells, and Ken Morrow scored, too, and Brooks, a pacer rather than a trotter, relaxed as the end of what he termed a "brutal" performance neared.

But, like the captain said, that's all right. A lot of nice things have happened to the Americans this week. They have become the stars of the XIII Winter Olympics, and deservedly so. The interviewers, the fans, the floaters, who once shunned them, now chase them. But, it appears that this hockey team can handle anything now—even defeat—because it is a team. All those six o'clock wake up calls for a bus trip to another exhibition game in another hamlet have created a bond.

"Amazing," says Eruzione, a Boston University product. "We're thrown together in September, and now we're incredibly close. I mean, a lot of us played together in school, but still it's a nice thing to see. We know we won't be together for the Winter Olympics in 1984. Lots of these guys will be pros. But we decided the other night to have a reunion every four years, anyway. We're going to have it here in Lake Placid, too. During the summer, when there's no snow. I just hope, ho, ho, we can get a bus."

The Americans' harmony is not lost on National Hockey League people, who are descending en masse on the village. The Montreal Canadiens locked up defenseman Bill Baker the other night. Dave Lucas, a Black Hawks' scout, is here to check out injured Jack O'Callahan (who may be held out again for Monday night's match versus Romania). And even the Pittsburgh Penguins are waking up on Johnson, whose small stature they fear certainly didn't restrict him from becoming the best college hockey player anywhere—maybe anytime—the last few years.

"I know one thing," said Minnesota North Stars' general manager Lou Nanne. "I'm glad *we* didn't have to play them the night they played the Czechs."

Jim Gregory, director of the NHL's Central Scouting Bureau, also witnessed Thursday night's 7–3 U.S. conquest.

"For a team that's been together six months to play that well against a team that's been together for six years . . . well, it's incredible," said Gregory. "It shows a lot of things. First of all, there may be more talent on the American team than a lot of people think. Secondly, they are tremendously well coached. Herb Brooks and his staff have really done it."

The American athletes, of course, can reap much by looking good here. But if you infer that they are working hard just because NHL people are in the stands, you insult them. First of all, the good players will make good money, medal or no medal. Secondly, ailing players such as Johnson and Morrow might gain more by sitting out than playing hurt. Morrow's shoulder is so bad he can barely shoot the puck. His "drive" from deep on the right was so slow Saturday that it fooled Martinsen.

Brooks, too, is on display. He is being chided in some circles for secluding his players so he may promote himself. But, in fact, they are available.

"Herbie wants us to think about hockey and nothing else," said Eruzione. "We understand that. Besides, after we beat the Czechs the other night, I was interviewed by everybody but *Hustler.*"

A few players, particularly Easterners such as goalie Jim Craig, question Brooks, but that is probably healthy, too. They have minds of their own. They have questions. They have personality. They are not robots. They act and react, relate and interrelate. That is part of their beauty.

When Eruzione's name was drawn to submit to the postgame doping test Saturday, he went to the medical room and requested a beer "just to make sure."

When Norway's Oeivind Loesaamoen lost his stick while jumping the U.S. net Saturday, Craig could have shunted it to the side. But no, Craig tapped it back to the defensemen so he could rejoin the play. "A gentleman," said the losing coach.

When you ask Buzz Schneider, the "old man" of the team, about his background, he asks if you know your geography. "One year I played for seven teams and three of them folded. I've been all over, and somewhere along the line I got married, too."

When Mark Pavelich, one of the few U.S. players who is a free agent, is asked which NHL team is his favorite, he replies, "this one."

And when Andrei Starovoitov, executive secretary for the Soviet Ice Hockey Federation, leaves his seat because he finds himself surrounded by fans cheering wildly for the boys in short pants, the boys in short pants notice.

Almost all of them have optimistic futures and great expectations. But for all of them, now is the moment. They are taking it all in, and taking it all in stride. Most enjoyably, they are working hard at playing hard and having fun while creating fun.

The boys in short pants are the stars of the XIII Winter Olympics. Only Kelly Brooks, the coach's 8-year-old daughter, doesn't quite understand.

She really wanted to give her dad a Valentine's Day card Thursday, but she couldn't.

When he left the arena past midnight, she was waiting outside.

"It's not Valentine's Day anymore, Daddy," she said. "It's the day after."

"That's okay, hon," said Herb. "I had a hockey game, and besides, you'll always be my Valentine."

A GOLD MEDAL

FEBRUARY 25, 1980

LAKE PLACID, NEW YORK—The United States Olympic hockey team, which came from nowhere and was supposed to go nowhere, Sunday exceeded its absolutely wildest expectations.

A gold medal.

"I couldn't sleep Friday night after we beat the Russians, and I won't sleep again tonight," said Rob McClanahan. "Because if I sleep, there'll always be the chance that this was a dream."

McClanahan, a left wing who is bound for the National Hockey League Buffalo Sabres, clicked for the winning goal at 6:05 of a stirring third period during which the Americans scored three times to defeat Finland 4–2.

The victory—which allowed the Americans to finish the XIII Winter Olympics with a record of six victories, no losses, one tie—guaranteed them this country's first hockey gold medal since 1960. Then, as this club did, a similarly obscure U.S. entry beat the Soviet Union in the next-to-last game before rallying in the closing period to clinch gold in its final match.

"I was the last player cut from that team 20 years ago," said U.S. Coach Herb Brooks. "And I remember being back home at some saloon in St. Paul, drinking beer and watching the team win the medal out in Squaw Valley. I much prefer this. What you saw on this club was a group of people who startled the athletic world. Not just the hockey world. I want to make that clear. They startled the athletic world."

The 42-year-old Brooks, who could pass for an anchorman on the 10 o'clock news, took a leave of absence last summer from the University of Minnesota, where he has won three NCAA titles. In early September, camp for the U.S. Olympic team convened and a grueling, 62-game, international exhibition training schedule ensued.

The byproduct was two weeks of excellence. The seventh-seeded Americans faced European powerhouses, beat them without any fights or without one penalty of more than two minutes. It was an uncommon accomplishment, one that has to embarrass the NHL. But Brooks, who can now write his professional ticket, did not gloat. Rather, he reacted as a teacher who finally got his lesson across.

"I'm not one to throw rocks at the pros," he said. "But I've said time and again there are other ways to play this game than the way it's played in the NHL. What our victory here does is prove, I think, that college hockey in the United States is better than a lot of people thought, and that the amateur program in this country is moving forward, not backwards."

Certainly, the overflow crowd in the 8,500-seat Olympic Fieldhouse on the closing day of the 1980 Winter Olympics was stirred. After Mark Johnson's short-handed goal with 4:35 remaining made it 4–2, the crescendo on "U-S-A, U-S-A," the flag waving and the impromptu choruses of "God Bless America" began. U.S. athletes from other Olympic teams arose from their seats clapping.

The Russian coaches—whose team, had America lost, would have had a chance at its fifth straight gold medal—ducked through the runway to prepare for a now-insignificant game against Sweden. A feeling engulfed the building. Here, after all, was a U.S. team so good that even Tass praised it.

Finally, with seconds remaining, goalie Jim Craig looked over to his bench and raised his gloved hand. His teammates, all standing, responded by banging their sticks onto the dashers. Then, Craig turned to Section 6, where players' parents and relatives were situated. He waved again. Then, even though the game had not officially ended, the Americans emptied onto the ice, heading for Craig.

At last, the moment arrived, the moment that made seven months of bumpy bus rides, greasy hamburgers, and threadbare hotel mattresses worthwhile.

00:00, the clock read.

"How do you describe something that's indescribable?" said team captain Mike Eruzione, son of a Boston sewage disposal worker. "I wish we could stay together forever. They say we were a group of college kids from Boston, and another group of college kids from Minnesota, but there are no groups on this team.

"We played for America. Maybe they can keep us as a team

and make us the 22nd franchise in the National Hockey League."

Downstairs, in the locker room, Vice President Mondale—from Minnesota, as were nine of the players—made the rounds. And then he handed the telephone to Eruzione. "It's President Carter," said the Vice President. Eruzione confirmed that the team will make good on the White House luncheon date Monday. Then President Carter wished Eruzione good luck.

"Good luck to you, too," concluded Eruzione, a plucky guy who never lacks for a rejoinder.

"What a team!" screamed Jack O'Callahan, the forever-loose Irishman who plans to drop the first puck at Wednesday night's Black Hawk game in Chicago. His ailing left knee hampered him this tournament, but Brooks praised the eager defenseman for his zeal.

"He was yelling so hard during the Russian game," said Brooks, "he coached the team during the last 10 minutes. Not me."

"What a team!" repeated O'Callahan.

It is all of that. When asked what this all meant to him, Craig mentioned Steve Janaszak, the backup goalie who hadn't played a minute here.

"He was as important to this club as anybody," said Craig. "The way he pushed me to play better, the way he carried himself, it made me a better person."

And they hugged. And when Johnson was asked if this was the happiest day of his life, he quite agreed.

"But Tuesday might just be the saddest," he said. "That's when we scatter. I'll never play with these guys again. I may never *see* a lot of these guys again."

For America's Team, nothing surpassed the importance of being earnest.

It was that way on the ice, too, of course. If they lacked talent, they did not lack pluck. How else do you explain the fact that they outscored opponents 11–2 in the second periods of their seven games and 16–3 in the third periods?

Splendid conditioning was part of it, and Brooks was so adamant in this area that his players growled, more than once muttering that "the real ayatollah is in Lake Placid, not Iran."

But the Russians and Swedes and Finns also are well honed.

No, it was more than wind sprints that did it. The body's most important muscle, after all, is the heart.

Sunday, all these truths were self-evident. For two periods, the Americans did not skate that well and because of it, did not play that well. They trailed 2–1. One might have ascribed their anguish at that juncture to the foibles of youth and inexperience, or to the motivated manner of their foe.

The answer lay somewhere between. Certainly, an American defeat would have been less an upset than upsetting. The Finns were playing well, closing off the middle smartly and being strong with the body.

"But I knew they couldn't skate with us in the long run," reasoned Eruzione. "I knew if they were going to win this game, it was going to be something like 2–1. They would not keep the pace."

Eruzione was correct. The Finns couldn't cope.

At 2:25 of the final period, Dave Christian—who will be a center for the Winnipeg Jets, but played defense for the Americans—collected his seventh assist when he fed Phil Verchota, a Brooks-trained Gopher, who jammed the tying puck past Finnish goalie Jorma Valtonen. It was 2–2, and for the next 10 minutes, the Finns would not have a shot.

"At that point," said Finnish coach Kari Makinen, "the Americans were possessed."

None was more possessed than Johnson, the 5–9 bumblebee whom the Pittsburgh Penguins are ignoring because of his size.

On the winner, he would not be stopped. Perched behind Finland's net, he passed out to McClanahan, who would not be moved from Valtonen's immediate left. The time was 6:05, the score was 3–2.

After this, the Americans were assessed three consecutive penalties by Czechoslovakian referee Vladimir Subrt, who, on the whole, was rather lenient this day.

At 6:48, Neal Broten went off for hooking. The Americans killed it. At 8:54, Christian went off for tripping. The Americans killed it. At 15:45, Verchota went off for roughing. The Americans did more than kill it.

A half minute into the penalty, Johnson came upon the puck just inside Finland's blue line. He drove for the net and would not be stopped again, or at least not until he stuffed in his own rebound for a shorthanded score at 16:25. The Americans' bench staged another evacuation drill.

"I'm so proud, so happy," said Mark's father, Bob, coach at the University of Wisconsin and coach of the 1976 Olympic team. "I was in Colorado last night for a game, and traveled all night to see this. A 4 a.m. bus from Albany. I would have walked to see this."

Craig could now take a deep breath. He had been beaten on a long drive 9:20 into the first period by Jukka Porvari, the Finnish captain who played and played and played. Just after they had survived their first penalty, the Americans evened it 1–1 when Steve Christoff slithered a tepid backhander between Valtonen's pads at 4:39 of the middle period.

But Buzz Schneider, the most veteran American player and the only returnee from the 1976 team, dug another hole at the six-minute mark. Inexplicably, the mild-mannered Schneider slashed Olli Saarinen, losing his stick in the process. Only 30 seconds later, on an exceptional powerplay pattern, Mikko Leinonen converted from Craig's left and it was 2–1.

Valtonen at this point was looking formidable. And the Americans were looking somewhat tentative.

"We were exhausted, emotionally and physically," said Craig. "I'm glad we don't have to go through this again. If we did, it might have a different result. I don't know anybody who expected us to come this far. I know I didn't. But to be 20 minutes away from the gold and not get it . . . God, we would never have forgiven ourselves."

As it was, America's Team—which had melded European ideals with Yankee ingenuity to effect Brooks' "system"—was understandably giddy as it trudged through the snow, en masse, still perspiring, to meet the press at a building next to the rink.

"They have hated me at times, I know," said Brooks. "But once in awhile, you have to spank your players as a father would spank his child. We didn't have to win a medal to prove our way of life is better, but we won anyway. And as I love my children, I love this team."

THE GREAT GRETZKY

FEBRUARY 11, 1982

EDMONTON, CANADA—Life in the fast lane finally has caught up with Wayne Gretzky. It is 33 below zero down-town—"But only 31 below at the airport," says the nervy TV weatherman—and the world's best hockey player has a cold.

"The Kid," which is what he is called when he isn't called "The Great One," is merely poking at his half-filled dinner plate, opting instead to sip from an assembly line of therapeutic liquids that includes tomato juice and hot tea. When he absolutely must, he swerves politely toward the wall of the restaurant to blow his nose.

It is the night before Gretzky and his Edmonton Oilers will challenge the Gallic thrusts of Montreal's Canadiens in a game that shall consume Canada as completely as winter, so, of course, he will be home in bed early. The raspy voice and heavy eyelids, though, tell you he should have been there long ago. It's just that, for all the records he breaks, he can't break a promise.

"I have an appearance to make," he explains. "How do you say no . . . especially after you say yes?"

The late and wonderful Red Smith, the best sports writer ever, forever cautioned himself and others in the reportorial business against "Godding up" athletes, making them seem better than they really are. But, in Gretzky's case, that is tough duty. Emissaries from Izvestia to the *New York Times,* and thousands of points in between, have probed The Kid in quest of his dark side. They come away with blank looks and matching notepads. What you see in Wayne Gretzky is what he is. A prince of a man who is still a boy.

The ingredients are there for him to be a spoiled brat. Just two weeks past his 21st birthday, Gretzky is the highest-paid athlete in North America, having recently signed a $20 million contract with bonus clauses and a shopping mall to be named later. Before his first "lifetime" pact was destroyed by Oilers' owner Peter Pocklington, the boss gave The Kid a $57,000 Ferrari to park beneath the $150,000 condominium he shares with teammate Kevin Lowe. At present, Gretzky does endorsements for nine major companies, but that figure, like his point total, is subject to almost daily upward revision.

But ask Gretzky to do a freebie speech before a gaggle of high school kids on the evils of smoking those funny little cigarettes, and he's got his coat on asking for directions. He is big on causes besides his own. The Oilers' yearbook, which lists his offseason home as "North America," acknowledges his frantic summer pace on behalf of charity. Gretzky has an aunt who is mentally retarded, and his steady girl—Edmonton nightclub entertainer Vickie Moss—has a similarly afflicted brother. Yet, when The Kid stages one of his benefit golf or tennis tournaments, he doesn't forget the blind, the Canadian Heart Fund, the United Way of Alberta or the Juvenile Diabetes Foundation.

It was such a commitment that curtailed a fun afternoon last Monday. The Oilers somehow corralled him for lunch, during which they surprised Gretzky with a gold pendant: crossed hockey sticks with the numbers "50" and "39" engraved above and below to signify the 50 goals he scored in his first 39 games this season—one of The Kid's many National Hockey League milestones.

"That probably meant more to him than all the money in the world," said Garry Unger, one of the few Edmonton players who is older than 25. "But Gretz couldn't stay long. He had to hop a plane to do something for someone. Beautiful. The Kid is beautiful."

Billy Harris, the Oilers' cerebral assistant coach, wholly agrees. He says Gretzky makes sure he doesn't dominate the locker room: that honor belongs to the Ping-Pong table that sits in the middle of the clubhouse, hosting impromptu tournaments whenever. Gretzky isn't the most talented at this game, but nobody can remember him losing very often, either.

The Oilers can remember preseason strength tests, when Gretzky failed introductory pushups, finished last in the class and wondered aloud whether he was stronger than his mother.

They also remember preparing for a game in Toronto, where The Kid's father would drive to from the family home in Brantford, Ontario, some 60 miles west, to watch. Fearful that dad wouldn't approve of a recent perm job, The Kid had his head decurled and came to the airport looking like a GI. He hasn't yet lived that one down.

"Despite who he is, Wayne can take a joke," says Harris. "Once in a while, there's a hint of jealousy in other players. You know, jesting that isn't really jesting. But they love him, and besides, Wayne is as much a genius in here as he is out there on the rink. Very mature. Don't forget, he's 21 going on 31."

Indeed, The Kid, who was nudged by father Walter to begin skating at age 3, didn't just become special. As a 10-year-old, he scored 378 goals, and Canada promptly labeled him the next Bobby Orr. Gretzky, then, has developed tact, social grace and the knack of calling all elders "mister" over a period of years. What he hasn't yet learned is the art of signing autographs while still moving toward the team bus. Often, that means the team bus doesn't move, either.

"It's in my new contract that this summer I'll be able to do nothing for 30 days," says Gretzky. "For that to happen, I guess Vickie and I will have to vanish somewhere. The only way you can't be around is if you're not around. But everybody makes too big a thing of how busy I am. I don't think it's half as bad as what Reggie Jackson went through in New York."

Trying to justify his role as Canada's greatest hero, Gretzky allows himself to be blitzed mercilessly by the media. At a Toronto press conference, 31 microphones almost caused the podium in front of him to tilt over. Yet, confidants can recall him nearing the breaking point only twice. Once, *Life* magazine turned a one-day photo session into six days. Another time, after Gretzky revealed he is Byelorussian-Ukrainian, a truth-seeker asked The Kid his feelings on the situation in Poland. Oiler publicity director Bill Tuele pulled the curtain then and there.

"He just never seems to get mad," says an awed Lowe. "Or tired. He'll sleep for an hour in the afternoon, then be ready to roll again. Must be all my good cooking or those days we spend watching *General Hospital* before games."

But Gretzky is more than a student of soap operas. Though shy, he is genuine with people. You will not feel uncomfortable in his company. And if he is laidback in casual discussion, he is a closet Britannica on hockey. The Hartford Whalers can recall an obscure minor leaguer, and The Kid will know all about him. The Kid also knows all about the perils of his sport, and is concerned that his visits represent the only guaranteed sellouts in too many NHL rinks.

"We've got to look after our game," says Gretzky, who is surprised that Orr ducked interviews during his playing days as a concession to his powers of concentration. Gretzky, it seems, wants to do everything his idols Gordie Howe, Bobby Hull and Orr did for hockey, on and off the ice, only better. Nothing less will satisfy The Kid's competitive urges.

Gretzky, who admits being awed in the presence of show biz celebrities, still would rather meet George Brett than anyone. The Kid, after all, is an all-sports freak who fondly remembers joining the defunct Indianapolis Racers of the equally defunct World Hockey Association at age 17.

"I went to Indianapolis in July before the season to complete grade 12," he says. "That was 1977, and we got all the baseball games on TV from Chicago. Both the Cubs and White Sox were hot there for a while. Do the Sox still have that crazy guy doing their games? Harry Caray, that's it. Great, he's great."

Though Gretzky might be even bigger if he played in, say, New York, he claims he is at ease in Edmonton, a boom oil town in western Canada. The city, like the Oilers, is young and vibrant, but the population of 570,000 is appreciative yet respectful of this blond prodigy. If you can't buy a Wayne Gretzky nightgown, it's only because they're sold out. Settle for a Wayne Gretzky purse instead? Still, on this particular night, the idol of 25 million Canadians can walk through the streets en route to dinner without being mobbed. To this bachelor, that constitutes getting lucky.

"The way I relax is playing hockey, and this is a nice place to play," he says, still sniffling and staring at a potato. "I did get pulled into a store coming over here, though. Somebody wanted me to buy a $45,000 fur coat. Can you believe that? I think I'll stick with my good old $90 job right here. It looks okay, doesn't it?"

REFORM UP TO PLAYERS

FEBRUARY 11, 1982

After he recently suspended a National Hockey League coach for ordering a player to fight, John Ziegler was accused by certain cynics of being a knee-jerk president.

This is absurd, of course. Everybody knows that Mr. Ziegler is not a knee.

What the doughty little leader did however, was underscore the inconsistencies of the league's penal system, such as it is. Hockey's great thinkers assure us that they are pledged to eliminate the game's seamy elements, but these speeches pack all the sincerity of Willie Sutton coming out in support of tighter security at the nation's banks during the Roaring '20s. After everything is said and left undone, hockey remains the only sport this side of boxing to condone fighting.

When Paul Holmgren attempted to rearrange the stripes on referee Andy Van Hellemond's shirt, it took the NHL court of justice too long to assess the Philadelphia Flyers' policeman too little punishment—five measly games. And when Jimmy Mann jumped off the bench in cold blood to break the jaw of Pittsburgh's Paul Gardner, Ziegler's Follies waited only two weeks to deprive the Winnipeg Jets of Mann's Herculean contributions—two goals in 30 games—for a paltry 10 games.

This was entirely predictable because Gardner, a 26-goal scorer when mugged, might miss only the rest of the season.

No doubt, NHL ostrich heads were duly prepared to stay sandbound last week when Don Perry, fight promoter for the Los Angeles Kings, commanded his Paul Mulvey to leave the bench for the expressed purpose of making a big brawl against the Vancouver Canucks just a bit bigger.

Mulvey not only refused, but he turned in his coach, then showed up frequently on national TV, which the NHL can't do unless it buys the time, folds, merges with the NFL or does something really ugly.

Well, it committed the latter, and Ziegler acted with such uncharacteristic quickness, one would have thought his opulent expense account had been slashed in half, or that someone had snatched the hanky from his suit jacket's breastpocket. He promptly suspended Perry 15 days, suggesting en route that never, ever, cross-his-heart could his league permit such a thing—particularly if such a thing were aired on *Good Morning, America.*

We were left to believe that no coach in NHL history had acted as Perry did. In truth, Perry simply was abiding by the clearly defined, 65-year-old rules of the NHL jungle.

But, some good may come of this yet. Obviously, the men who run the NHL aren't able or willing to make hockey the major-league sport it deserves to be.

Ziegler is occupied knitting jerseys to present President Reagan. And Chairman of the Board William Wirtz, who pulls a lot of NHL strings, including several attached to Ziegler's backside, is even busier. You can't count the number of companies he operates efficiently, although, if you've got two hands free, you can count the number of coaching changes his Black Hawks have undergone in the last six seasons. Six.

So, it is up to the Paul Mulveys of the world to develop some rules of order. The players who are supposed to do the dirty work are infinitely more qualified than the owners to suggest that it isn't working. And, apparently, the players are more sensitive than their bosses to the stagnant plight of the game.

If the athletes were to demand an end to needless violence, it wouldn't mean the inmates are trying to run the asylum. Rather, it would mean they're trying, at long last, to straighten out the asylum.

Fortunately, the time is perfect, because the NHL Players Association's collective bargaining agreement will expire in September. And, fortunately, the players whose livelihood hockey is are making encouraging noises in that direction. Enough is just about enough, they told the owners at the recent All-Star conclave in Washington.

"There wasn't a lot of discussion about what's been going on, but there was some, and there'll be more," NHLPA president and Chicago goalie Tony Esposito was saying Wednesday.

"I got the feeling that the owners are pretty satisfied with the way things are. But I'm not, a lot of other players aren't, and we're going to do something about it. The average career of an NHL player now is down to only 4.09 years per man. That's not very long. We can't have our guys endangered with disability because some guy decides to get angry and goon it up."

The NHL's so-called administrators contend that fights are a natural offshoot of their emotional sport and that the man-to-man combat is a safety valve. Safety valve against what, they never quite explain. They also maintain that, in a one-on-one rumble, nobody ever gets hurt.

If Paul Gardner could talk today, he'd probably disagree, but Esposito will buy the owners' line—at least to a point.

"I don't think the occasional fight is wrong . . . it may even add something," he says. "But when a guy gets in a fight every other night and winds up with 300 and 400 penalty minutes, that's not right.

"First of all, we need harder punishment. When there's flagrant intent to injure, when there's a chance a player might be permanently hurt, the guy who's guilty has to really be hit with a strong suspension.

"And during that suspension, he can't be paid. A lot of times, I'm afraid that players who start a fight 'for the good of the team' are reimbursed by their own club.

"We don't blame the owners for all of this. A lot of owners will go according to what their general managers tell them, and a lot of GMs are worried about long suspensions because they never know when the guy who gets in trouble will be one of their own players.

"But we've got to make some improvements in this area. We don't want to take the contact out of the game any more that it is; we don't want to eliminate the good body check. We just want severe deterrents against the cheap shots, the stick-swinging, and now we're in a position to have a voice.

"The day of the goon is gone. We just want to get rid of some of the other foolishness by some players. We have to, to protect ourselves."

From each other, or from the blood-thirsty owners?

Horse Racing

A MS. MATCH

MAY 4, 1980

LOUISVILLE—First it was Billie Jean King winning game, set, match from Bobby Riggs. Then it was Title IX, meaning that a women's college rugby team made as much cents as a men's college rugby team. Next, the gals took to building their bodies by pumping iron just like Arnold Schwarzenegger.

Now this. Pretty soon, ERA isn't going to mean earned run average anymore.

For all you fellows who were out in the kitchen washing dishes Saturday afternoon, a filly won the 106th Kentucky Derby. Genuine Risk doesn't curtsy very well, but she sure can run. Ask the 12 guys who followed her to the finish line with crushed egos and dust in their eyes. The last time such a thing happened was in 1915, when stewardesses hadn't dreamed of becoming flight attendants.

"Disgusting, disgusting," said Johnny Oldham. "I hope this doesn't make the women of the world any tougher to live with. They're tough enough already."

Oldham was aboard Rockhill Native, a speed horse that was the 2–1 favorite. For a while, it appeared the safe money was safe. But then, as they came to the three-sixteenths pole, Oldham asked of Rocky what Jacinto Vasquez asked of Genuine Risk. It was a Ms. match. The favorite faded to fifth, while the lady of the hour, at 13–1, beat Rumbo by a length.

Moreover, the winning time—which was supposed to be bad for this race of nonentities—wasn't. It was 2:02. Not a record, but well better than the Derby's worst (2:52¼), established in 1891 by Kingman (no wisecracks, please).

"I really can't say I'm surprised," said Laffitt Pincay, who was aboard runner-up Rumbo. "I rode the filly in New York last fall, and knew she had a good chance today. I feared her more than any horse here."

Rumbo, as unpredictable as the youths among the throng of 131,859 who paid 10 bucks to graze the infield, had a shot at

Genuine Risk in the stretch. But Rumbo did a sidestep. When Pincay hit him left handed, Rumbo lugged out. When Pincay hit him right handed, Rumbo lugged in. They say if you cut Rumbo's head off, he'd be a Triple Crown winner. Of course, then he could never win by a nose.

"Still," said Pincay, "even if my horse had gone for it the way I would have liked, he might not have won. The way that filly ran, she would have been hard to catch. I was getting close, then I could see her really dig in. She wouldn't stop. There was no catching her today."

Rockhill Native established an early pace, taking a relaxed lead going between rivals entering the backstretch.

"I hadn't planned it that way," said Oldham, "but it happened that way. I really wasn't pushing him, but he felt good and sure underneath me. Once, by the three-quarter pole, I think, he ducked out on me. I don't know why. There was no crowd of people around there, or anything, but I snatched him back and I still felt good about the race, still confident.

"Then, right past the quarter pole, when I thought I had the race still in command, I wanted it, but my little baby just didn't have it. He had come up on empty. It just wasn't there. He gave Ma a run, but not like he could. There wasn't much left.

"I don't know whether this makes the 3-year-old picture clearer or whether this confuses it. I thought I had the best of the bunch, but I guess that's debatable now. I guess Genuine Risk was the best today, if not the best overall.

"Obviously, sex has nothing to do with winning the Derby, unless you count that she was five pounds lighter because she was a filly. You look at what she's done on paper, and you gotta give her credit. She won six races in a row, and they were nice races. She got lucky today, and won a seventh. Will my horse run in the Preakness? I don't know. I'm not the trainer."

Herb Stevens is, and he wasn't saying anything Saturday. He says to do what he does, you must be part ogre. Mr. Stevens seems overqualified for his job.

The others who also ran were more amenable to discussion, if not terribly enlightening stuff.

Said Buck Thornburg, who rode 5–2 Plugged Nickel to a dismal seventh: "We got beat and beat bad. My horse never got a hold of the track, which was cuppy. But others did, I guess."

Said Darrell McHargue, who took Jacklin Klugman to a show

finish: "I thought fillies weren't supposed to keep going, but this one did. Nobody told her to stop. I couldn't believe it. But if this same group of horses goes to the Preakness, there will be a different outcome."

Actor Jack Klugman, who owns half of Jacklin (he wouldn't say which half), quite agreed. He thinks if Codex, a talented 3-year-old who wasn't even nominated for the Derby, had been, it would have won.

Even Vasquez, out of Genuine Risk's earshot, was tickled by his damsel's victory over a clumsy field. Asked if she could someday run a mile-and-a-half, he quipped, "Against this competition, she could run two miles."

But Saturday, against a bunch of chauvinist nags, it didn't much matter what anybody said. A filly won the 106th Kentucky Derby. President Carter did not telephone his congratulations. He might be worried. The White House could be next.

DEVIL'S BAG
BARES HIS SOUL

MAY 3, 1984

LOUISVILLE—"Uh, Devil's Bag . . . have you got a minute? I'm from the Chic. . . ."

"What do you think this is, Mister Ed? I haven't given interviews for three years, and I'm not gonna start now."

"Yes, But Big D, you owe it to the public. You've been scratched from Saturday's 110th Kentucky Derby. You were supposed to be the next super horse. Secretariat all over again. Now look at you."

"You heard what my agent, Woody Stephens, said. I'm not in shape. I'm tired, bored, burned out. I've been doing this all my life, and they've already paid $36 million for me just to find a wife, settle down and have a family. Who needs the aggravation? Burp. You, over there. More hay."

"But Big D, where's your intensity?"

"Look, I've got all the money I need. Deferrals, annuities, endorsements, a new farm in Florida. It's all part of the contract I negotiated after I won my first race at Saratoga. Steve Young's getting $40 million, but his league might not last longer than Saturday's race. I'm getting out while the getting's good, while I can still walk. Maybe I'll try TV."

"No more racing, Big D?"

"Maybe the Preakness. Depends. I've got a guaranteed no-whip clause. I'll talk it over with my agent. They can't force me to do anything. If they try, I'll file a grievance with our association. Hey, for a long time the owners had it their way. Now, the pendulum has swung back to us horses."

"But even Woody Stephens said you were a Triple Crown horse if ever he saw one."

"Oh, that's just part of the hype. He was just trying to drive up my price. It happens all the time in sports now. You remember that guy Cooney. He got $10 million for losing to Larry

Holmes. Where's Cooney now? See what I mean? It's all show biz."

"In other words, Big D, you never were any good?"

"Oh, I could run when I felt like it. But the traveling got to me, the lack of privacy, all that lying around waiting for race day. Sooner or later, you gotta prepare for the rest of your life, get your priorities straight. I want to stop and smell the roses, although I won't be able to on Saturday."

"The odds-on favorite to win the Kentucky Derby, burned out? It's unheard of."

"Humanfeathers. My pals Rockhill Native, Proud Appeal, Air Forbes Won, and that crazy dame, Marfa. You know what they all have in common? They were all favored to win the last four Kentucky Derbys. Well, they not only didn't win, they all finished out of the money. Furthermore, they didn't even win a single race since they got beat here. Hype, all hype."

"Yeah, Big D, but you're supposed to be different. Besides, you won the Derby Trial last week."

"I wasn't into it, though, couldn't get up for it. I just barely beat Biloxi Indian, who's fatter than I am. I was exhausted after that race. You think I'm gonna try Saturday, and risk the embarrassment of losing to a *filly*? I'll rest on my laurels. You, over there, more hay."

"Tell me, Big D. Is there something funny here? I mean, this syndicate thing. The same guys who have you, have Swale. Could it be they don't want you in the same race because whichever one loses, the value goes down?"

"I can't comment on Swale. Go ask him, he's in the next barn. I know I've got my money secured. I could live off the interest. Now, you ask me whether thoroughbred racing is completely clean . . . well, what do they call it? The sport of kinks? Burp."

"Before Woody announced you won't race Saturday, he said he thought Swale was a better bet to win the Derby anyway."

"I read that in the paper, and wasn't too happy about it. I demanded a retraction. He said he was misquoted. He might have been trying to motivate me, but that affected me mentally. He's 70, and I'm 3. We don't communicate like we should. You know, you gotta have that in professional sports now. You tell a horse something, the horse has a right to know why."

"Big D, that's what a lot of athletes say."

"Of course. Basically, we're all just pieces of meat. When you can't produce anymore, people have no use for you. I've been getting up at all hours since I was 2, racing hurt, sweating when other horses were living like normal horses. Owners don't care if you have your head on straight. As long as you've got the saddle on straight."

"Big D, you're one confused colt, aren't you?"

"I've missed a lot in life. My dad, Halo, made me run before I could walk. These owners can trade me to another stable, as long as I approve it. You over there, more hay. I don't need Saturday with Howard Cosell in the winner's circle. And, I'm not on drugs. I just want to be treated right. This isn't sports to me. It's a business. These owners, they're in it for the ego. But us athletes, we know what's going on. What do the owners think? They think we wear blinders?"

FATE TAKES PINCAY FOR A RIDE

MAY 28, 1985

CHERRY HILL, NEW JERSEY—Having to settle for Laffitt Pincay Jr. as a substitute jockey is like taking your car into the shop and getting a Rolls Royce as a loaner. Or like finding out your long-lost aunt is Morgan Fairchild. You should be so lucky.

Yet, as the debonair Panamanian emerged from his quarters at Garden State Park Monday, neat as could be in a black three-piece suit with red pinstripes, his dark eyes hidden by even darker sunglasses, it was he who felt blessed by one of life's peculiar twists of faith.

"Where do I sign the check?" Pincay said, wielding a pen. "I bought champagne for the guys, 10 bottles. Unbelievable. Last time I saw this horse, I was looking at it from six lengths back. I like it better, the view I got today."

Spend a Buck, by a neck, captured the Jersey Derby this scalding afternoon, and with it, thoroughbred racing's most opulent reward ever—$2.6 million. For owner Dennis Diaz, who purchased the colt for a mere $12,500, that was another reasonable return on his gamble. Only John Henry has won more than Spend a Buck's career haul of nearly $4 million, and the former, being a gelding, has had fewer distractions.

But when Diaz adds up all the honorariums on top of stud fees to go with syndication promises, he might come to realize that his second wisest investment was the thin dime used to hire Pincay. If ever a splendid animal required the legerdemain of a great jockey, it was Monday. Pincay, then, might have been the biggest bonus of all.

During his three previous races—the Kentucky Derby last

month, preceded by two at Garden State—Spend a Buck had romped by a total of 25¹/₄ lengths, all with Angel Cordero Jr. aboard. But Cordero, who can be a brat, hedged about his Monday commitment, for he had an assignment at nearby Belmont. He suggested they move back the post time of the Jersey Derby, so he might handle two horses in two states within the same hour.

"Finally, we decided Cordero was screwing around too much," huffed Spend a Buck's trainer, Cam Gambolati. A second choice was no choice at all. Pincay, a street thug as a kid who recently won his 7,000th race, was asked to forget his fear of airplanes and make the trip from California. Being of sound mind and body at age 38, Pincay accepted.

At the Kentucky Derby, where he finished a distant second on Stephan's Odyssey, Pincay sensed there was a superhorse up ahead. What Pincay didn't know, but was subsequently told by Gambolati, was that Spend a Buck is as game, as competitive, as this business is treacherously cutthroat. Monday, Pincay discovered for himself.

"I know what Cam meant now," he said. "He won this race on guts. I would like to have won easy, but it wasn't easy. My horse was challenged three, four times. I was worried once. But this is a real athlete."

For starters, Spend a Buck, at 1 to 20 in the betting, broke badly, stumbling from the gate. Now, Pincay had to drop plans to lay the horse second. He had to let Spend a Buck go, and go he did to the lead, but at burnout speed. For three-quarters of a mile, 1 minute 9 seconds, with a half-mile remaining. "No question," Pincay said, "that was too fast a pace."

Plots and schemes developed. Trainer Wayne Lukas, aiming to enhance the status of his Preakness winner Tank's Prospect, had entered Huddle Up here to wear out Spend a Buck. And Huddle Up was right there. Then there was rabbit Purple Mountain on the dance card, designed to make way for trainer Woody Sedlacek's better half, El Basco, who came from behind on cue. And Woody Stephens' Creme Fraiche roared toward the finish too.

"They came from all over," Pincay said. "The one horse [Creme Fraiche] passed me by a head at the quarter pole. That's when I thought I might not win. I didn't know if I had any horse left. But I gave it [Spend a Buck] the whip three times with the right hand, four or five with the left, and he responded. Most horses, they have nothing left to give at that point. That's why I say he ran a great race. Not easy, but great."

And with a great jockey above. Cordero had been praised for knowing how to relax Spend a Buck. Pincay will be remembered by his usual calling card.

"If ever you wanted anybody on your horse in a tough stretch run," Diaz concluded, "you want Laffitt. He's our man for our horse from now on, wherever we go."

One can debate the purity of tendering bonuses for this or that sporting feat. Monday's booty certainly diminished the tradition of the Triple Crown. But this sort of thing is happening everywhere now. In golf, in tennis, the green is always greener somewhere else. Money doesn't just talk anymore. It screams.

"I have no opinion on that," Pincay said, addressing the tender subject. "I know that I had a big payday at the Kentucky Derby last year with Swale. But nothing like this."

This, the Jersey Derby, was worth $260,000, a 10 percent cut, for Pincay, the relief rider who watches his weight by eating dry cereal and sunflower seeds—"squirrel food," he quips. He spoke again of his good fortune, no pun intended. Then he spoke of last winter, when he was at the other end of the spectrum, when wife Linda, in ill health, committed suicide.

"I did nothing for two weeks," Pincay said. "I just stayed in the house. Before the funeral, after the funeral. I was very sad. Some days, I think of it. Some days, I have to put it out of my mind."

Laffitt Pincay Jr. paid for the champagne and walked away.

IT'S THE ONLY RACE

MAY 4, 1987

LOUISVILLE—His office is his suitcase, his monthly telephone bill averages $4,000, his airplane tickets cost $70,000 a year and his name is Jack. Above all, his name is Jack.

"Congratulations, Mr. Van Berg," someone yelled from a distance early this gray Sunday morning.

"Jack," he corrected. "It's Jack, not Mister. Nothing's changed."

Almost. On Saturday afternoon, when his Alysheba won a Kentucky Derby that resembled the Kentucky 500, Jack Van Berg was all spiffed up in a light brown suit and necktie—uncomfortable attire for this 50-year-old hulk of a Hall-of-Fame trainer, though that's not why his voice cracked and his eyes watered. But now, propped up on a rail beside Barn 32 at Churchill Downs shortly before 7 a.m., Van Berg was back in his element: blue jeans, boots, plaid shirt, spinning stories, mostly about Dad.

"Marion," said Van Berg. "Died exactly 16 years ago today. Greatest horseman that ever lived. He din't have to take a back seat to nobody. He could learn more about a horse in two minutes than most people could learn in two weeks. Even after his stroke, when he couldn't talk, he'd be pointing out things that we couldn't see after being with the horse all the time.

"And what a worker. He had me convinced when I was a kid that I was too dumb to make it. Tried to quit working for him, but he'd always sweet-talk you out of it. Wound up making you feel sorry for getting mad at him. We got close toward the end. He'll be happy today."

Jack Van Berg was delighted, too, of course. He'd rung up some 5,000 winners, more than any living trainer, but never a winner in the Run for the Roses. Lots of claimers at too many remote tracks in hundreds of faraway places, but at previous Kentucky Derbies, his best shot was with Gate Dancer in '84. The horse came in fourth, then was disqualified to fifth. Dad hadn't fared well here, either, in one failed attempt, 1960. Spring Broker cracked his head on the starting gate, which isn't easy, and finished eighth.

"Mr. Van Berg . . . " someone began from the back.

"Jack," said Van Berg. "It's Jack. Only thing that's changed is that I slept in a little late this morning. Called in here from the mobile phone, telling them I'd been out on the farm, checking some legs. Truth is, I just rolled out of bed. Jack. It's Jack."

"Jack," the interrogator continued. "Is this different? Charlie Whittingham won the Derby last year at 73, and he said he didn't realize how much it meant."

"It's the only race," Van Berg went on. "This is awfully hard, you know, to get a horse ready for the first Saturday in May. Horses are like tomatoes. They spoil easily. That's why I broke down yesterday. There's no greater feeling."

Jack Van Berg's map is full of stickpins. He has about 170 horses, works for about 35 different owners, employs about 200 people, and has divisions throughout the country. If he must have a base of operations, call it the modern layout at Skylight, in Goshen, not far from here. But better you try him at his 800 number because he's busy with that new training operation in the California desert, just outside San Bernardino.

"We're not in the earthquake belt, though," Van Berg said. "Checked that out. But if it happens, where we are inland, we might just have us some beachfront property all of a sudden. Think what the land would be worth then. Good thing I can sleep whenever I want to. God blessed me that way. When I get into an airplane seat, it's like somebody pressed a button. Heck, I took a nap yesterday, before the race. I'll do the same thing if you come to my house. When I'm tired, I'll fall asleep, I don't care what you're talking about."

Sunday morning, everybody was talking about Alysheba, survivor of a rough Kentucky Derby in something less than lightning fractions.

"Time only matters in prison," Van Berg said. "They tell me my horse almost went down. Lot of bumping and stumbling. Well, I haven't seen it yet. Haven't seen the tapes, and from where I was sitting, front row, Box 30, people kept standing up blocking my view. I didn't want to lean out too far, or I might have bailed out.

"This is a good horse, though. Nothing bothers him, and maybe if he got hit, that woke him up some. This is a real athlete, though. He's agile like me. He could flip up in the air and land on his feet. And to get him ready for the Preakness, we won't have to do much. He's had some bad luck. When you get beat by noses, you got bad luck. Plus, he had a virus, and surgery for an entrapped epiglottis. I ain't a vet, but I know it affects a horse's breathing."

Pat Day, the jockey aboard starcrossed favorite Demons Begone and once Alysheba's rider, hailed Van Berg as the hardest working trainer in the sport.

"Well, I've got a lot of miles on me and been blessed with some horse sense, I guess," Van Berg said. "Dad was a great teacher, starting with when I got into this in Nebraska. Columbus. Three things I don't like to do, and that's walk a horse, hold for the blacksmith and milk a cow. That's the biggest whipping I ever got. I was about 12 or 13, supposed to milk a cow while the rest of the family went to eat. Well, I wanted to go eat, too.

"So, I went and bought some milk from the grocery store and put it in the pail. Thing is, it was homogenized already. And cold. Hell of a cow I had there. Milk you get from milking is warm and foamy. Mine was like it just came from a carton, because it did. He took one sniff of that, my dad did, and did I ever get the strap. He was right. He told me I was dumb, and I was dumb. But today, I'm dumb happy. I don't go to church as often as I should, but I want to go today, to thank the man. Lord was awfully good to me yesterday. He's been awfully good to me right along, actually."

Olympics

TOUGH SLEDDING FOR ONE-MAN TEAM

FEBRUARY 5, 1984

SARAJEVO, YUGOSLAVIA—As we all know, this luge business is no day at the beach. For sheer danger, it is an international version of Friday nights on the Dan Rayn Distressway. Strap yourself onto a sled, and you are unsafe at any speed. You also get a vague idea of what it's like to pitch for the Cubs.

When the luge competition was introduced to the Winter Olympics at Innsbruck, Austria, in 1964, one participant was killed and two others were seriously injured. Lugers routinely suffer cracked tailbones, shattered dreams, headaches, neuritis and neuralgia.

None of this seems to annoy George Tucker, a member of Puerto Rico's Olympic team. Make that George Tucker, Puerto Rico's Olympic team. He's it. The only one. During Wednesday's opening ceremony for the XIV Winter Games, he'll be carrying the flag of Puerto Rico. And if he drops it, there will be nobody behind him to pick it up.

That's if Geroge Tucker makes it to Wednesday. As you read this, he's out practicing along Trebevic Mountain.

"I have a completion percentage of about 75 percent," Tucker said. That's pretty good in the National Football League, but not so good in the luge.

Tucker, who is legally sane, is also an American. He's 6-foot-1 and sturdy enough to make you believe he once played some college football. He also carries enough excess padding to confirm that he's 36 years old, and he's quite devoted to completing his doctorate in physics.

It's only when he's on horizontal hold, whooshing down a 4,084-foot track at 65 miles an hour, that you wonder whether George Tucker isn't also working on something else. Like getting knocked senseless.

"I'm not worried," says Tucker. "It's a labor of love."

Tucker, who lives in Albany, New York, caught the luge bug at the 1980 Winter Olympics in Lake Placid, where most normal beings were sufficiently occupied merely trying to catch a bus. He hung around the American athletes, leaning always to the American lugers.

"I became hooked," says Tucker, hooking his index finger in his right cheek so as to impersonate a fish in distress.

Not long after, Tucker read a story in the *New York Times* containing the name of the president of the Puerto Rican Olympic Committee, such as it is. Tucker was familiar with Puerto Rico, having been born there to American parents. His father worked for RKO Pictures, and George didn't move to the United States until he was 6.

"I wrote the president a letter and told him what I had on my mind," Tucker recalled. "What I had in mind was representing Puerto Rico in the luge at these Olympic Games in Sarajevo. They had never had anybody in the Winter Olympics. I didn't know what he would think.

"Well, he was very excited. He wrote back and sent me a red beret. The rest of the uniform would be up to me. I was the first one, so I would design it. I did. Bought my stuff from off the shelf. And here I am."

When Tucker arrived in this town which is long on hospitality but short on snow, there was no credential waiting. He had to find makeshift living quarters for two nights, all the while losing valuable practice time. Finally, he got angry.

"I told the Yugoslavian Olympic officials that if they didn't let me participate immediately, I was going home," Tucker said. "We cleared things up. And then, when they saw me take a few runs, I think they realized that I wasn't going to be a threat to make off with the gold medal. I crashed.

"That's the hard part. When you crash, you not only have to check and see if you're still in one piece, you gotta go find the sled, too."

Tucker's scarred warmup togs indicate that he is as far away from perfection as he is from home. But, also, he is as undaunted as he is unpolished. The only Olympic-sized luge run in the United States is at Lake Placid, and Tucker has been taking his plunges there for two years.

"I feel very lucky," Tucker said. "I once considered trying out for the Puerto Rican basketball team, but then I realized the luge was my calling.

"I don't think I could have qualified for the American team, and I feel bad for the Americans who are better than me, but couldn't qualify either. I took one tumble here earlier this week, and the natives thought they were going to have an Olympic funeral on their hands."

Before that practice session the other day, the attending official cleared his Serbo-Croatian throat and announced George Tucker as George Turkey.

Tucker, who is not afraid to laugh at himself, said, "I think that guy knows a lot more English than he's letting on."

Lugers lie face up on their sleds, lifting their eyes only to survey oncoming problems. Lifting one's head too much to offer wind resistance decreases one's horsepower. Negotiating the labyrinth of curves, walls and hairpin turns is the essence of success. But, then, as we all know, you've got to start quickly, or be done.

"Didn't have any teammates to push me off, of course," Tucker said. "So the other day, I asked a sportswriter to give me a nudge."

Strap George Tucker in. And light a candle for him.

ALL THE COMFORTS OF HOME—ALMOST

FEBRUARY 9, 1984

SARAJEVO, YUGOSLAVIA—What you hold in your hands at this very moment I would kill for. An American sports section. The local daily newspaper, *Oslobodenje,* shows no interest in the Crosby golf results. Then again, the natives don't have much interest in golf, period. There's only one course in the entire *country.* And it's closed.

What else is missed after a week away from home on assignment at the XIV Winter Olympics? Orange juice, country music, Dan Rather, Miller Lite and shower curtains. Especially shower curtains. They have showers, or at least movable, handheld spray things that you can operate like a garden hose. But no shower curtains.

I asked Berka about this. She runs the front desk in our building at the press compound.

"Berka, without a shower curtain there's a lot of water that winds up on the floor every morning."

"Okay. There is a drain outside tub for that."

"But Berka, the water is still on the floor at night."

"Okay. There is no worry about that."

"Berka, tomorrow morning I'm going to try something new. I will keep more water inside the tub. I'll shower on my knees."

"Okay. But when do you wash your knees?"

"Chicago. When I get back to Chicago."

Otherwise, no complaints. The nabobs of the International Olympic Committee, also known as the "Earls of Dandruff," have tried to ruin the show with this business about professionalism. That's one problem they don't have to deal with on a personal level. The guys in blue blazers will never, ever lose their amateur standing.

But the natives, despite the language barrier, are as gracious and helpful as they can be. So far, and it is early yet, they've put ·he people of Lake Placid to shame. The 1980 Winter Games were treated like a nuisance by the folks in upstate New York. Here in the middle of Bosnia-Herzegovina, citizens bend over backwards. Except when they take a shower.

The food is a little spicy and a lot greasy. I ordered chicken for dinner and the waiter brought a whole chicken. I asked him for a doggie bag and he brought me a hot dog. I didn't ask for anything after that, but he brought me the check, anyway. I felt right at home.

They say there's a terrible drinking problem in Yugoslavia, and here's why. The beer, or *pivo*, contains 13 percent alcohol. Four of those and it's a lot easier to sleep, even though the beds are no bigger than desktops. The other favorite liquid is a plum brandy called *slivovitz*. It's 121 proof and works better in your Zippo lighter than in your stomach.

Otherwise, no complaints. Except for the telephones. It's hard to secure one, and even harder to make one work. If you succeed at both, it's really hard on the bank account. Ma Bellski shows no mercy. Before Wednesday's opening ceremonies, I was already down $600.

"It's three bucks a minute to the United States," noted cellmate John Husar, "but that's still unbelievable. What have you been doing? Calling Sports Phone in Chicago every night?"

I pleaded guilty on two counts, but I still don't know who won the Crosby.

Otherwise, no complaints. Except for the television. It's pretty limited, even if you can handle *Red River* starring John Wayne. Somehow, "Duke" loses a little impact when he tells the bad guys to put away their guns in Serbo-Croatian. On the train ride from Zagreb to Sarajevo, each car had a TV that was tuned to a Bugs Bunny cartoon, with somebody dubbing for Mel Blanc.

The city of Sarajevo is rich in history. ABC-TV president Roone Arledge, who must want to commit suicide now that the U.S. hockey team has lost its first game, is staying in the same hotel suite where Archduke Franz Ferdinand spent his last night on earth.

At least, Arledge has a choice. The archduke didn't. He was fixing to take over the country when a young rebel killed him. That was the shot that started World War I. The assassin had a bridge named after him, but the real hero here is Marshal Tito, who looked the Soviets eye-to-eye for 30 years until his death in 1980.

There are murals of Tito everywhere. The people of Yugoslavia cherish his memory and their independence, such as it is. They don't take kindly to your calling this country communist. It is socialist, an East-West intersection, they say.

"You have your freedoms in United States," Berka explained. "We have our freedoms. We walk streets alone at night. No trouble."

To be sure, security is awesome. Guards carrying Kalashnikov AK-47 submachine guns are everywhere, stalking mountain tops near the Olympic Village, flanking metal detectors through which all hockey ticketholders at Zetra Arena must pass. Even parents of participating athletes cannot enter the Olympic Village. Only the press.

"Munich," says a member of the militia, when asked why. "Munich." But the residents live on, stoically, hoping that the Olympics will buoy their ravaged economy. Women walk arm-in-arm along the sidewalks; men kiss each other hello and goodbye; cabbies assume Grand Prix speeds around corners, trying to conserve precious fuel. Everybody smokes cigarettes.

"Your laundry?" Berka said. "Not ready yet. Five days. Unless you pay double. Then one day. Want to pay double?"

"I can't Berka," I said. "I've got this $600 phone bill."

Otherwise, no complaints. Except, who won the Crosby?

A THRILL FOR MR. AGONY

FEBRUARY 13, 1984

SARAJEVO, YUGOSLAVIA—If only Vinko Bogataj lived in the United States, could we ever make an antihero out of him.

Just like Marvelous Marv Throneberry. Think of it. Boom-Boom Bogataj. An enduring monument to ineptitude. A textbook example of how not to do it. A living, breathing, talking pratfall.

Marvelous Marv, the former first baseman with hands of asbestos, could continue to do his beer commercials, but not Boom-Boom Bogataj. He could sell Blue Cross or Band-Aids, or be the sad guy in the white suit who regrets to inform you that there is no tomorrow. But only in America. Not here.

"That wouldn't work here in Yugoslavia," says Bogataj. "Here, my countrymen don't know who I am. It is just as well."

Indeed, at the Malo Polje ski jump Sunday morning, Vinko Bogataj was just another frozen face in the crowd. He's a volunteer at the XIV Winter Olympics, a starter this particular morning at the 70-meter event. Imagine that. One of the most notorious nonfinishers in the world of athletics a starter.

"They still show that film in America, do they?" says Bogataj, grinning.

Do they ever. Bogataj stars in the longest-running disaster flick on U.S. television. He's the human Frisbee you see on ABC's *Wide World of Sports* every weekend. He starts the show by losing balance, sliding beneath his skis, cartwheeling sideways, careening into a wall, then dropping off toward your living room rug. And, in case you miss it, he does it again to end the show.

Vinko Bogataj is sole author, leading man and lone survivor of an all-time gaffe in sports. He ranks right down there with Roy Riegels running the wrong way in the 1929 Rose Bowl,

Mickey Owen dropping a third strike in the 1941 World Series and any 1969 Cub. Vinko Bogataj is "The Agony of Defeat." And ABC is not about to let you forget it.

Bogataj was competing at Oberstdorf, West Germany, in 1970. He recalls there being inclement weather, and then a delay of several seconds before he was to initiate his first jump that day. Bogataj lost his concentration. How is it that he didn't also lose his life?

"I don't recall exactly what happened, because I was knocked unconscious for a couple of minutes," he says. "When I saw people coming around me, they were afraid to touch me. They were sure that I would be seriously hurt after all the things I had hit. But I had only a broken ankle, concussions, bruises and a headache."

And ABC had itself a star. Shortly after the clips of Vinko's aborted trip were viewed, the network taped him into position. Boom-Boom Bogataj went bingo-bango-bongo and lived to talk about it. ABC has changed "The Thrill of Victory" scene since, but Bogataj appears to be a fixture until another ski jumper can forge a greater crash.

"I do not wish that to happen," says Bogataj. "I don't want anybody to be in the danger I was in. Every time I see a skier go down now, I feel it. Besides, I am happy they have used me on the show so often. I realize it has made me popular in America and that I enjoy."

Bogataj began to comprehend the extent of his fame in 1981, when ABC invited him to New York for a 20th anniversary dinner of the *Wide World* program. When Vinko was announced, he was accorded a standing ovation. Only the 1980 U.S. Olympic hockey team elicited a louder reaction.

"I couldn't believe it," Bogataj says. "Ali was there, Jackie Stewart was there. But, they applaud me. That trip to the United States was my first, and one of the highlights of my life."

Those are few and far between for Vinko. He drives a forklift at a factory and paints landscapes in his free time. He has dreams about traveling throughout the world, but that will require more money. He has a cassette of his problem in Germany, but nothing on which to show it. That, too, will take more money. At 36, then, Bogataj admits he's still searching for that perfect landing.

"I was pretty good as a skier," he says. "Never good enough

to make the Olympic team, though. After the fall I took, I spent two weeks in the hospital and jumped again a few months later. But I didn't feel the same as I used to, and soon, I gave it up.

"I don't make a big thing about what happened. When I lost control that day, it happened so fast I didn't have time to be afraid. Now, I'm not embarrassed by it. I talk about it with my daughter sometimes, but no big thing. It was just one of the things that you do in life. This one, I did it, and the cameras were there."

To millions of Americans, Vinko Bogataj is an everyday symbol of failure, and twice a day on weekends. It has been that way for almost 14 years. But, by next week, Mr. Agony of Defeat could be in big trouble again. ABC just might replace him with a U.S. Olympic team picture.

SOVIETS WHINE WAY TO L.A.

APRIL 22, 1984

Given their current state of distress concerning the upcoming Olympic Games in Los Angeles, the Soviets have two rather obvious courses of action. Possibly they could shut up. Or possibly they could stay home.

But, off past performances, the Soviets are no easier to deal with than they are to gauge. One would surmise, then, that they will opt for a third alternative to satisfy their peculiar sense of logic. They will not refrain from bombast. But they will not bypass an opportunity for their "amateur" athletes to strut their stuff come July 28, either.

International sports and politics don't mix, or so goes the notion. The reality is that they are awkward but inevitable cellmates. By June 2, which is the deadline for the Soviets to accept the invitation to participate, their bluster will be so loud, their posturing so incessant, that what's left of the Olympic ideal will be lost forever in a cloud of their smoke.

What we're hearing is not hastily prepared rhetoric, mind you. Dumb, the Soviets aren't. Since 1978, when the 23rd Summer Games were awarded to Los Angeles, the Soviets have been making ominous noises. When the United States boycotted the 1980 Olympics in Moscow, the Soviets were angered, but they would have their days.

Now, hardly a day passes without some message from the Soviet Union about what's already wrong, or what could go wrong, or what probably will go wrong in Los Angeles. The tirades are tiresome, to be sure. But, again, there is method to the Soviets' propaganda madness.

With athletes from 150 nations converging on a densely populated metropolis for two weeks, moving from one venue to another at all hours, there is every chance for an unwieldy spectacle. It is the nature of the event, no matter where it is staged or when. There is reason to expect congestion, discomfort and even breakdowns bordering on chaos.

As though they are the only delegates who might be subjected to difficulty, the Soviets are pointing out all the imperfections so as to place themselves in a perfect position. If one of their buses gets a flat tire, they told us it wouldn't work. If everything proceeds smoothly, they made it that way by threatening and cautioning in advance.

The Soviets have demanded an emergency meeting of the International Olympic Committee, even though its executive committee is scheduled to convene in Switzerland next month to discuss any potential logistical problems. The Soviets contend that the United States is the problem, that the Americans have broken the Olympic charter, that the Americans have violated the code of "fair play."

This is a brazen but predictable accusation from a country that shoots down civilian airplanes, then officially hails the action. But the Soviets are relentless, charging that the U.S. is more concerned about "uncontrollable commercialization" at Los Angeles than protecting the Soviet Union's athletes, coaches and journalists.

What the Soviets don't mention is that their "amateur" pole-vaulters will be charged $35 daily for housing, transportation, 24-hour meal service, medical attention and entertainment. That is $2 more a day than all participants were charged at the Winter Olympics in Sarajevo, Yugoslavia, last February. This is uncontrollable commercialism?

The Soviets are not alone in their concern about the possibility that persons or groups will demonstrate or even attempt violence before a worldwide audience. As Los Angeles Olympic Organizing Committee President Peter Ueberroth remarked in Yugoslavia, "We cannot decree that all private cars stay off the freeways of Los Angeles, and we can't put a law officer at every streetcorner with a machine gun . . . We're a free country."

But the Soviets' charge that the U.S. will assist or condone any terrorist action against Soviet-bloc representatives in Los Angeles is patently absurd. The security force of 17,000 to protect 10,000 athletes from harassment or harm is not exactly a cavalier attempt to insure the "safe Olympics" that Ueberroth envisions.

The Soviets complain about media accreditation. The Soviets complain about capitalist plots to have their athletes defect. The Soviets complain about too many call girls on the streets of Los Angeles. The Soviets complain about everything. They even complain that the Americans ignore the charter's clause "to spread Olympic principles throughout the world, thereby creating goodwill." Would you believe.

Ueberroth is too polite when he chides the Soviets for "nit-picking." But he still is contemplating a trip to the Soviet Union to make some sense out of all the nonsense. Surely, if the Soviets boycott—although that's one of few menacing words they haven't employed—it would reduce the impact of the 23rd Summer Games.

But when they aren't making speeches, the Soviets are making plans. Their rooms in Los Angeles are paid for, their TV crews have staked out broadcast locations, their 6,000 citizen fans have purchased plane tickets and, rest assured, their "amateur" athletes are training at this very minute.

The Soviets won't stay quiet, but they won't stay away.

VIEW FROM
MEN OF TASS

AUGUST 1, 1984

LOS ANGELES—"Take this as an example," said the man across the table. "It is supposed to be shrimp salad. It looks beautiful, but there's hardly any shrimp. Back home, if I order shrimp salad, I get shrimp salad. This is like the Games themselves. More style than substance."

It was midnight in Moscow but lunch hour at the XXIII Olympics. Yuri Ustimenko and Mikhail Beglov of Tass, the official news agency for the Soviet Union, had to eat, so why not eat with someone new and different, personable and worldly, young and handsome? We did not talk about the Cubs.

"We write what we see," said Ustimenko, in excellent English. "So far, we have had no problems. But I do not deny that we criticized the opening ceremony Saturday. It was show girls, Hollywood, too commercial like everything.

"America's the best, America the beautiful. Nothing about the other countries, little to do with sport. Can you imagine if, at Moscow in 1980, we devoted the whole ceremony to our revolution?"

"This does not mean everything is bad in Los Angeles," suggested Beglov. "Peter Ueberroth, the president of your Olympic committee, is a great guy. We reported that. A great politician. Instead of becoming commissioner of baseball, he should become president of the United States. Better for all."

Between bites, Ustimenko and Beglov were a lot tougher than the veal piccatta they both ordered. Yuri is based in San Francisco and his comrade in Washington. Beglov smokes Winstons, and Ustimenko drives an Oldsmobile. So much for their Americanization.

"There is interest back home in the Olympics, of course," said Yuri. "But the medals won here do not mean much. If our boys and girls were here, they would win a majority. They are better. They don't make a million dollars to run. America, it is too soft. Hard in the sense that everybody dies for the buck, but otherwise, soft."

Swear on their vodka, Ustimenko and Beglov claimed they believe in international understanding through sports. They said they wish their athletes were here. They think American athletes wish likewise. They hope it can happen at a future Olympics. But there is no way it could have happened in Los Angeles.

"You ask, how can we relate the crazy man who killed those people in his car the other night with these Games?" said Belov. "That is not freedom. That is lack of security. A couple of Olympic guards were arrested for smoking pot. I would not want my life entrusted with that type of protection.

"Our athletes, who have been threatened by terrorists? Absolutely, they made the right decision in not coming. A madman in the streets of San Diego kills 21 innocent people, and we are criticized for keeping our athletes home where they are safe? Let's be realistic."

No, Yuri, let's be honest. When stationed in Ireland, you were identified in a book, *The Terror Network,* by Claire Sterling, as a member of the KGB.

"Absolutely not," he said. "I am a journalist, and I'm disappointed in your journalists. They twist things. How do I know you won't do the same? But if we don't talk, if we close our office here, then you crucify us anyway. You'll write that the two Russian reporters at the Olympics don't speak. We can't win. That is not comfortable, but it comes with our territory."

So does Romania, the only Soviet-bloc nation to defy the boycott. Has Tass given the Romanians a fair shake?

"Of course, we write the facts," said Ustimenko. "There is a story in the local paper today that the Los Angeles Olympic Committee paid the Romanians to come here. We report it to Moscow, but we have no comment. We cannot substantiate it."

But Tass can and did substantiate that the Romanians received a warm ovation at Saturday's opening ceremony, while Nicaragua was greeted with virtual silence.

"That is politics, and Americans are so brainwashed about good guys versus bad guys," said Beglov. "In Moscow, it would be pure sport. Russian people would separate the American athletes, whom they respect, from the government. All delegations would receive a cordial welcome."

"I don't believe that," I said.

"It is a fact," said Ustimenko. "Just like it is a fact that we have been treated fine as members of the Russian press. Just like it is a fact that this whole thing in Los Angeles is staged for your TV."

Meal over. The waiter brought coffee. Yuri wondered why a country born in 1776 still hasn't learned how to make good coffee. Then, the waiter brought dessert. Apple pie, would you believe, with a small American flag stuck in the middle. Yuri winced. I figured, if they don't like it, let them eat cake. I thought again, be the good host. So I grabbed the check.

"Are you on expense account?" Yuri asked. Yes, he was assured. "Ahh, my son, who I starve for, is back in Moscow studying to be a journalist. I have tried to talk him out of it, but . . ."

Finally we agreed on something. Shrimp salad in Moscow?

TIME TO END 5-RING CIRCUS

AUGUST 5, 1984

LOS ANGELES—Way back when, the five Olympic rings represented the participating continents—Africa, America, Asia, Europe, and Oceania, in alphabetical order.

But now, the five rings stand for the prevailing forces— Hypocrisy, Greed, Politics, Stubbornness and Stupidity—not necessarily according to the impact each has toward the corruption and contamination of the Olympic ideal, such as it is.

History insists that, in simpler times, it was saner. Ancient thinclads actually interrupted wars for these Games, so as to throw javelins instead of sticks and stones. But, now, no matter how often Jim McKay tells us that synchronized swimming is what life is all about, the Olympics fail everywhere except on the Nielsen ratings.

Oh, this quadrennial track meet has an international flavor, all right. But the flavor is rotten. It was that way in 1932, when Finnish runner Paavo Nurmi was disqualified for padding his expense account. It was that way in 1936, when maniacal Adolf Hitler and his goose-stepping murderers served as "hosts." It was that way in 1972, when the Games went on as an addendum to funeral processions for 11 slain Israelis.

There have been no catastrophes, yet, at the current Olympiad—only more reasons why the Games, as we know them, need not go on anymore. It is time to revise the Olympics, or reject the Olympics forever.

It has become painfully evident that the Games are too costly, too unwieldy and too vulnerable to world tensions. The Games should belong to the athletes. Instead, the Games belong to the governments that can't support them but want to meddle anyway, and to businesses that will exchange money for logos and influence.

This is pure? This is pure pollution. The common hue and

cry now is to find a permanent site for the Olympics. But the answer is to spread events throughout the world—swimming, say in the United States; gymnastics in China; field hockey in India; basketball in Yugoslavia; track in the Soviet Union, and so on. Four years later, rotate.

If there is any Olympic spirit left to be felt, all participating nations could feel it. No singular locale would have to shoulder the logistical nightmare or the subsequent red ink. Boycotts would be fewer, costs—and perhaps even complaints—reduced. To have a true Olympics, the Olympics need total representation.

Should such an international spectacular diminish the importance of medals (i.e., winning), so be it. There's too much of that now. Let presidents and premiers worry about domination; let the world's athletes worry about participation. Pole vaulters can keep their gold, silver or bronze; why do we have to keep score? Wouldn't you rather read about Olympic datelines than Olympic standings?

There is yet another way to open the Olympics. Make everybody eligible and eliminate those flimsy, meaningless labels— "amateur" and "professional"—which aren't worth any more than the governing bodies that define them. No longer would the Olympics be sullied by such squirrels as Joe Douglas, the sawed-off alter ego for Carl Lewis.

If Lewis is America's fastest human being, Douglas isn't far behind. He masquerades as a father protector, claiming how "we want to be loved by all." We're here for the sport, not the money. But, when asked to pose for a family portrait, Lewis refuses. After he wins four gold medals, of course, *People* magazine will pay him dearly for it.

Decentralization of the Games also might spell a fitting end to the International Olympic Committee, which spends 1984 dollars to live in the past. Its doddering president, Juan Antonio Samaranch, criticized ABC for its chauvinistic coverage. Yet he gladly sleeps in a hotel suite and nibbles on caviar that TV made possible. Mr. Samaranch belongs in his Barcelona cabana, babbling into the hearing aids of the other IOC fossils.

The Los Angeles Olympic Organizing Committee has done its best to make these Games work. But the problem is, the Games can't work. Helicopters hover over venues, searching for terrorists. As the "Star Spangled Banner" hails another gold medal at poolside, police stand atop buildings with binoculars and guns poised. Sorry to report, it's not as pretty as ABC's picture. It is the cruel world, dressed up in short pants or leotards.

The LAOOC hasn't explained the absence at the opening ceremonies of Mark Spitz, who had to buy his tickets, or of Bob Mathias. Neither has the LAOOC explained how the Games that are supposed to cost the public nothing probably will cost taxpayers $100 million.

For those who don't have a salary to tax, the Games are a sham, too. To put on a pretty face, local police on horseback have shooed winos away from public parks at night. Where the street people sleep now, nobody knows. Where their belongings are now, nobody knows.

"The bag with everything I own, they took it," said one poor soul along Grand and 5th the other day. "I have to start all over."

So do the Olympic Games, a five-ring circus. There are a lot of nice stories here; there are a lot more harsh realities. The Olympics must be changed, or be gone.

WHOLLY MOSES

AUGUST 6, 1984

LOS ANGELES—He lay down for a spell by the starting blocks before it began, and then ambled calmly around the track after it was over. That's typical of Edwin Moses, an understated champion.

So was what transpired in between. With remarkable ease, and elan, Moses captured a gold medal Sunday evening, winning the 400-meter intermediate hurdles at the XXIII Summer Olympics. It wasn't the time of his life, this clocking of 47.75 seconds, but it was his moment.

Moses didn't grab for an American flag, and he didn't solicit a reaction from the elbow-to-elbow gathering that came to watch him perpetuate history. All Moses did was be himself, which might be why he is the most respected athlete in the huge U.S. contingent. The world is his oyster, but there's nothing fishy about him, and surely nothing phony.

Carl Lewis, on merit and medals, is the superstar of the U.S. track team. He wears makeup, preens in unisex clothes, arrives uncommonly early to every finish line, but fashionably late to everything else. He was born in Alabama, he grew up in New Jersey, he lives in a mansion in Houston, but make no mistake about it. He was made in, and for, Hollywood.

Edwin Moses, on the contrary, is more one of us. He has class, dignity, humility and, best of all, a bald spot. He doesn't like to talk about himself, leaving that chore to his bubbly wife, Myrella. She says that, with a little less hair on his head and a little more on his chin, hubby "would look like a king."

Edwin Moses certainly is king of his event. He could be the reason why the 400-meter intermediate hurdles is a bore; instead, he's the reason why it isn't. He is the Johnny Carson of his business, and everybody else in the world is Alan Thicke. Moses says every time he goes to the post, he feels like he's being led to the electric chair.

"Pressure," he says. "Race by race. I take it race by race. I feel pressure more than you think. And tonight's—which I dedicate to my father, who passed away last winter—I'm glad it's over."

Sunday's exercise at Los Angeles Memorial Coliseum was Moses' 105th victory in succession, heats included. The last time he lost, we were all seven years younger. August 26, 1977, to Harald Schmid of West Germany. In those days, a joint wasn't something you smoked. It was a place you went for beer and pretzels. That's how long it has been since Moses came to a finish line looking at someone else's backside.

On four occasions, Moses has broken the world record. Of the 18 fastest times in the somewhat fameless history of his event, Moses owns 17. Most of his contemporaries consider it a day in the sun to better the 48-second mark; Moses has breezed through 28 such days in the sun.

Literally, Moses, who has a degree in physics, has those 400 meters, those 10 hurdles, down to a science. He glides from the blocks, he unfailingly takes 13 strides between hurdles and he wins—always. Like many of the great ones, in any endeavor, his frame of reference is himself. Success, he says, is achieving the fastest possible time with the least possible exhaustion.

Moses, for sure, will not expend much energy patting himself on the back, or indulging himself in the trappings of his new-found fame. When he was the only member of the U.S. team to garner an individual gold medal in a track event at the 1976 Olympics in Montreal, he was quiet—and virtually ignored because of it.

Now, Moses' personality glows almost as brightly as his streak, but he does not curry favor. Fellow American Andrew Phillips, a staunch admirer, calls Moses "the Lone Ranger" because he comes, he conquers, he disappears. Like Michael Jackson, theorizes Phillips, Moses knows he's a celebrity but he doesn't quite know whether he likes it.

"When you're known for one thing, you're not always regarded as a normal human being," Moses says. "I'm a hurdler. Period. You have to stop and step back a lot of times when you talk to people about sports.

"I can meet someone on even terms, and have a basic relationship. But, once he or she finds out I'm Ed Moses, well, then, everything is changed. And, that can ruin everything. It's hard to act normal then, because people don't expect you to act normal."

Perhaps, that is why Edwin Moses is not a follower. And perhaps, that is why everybody follows Edwin Moses, on and off the track. He wanted to retire after the 1980 Olympics, but President Carter changed his mind. Then Moses was named to the Athlete's Advisory Board, a blue-ribbon panel of thinkers who are trying to open Olympic eyes on shamateurism.

"I make a good living, within the rules," he says. "We are in a delicate position. Nobody runs the 400-meter hurdles faster than I, so I am, in effect, a professional in the field."

So, Edwin Moses just kept on training, hurdling, winning. And Sunday night, after his moment, he said, "I'm not gonna quit, and I'm not gonna think about trying any other events. I just want to savor this for a while . . . and go with the flow. I feel real good about this. Real good."

If anyone deserves to feel good about himself, it's Edwin Moses.

NO PLACE FOR 'COURAGE'

AUGUST 7, 1984

LOS ANGELES—A short run, maybe a swim, then dinner. That's how Gabrielle Andersen-Schiess would spend Monday evening. She had no time to watch TV, or look at the newspapers. She would make sure she would have no time.

Gabrielle Andersen-Schiess is lucky. Unlike thousands of spectators and millions of viewers around the world, she wouldn't have to see how she had wobbled into Los Angeles Coliseum Sunday morning, a twisted and contorted wreck trying to complete the first Olympic marathon for women.

Like the Games themselves, this grotesque incident was not necessary. Doctors on the scene will justify it, saying all's well that ends well. Look, she was up and around hours after the race. See, she is healthy the day after. Wait, this 39-year-old ski instructor from Idaho, performing "courageously" for her native Switzerland, will be okay Tuesday, too.

But Gabrielle was not okay on Sunday. You did not need a medical degree on your wall or a shingle hanging from your lamppost to realize that she was in serious trouble. All you needed was common sense and compassion. It was time for doctors to err on the side of caution; they simply erred. They had no reason to be irrational; but she did, and was.

"I was blacking out . . . I didn't really know where I was," Andersen-Schiess recalled Monday. "I remember being in a lot of pain, cramped up, my body was on fire. In another marathon, I might have pulled out before the end. But this was historic."

It was almost historic in the worst way. A Canadian doctor said Andersen-Schiess was virtually paralyzed on the left side and in danger of dying. But he didn't have a vote, and neither did Dr. Bernard Segessel of Switzerland. He said Monday that

225

Gabrielle should have been stopped. "Crazy," added Grete Waitz, runner-up to winner Joan Benoit.

Yet, doctors on duty defended themselves Monday because, lest we forget, all's well that ends well. Dr. Richard Greenspun, chief medical officer for the Los Angeles Olympic Organizing Committee, again said there was no need to interfere. Meanwhile, sidekick Dr. Gene Osher shed new and inconsequential light on why Gabrielle's left leg might have been dragging, her right arm flailing, her face twitching.

"She told me when it was over that she had missed her last water stop," said Dr. Osher. But Monday, Gabrielle said she didn't remember whether she saw water, took water, or by-passed water. She couldn't think. She needed somebody to think for her. Nobody did.

In defense of the good doctors, who could certainly use some, the prevailing rule makes no sense. Touch a runner and he or she is disqualified. Gabrielle, dazed, instinctively lurched away from their three attempts to approach her. That may have influenced the doctors. It is to be hoped that the ghoulish entreaties of 70,000-plus clapping fans did not.

"When I saw her first come into the stadium, my first reaction was, 'Oh, God,' " said Gabrielle's husband, Dick. "I wanted them to stop it. I broke out crying."

Gabrielle said she thought she was closer to the finish than she was when she emerged from the Coliseum tunnel. She said she thought that, for such a prestigious event, surely she would be accorded the best medical attention. She said she thought it would be embarrassing if she didn't make it. At least, she thought she thought those thoughts.

"But," Gabrielle admitted Monday, "I probably wasn't really able to think at that point."

One day later, she was not alone. Doctors' disciples point out that, after all, Gabrielle did beat seven other women, even though it took her 16 minutes to stagger the last mile. And they point out that she was still sweating, blinking, moving forward. This sort of thing happens all the time to fatigued marathoners, they say. And so yawn.

"She should have been stopped before she got to the Coliseum," said Katherine Switzer, the first female entry in the Boston Marathon. "She didn't suddenly get into trouble. But I hope this controversy isn't because she's a woman. Equal rights mean equal responsibility."

But if athletes accept the possibility that they will die in action, does that mean authorities abandon their responsibility to prevent tragedy?

Would an injured horse be allowed to continue as far as Gabrielle on Sunday? Would a helpless fighter be permitted to absorb such abuse? If a drunk driver doesn't kill anybody, does he still deserve a ticket?

"If it's as hot next Sunday," said Benoit, "let's see how the men look when they finish their marathon."

Please. This issue has nothing to do with NOW or ERA or the LAOOC, which has earned raves for its efforts. Neither did Sunday have anything to do with courage. Gabrielle didn't have to finish to be noble.

As she bobbed and weaved into the Coliseum, she needed a second opinion. She didn't get one, and now the self-congratulating medics say that she's out of danger, forever.

Who knows? We do know that Gabrielle Andersen-Schiess is lucky. And so are the doctors.

LIKE HOCKEY IN A BIG BATHTUB

AUGUST 8, 1984

MALIBU, CALIFORNIA—All the guys look like they've been sired by Mr. Clean and foaled by the Coppertone Lady, but that's not the reason you've got to dig water polo. They play quickly, and you would, too, if the Pacific Ocean were across the street.

Tuesday, for instance, the United States Olympic team scored more—12—within an hour than the Bears usually do in 3¹/₂ hours. The other squad, Australia, had seven, which means the undefeated Americans are closing in on their first medal since 1972. All this by 9:30 on a California morning.

"Gives us the rest of the day to relax," explained goalie Craig Wilson, a blond toothpaste ad. "We work hard, and we play hard, although a couple of our most raucous partygoers have been on the wagon for months because of this. Gotta sacrifice."

They sacrifice everything except fun. These beach boys in a basic California sport are having a ball, which is what they attempt to throw above water, around traffic and into the opponents' net. Four seven-minute periods plus a two-minute halftime intermission, and it's game over. Can you beat that?

Possibly. These water polomaniacs marketed a group poster in not-so-full uniform. It sold out. But sadly for the gals in the audience, they can't have their beefcake and watch it move, too. Most of the action is submerged. All you see are heads, arms and half-Nelsons. Hockey in a bathtub.

"Funny you brought that up," said team captain Terry Schroeder. "At a recent game against Italy, my dad's in the stands explaining our sport to friends. It's a lot like hockey, he says, except for those silly fights. Bingo, we have two bench-emptying brawls."

The most unruly Olympic water polo match occurred at Melbourne, Australia, during the Soviet invasion of Hungary in 1956. To make a long argument short, those two squads started one day but didn't finish. The Hungarians beat upon their Big Bear foes until the blue swimming pool turned Red. The referee called the game, then the riot police.

"Hungary still has one guy who's pretty rough," said Peter Campbell, who had two goals against Australia. "He grabs you under water and throws the ball with his other hand. You gotta rip that hand underneath away, or else."

Or else?

"Or else," said Campbell.

Tuesday's affair was relatively civilized. Classical music graced the Pepperdine University compound during the warmup, players from both sides joked, and the scoresheet listed no felonies, assaults or batteries.

Still, precautions had to be taken. Refs checked the length of everybody's fingernails beforehand, and all the Americans wore two Speedo suits. One to swim in, another in case an Australian elected to become overzealous when an official was looking the other way. In water polo, sometimes anything goes, even your wardrobe.

"Broken noses, fingers, cut eyelids," said Schroeder. "They all happen. Especially broken noses. Once, my neck sort of popped out. But I was prepared for it. I'm going to school to be a chiropractor, like my dad."

All the Americans are Californians hoping that their Olympic success will spread water polo's gospel, particularly throughout the unenlightened East. Most of the Americans are converted swimmers who opted not to endure the tedium of doing laps.

"I didn't want to spend four hours a day looking down at a dark line in the pool," said Wilson. "Even marathon runners have diversions. Swimmers see nothing, hear nothing. They're just in there to hurt themselves.

"I like our team concept. You gotta be in shape. I may be crazy to be a goalie. I get kicked a lot, but the guys up front are really crazy. That's war."

Schroeder, 25, is Team America's pin-up boy. On next year's "Superstar Buns Calendar," he is the one and only Mr. November. "I did nothing wrong," he said, correctly. At least he had clothes on. When he posed for a statue that now stands before the Los Angeles Coliseum, they told him just to bring a comb.

"One of a woman, one of a man, just for the Olympics," he said, blushing. "I stood naked for 60 hours. I'd never done anything like *that* before. I was a little embarrassed, but someday I'll take my grandchildren there and tell 'em that's me. They'll look at my pot-belly and say, 'Oh, sure.' At least they cut the head off the statue. Gives the pigeons a better place to land."

All of this, um, exposure, gives America's aquanuts some extra money for their program.

Peter Ueberroth, boss of these superbly orchestrated Games, is a former water polo devotee, with the nose to prove it. But nothing could further the cause more than a gold medal.

"The poster, the calendar, the statue . . . that doesn't mean anything," said Schroeder. "That's publicity. We've given up a lot for this. Drinking, wives, school for a while. The girl I went out with for five years, I broke up with. I don't want to blame it all on water polo. But this has been my life since March. I can taste it."

Chlorine?

THE LAST ANTHEM BELONGS TO L.A.

AUGUST 13, 1984

LOS ANGELES—On April 1, 1979, a rather nebulous outfit called the Los Angeles Olympic Organizing Committee anointed one Peter V. Ueberroth as president. He joked about being installed on April Fool's Day, for you wouldn't wish his spot on a leopard.

Now, some 1,957 days later, this former travel agent and baseball commissioner-to-be has emerged as the star of the XXIII Summer Games. What he did and how he did it should be remembered long after who won the 1,000-meter kayak, or why. Peter V. Ueberroth was the true marathon man.

Ueberroth maintains a low profile, deflecting praise to his staff and the thousands of volunteers. "We've all just been stagehands," he says, repeating that the stage belongs to the world's athletes. On that score, Ueberroth is right and wrong.

The players played their games in peace and comfort, but only because Ueberroth and his foot soldiers made everything work. Security was omnipresent, but not oppressive. Volunteers were remarkably informed and genial. And the 10:15 bus to the volleyball venue left at 10:15, not 10:14 or 10:16.

Traffic was supposed to be a problem, but wasn't. As requested, trucking companies delivered their goods at night. Record numbers of citizens abandoned their beloved automobiles for buses to attend events, and price gouging, like the smog, never justified pre-Olympic fear and trepidation.

The impossible was also made believable by southern Califor-

231

nians, who are oft-dismissed as jaded or ultra-mellow folk, their minds addled by too many hours on the beaches and freeways. But no longer can we say of Los Angeles that there is no there there. For these Games, this megalopolis of sand, surf and Taco Bells exhibited the pride of Peoria. Civic duty demands that they congratulate themselves.

Despite his denials, it is rumored that Ueberroth will not carry this after-glow to baseball, that he'll reject the commissioner's job at the 11th hour. Though his horizons and gainful employment possibilities seem limitless now, one can only hope he shows up in New York on October 1, as planned.

After pulling off this miracle, dealing with stubborn Soviets and the hopelessly inept simpletons on the International Olympic Committee, baseball should be a cupcake. With a stern but pragmatic Ueberroth as boss, fickle franchise owners might learn to agree on something other than when to break for lunch.

Besides nearly flawless execution, these Olympics will be chronicled as the Games that veered from status quo. For instance, soccer can't make it in the United States, but you couldn't get a ticket here. On the other hand, this XXIII Olympiad gave us unfortunate excuses for sport, such as synchronized swimming and rhythmic gymnastics, a wearisome ode to the hula-hoop. Better the IOC dunderheads bring back rope climbing, which disappeared in 1932 for lack of interest.

And, though a man was calling signals, the Los Angeles Games also will be recorded as a triumph for women. In all shapes and sizes, from all countries, they excelled. Then there was Swiss runner Gabrielle Andersen-Schiess, who was noble in defeat. And then there was Mary Decker, whose incessant bawling we should remember to forget.

The Los Angeles Games did nothing to solve the official Olympic riddle—when is an amateur not an amateur?—but that is an ongoing dilemma. Whether the Los Angeles Games created a new mode of financing and operating the world's gaudiest sports festival is debatable. Because it worked here doesn't mean it will work again.

Americans should feel no guilt about the manner in which U.S. athletes dominated this quadrennial picnic. And ABC should extend not one apology for paying $225 million to broadcast whatever pictures it pleases. But sooner or later, the

16-day patriotic fix will wear off, at which point reality will supersede America's cache of medals.

The world still spins along, perilously. A boxer from Iraq noticed that the other day. As soon as his tournament ended, he had to return home to rejoin his country's war with Iran. Likewise, on the same afternoon that the American basketball team was beating up on France, the Soviets were beating up on a U.S. Marine in Leningrad.

So, then, this fabulous lawn party with all its parades and anthems and euphoric flag waving and smiling youngsters in leotards has nothing to do with anything consequential. The Games are games, and no matter how well they were organized by Peter Ueberroth and his stagehands, international understanding through sport is an anachronism, as are the Olympics.

Already, the IOC has scheduled meetings with the Soviets to determine whether they will participate in four years at Seoul, South Korea. Movers and shakers around the globe will devote time and money to the cause, all the while blithely assuming that a track meet is the answer, or even part of the answer.

But it isn't, and it doesn't matter. Instead of everybody worrying about whether there will be a 1988 Olympics, the people of the world should be wondering about whether there will be a 1988.

Miscellany

BILLIE JEAN ISN'T LETTING UP

For every movement, there must be a prime mover, a rebel with a cause who fights no with no, a hellion who figures the best polish of all is elbow grease.

The English Channel was just another body of water until somebody swam it, and the moon, for all the lovers' lanes it brightened, never really became boffo until the first astronaut walked it.

Similarly, women had been thwacking tennis balls around for eons until one and only one person took the sport from the broom closet to center court.

Billie Jean King. She may have been in the right place at the right time, but she was also the right individual. She played the game, promoted the game, barnstormed the game, revised the game, enhanced the game, and the game has never been the same since, on one memorable evening in Houston, she silenced Bobby Riggs' racket.

Now, watching good female players play for good money in a good Avon Tournament on a gray Tuesday afternoon in Chicago, Billie Jean King can say it was all worthwhile. Having transcended your sport means never having to say you're sorry.

"A pioneer? Yeah, I guess I was," she says. "I guess I put my neck on the line. But I did it because I believed in it, not because I was forced into it. It was conviction, not coercion. I had to chuckle the other day in the interview room when all the TV cameras and reporters crowded in. I used to have to come to town and go to *them*. Now they come to us. Do you know how much time I spent just going from newspaper office to newspaper office?"

The tennis boom undoubtedly was the sports story of the '70s. Until then, the men had experienced only limited exposure while the women endured an indecent lack of exposure.

"They used to play on Court 35," Billie Jean recalled, "and we'd play on Court 55."

The advent of open tennis in 1968 was historic, but women were still treated like a side dish that hadn't been ordered. Billie Jean King kicked and screamed and with precious few side-kicks—Rosie Casals, Francoise Durr, Ann Jones—lobbied for a piece of the pie. To disparage the sport was unfair, Billie Jean felt. To dismiss the sport when it was played by women, she insisted, was a double fault.

"I had seen us get pushed into the background ever since I was a kid in California," she says, "when the men got whatever they wanted and when the girls got nothing. If I wanted to get into tournaments then, I had to pay. My parents couldn't afford that every week."

The break occurred in the early '70s, when the women went their own way. Virginia Slims provided money and Billie Jean King provided identity. She won 19 tournaments in 1971 for $117,000; she had become the first woman to earn six figures playing anything. Today, 19 tournament victories would mean seven figures, easily.

No wonder then, when the pompous USTA threatened her with suspension, Billie Jean signed anyway to join the daring new women's tour—for the grand sum of $1. Talk about conviction. Prize money for the first WTA tournament in Houston was $7,200. A decade later, on Wednesday night at the Amphitheatre, Billie Jean will play Renee Richards in a second round singles match of a tournament worth $200,000.

Of course, if Billie Jean hadn't won a significant satellite match seven years ago, the Amphitheatre might have been booking roller derby this week. But Bobby Riggs, whose bark had more bite than his serve, couldn't handle her in the Astrodome's landmark battle of the sexes.

"I really wasn't going to play him," said Billie Jean. "But he just kept bugging me and bugging me. Finally, I was just getting on a plane coming home from Japan earlier that year when I heard that he had beaten Margaret [Court]. I said to myself, 'That's it . . . I've got to play him and beat him.' If I hadn't won that match, I'd have killed myself.

"I like Bobby, believe me. Some of my best friends are male chauvanist pigs. Plus, that match might have put the seal of approval on women's tennis. And the rise of women's tennis has gone hand-in-hand with the rise of women, period. Women entertainers in other fields—music, dance, theater—can be judged subjectively. But sports is objective. You either win or lose."

Nowadays, tennis is tennis. What's good for the goose is good for the gander. The men muscle it more and win maybe 30 percent of their points on serves. The women finesse it. Both sides are thriving.

"But the last thing we can do is to stop working," says Billie Jean. "So much time in life is spent on taking short-cuts. We have a long way to go, and I always worry about the fact that we may have peaked. It's gratifying to see how far we've come, but we can't be happy until every seat in this place is full for every match every day.

"And when that happens, you keep on busting your tail. I talk to the younger girls who play—I think there is that respect for me there—and I encourage them to do whatever they can to make tennis happen. The moment you think you have it made is the moment you are done. Not only in sports. In life. They don't need someone with my gumption anymore. The forum is there. The vehicle is there."

It is there because Billie Jean King put it there. Joe Namath made the American Football League go, and Bobby Hull made the World Hockey Association go, but they had ready markets. Billie Jean King had little to work with other than a vision, which is why women admire her openly, and men, quietly.

At 36, though, she is far from jaded.

"How can you get bored with tennis?" she says. "In all the years I've been playing, you know I've never seen the ball come over the net the same way twice?"

REAGAN A CUB FAN

NOVEMBER 6, 1980

You may disapprove of the results from Tuesday's Presidential election, but rest assured of one thing, my fellow Americans. With Ronald Reagan moving into the White House, sports and politics will not mix.

Ronald Reagan, you see, is a Cub fan. Case closed.

If Reagan wants to stay in office, he had best keep this personality flaw a military secret. After all, during preparations last February for the boycott of the Moscow Olympics, Jimmy Carter was widely criticized for jumping on the bandwagon and inviting the United States hockey team to Washington after its exhilarating gold medal victory in Lake Placid. But, really now, can you imagine Ronald Reagan inviting his beloved Cubs to the White House steps for any reason other than to sweep them? Can you imagine Reagan telephoning Joey Amalfitano in the Wrigley Field clubhouse next April after the Cubs beat the Mets to take over third place? It would be political suicide.

The temptations for Reagan to show favoritism will be acute. First of all, he was raised in Dixon, Illinois, a lovely town 100 miles away which, every summer, organizes bus trips to see the Cubs play baseball, or whatever it is they play in Chicago. Moreover—and it is amazing that Mr. Carter didn't pounce on this subject during the debate—Reagan once broadcast Cub games.

"It was back in the 1930s, I guess," Jack Brickhouse was saying Wednesday. "He was working for a big radio station in Des Moines, Iowa, called WHO. A 50,000-watt station. Des Moines had a Cub farm team then, and whenever the minor league team wasn't playing, Ronald Reagan would do the Cub game. He didn't do it live, of course. He did a re-creation."

That means Reagan had to sit in a studio in Des Moines and digest ticker-tape reports from whatever ballpark the Cubs were playing at that day. It was common practice in that era. Reagan would pretend he was actually at the game by describing it in detail ("The wind is starting to blow out to left now, fans, and with the meat of our order coming up in the bottom of the ninth, there's no reason we can't cut into Brooklyn's 12−1 lead.") Or something like that.

The essence of Reagan's job meant that, even though the Cubs were a thousand miles away, he had to make them sound like they were real life and exciting. After that assignment, negotiating with the Kremlin now will seem like a cupcake. And, with that type of preparation, Ronald Reagan was adequately prepared for his next occupation. Acting.

"The Cubs, in a way, helped him get into the movies, too," Brickhouse continued. "They had spring training in those days at Catalina Island in California. And, as a man who covered the Cubs, Ronald Reagan would go out there to report on how they were shaping up for the upcoming season. Well, it was during one of his visits out there that he arranged to have his first screen test. The rest is history.

"Anyway, I got to know him a little bit in subsquent years. On a trip to Chicago, we were doing a Notre Dame football game, and he dropped up to our booth and did play-by-play for a quarter. Did a good job, too.

"I don't think he ever has lost his love of sports or broadcasting sports, and I can guarantee you that he has not lost his love for the Cubs. He is a diehard Cubs fan. I'm privileged to call him a friend. And, you know, because one thing led to another, the Cubs actually sort of helped Ronald Reagan make it to the White House as president."

Not after releasing an incriminating statement like that, you won't be his friend, Brickhouse.

Of course, Reagan's life as a Cub fan will assist him immeasurably in many facets of being a good president. For one thing, he knows what it means to be a hostage. He should have a clearer understanding of energy shortages every summer. He should be especially sympathetic to needy cases. He should be particulary hard on big business firms that try to placate the public with talk of 36-year rebuilding plans. Moreover, by talking with the company whose main account is printing Cub World Series programs and tickets, Mr. Reagan can get an immediate feel for what the unemployment rate is all about.

"I'm going to change things around," President-elect Reagan said Tuesday night. "We're going to do things differently."

Now, frankly, that might be cause for some concern. If, for instance, he names Juicy Fruit the national food so the Cubs can afford to buy some free agents, then Reagan might be subject to some suspicion. If he sends the Philadelphia Phillies or Montreal Expos or Pittsburgh Pirates to Japan for a goodwill tour, and then confiscates their passports so they must remain overseas, I suspect Ed DeBartolo's good pal, Bowie Kuhn, might issue a protest. If Reagan uses federal funds to put a dome over Wrigley Field on the pretense that it is an American treasure in danger of becoming an endangered species, National League opponents who watch the Cub players perspire all the way to sixth place every August are sure to launch impeachment proceedings.

The ultimate betrayal of Reagan's Cubbish tendencies, of course, could occur when he appoints his Cabinet and other high officials. Considering the Cubs' abysmal farm system, be quizzical if Bob Kennedy is named Secretary of Argiculture. Mindful of Dave Kingman's glovework, worry if he is named Secretary of Defense. Women who have observed Willie Hernandez surrender five or six runs in relief should take umbrage if he is entrusted with progress of the ERA amendment.

Naturally, being of sound mind and body, Reagan is likely to be very professional in his new job. Old Cub fans don't die, they just go to the White House, and it's not his fault that he grew up trying to make the Cubs sound exciting. Jack Brickhouse has been doing that for three decades, and he's a very nice man, too.

In fact, it might be the proper gesture to invite President-elect Reagan to Chicago for the Cubs' home opener next season. No doubt, he will be thrilled to throw out the ceremonial first ball. After six weeks of spring training, at least one of the Cubs ought to be able to catch it.

RUMORIZING WITH THE KING'S ENGLISH

MARCH 11, 1984

Don King treats his latest prized client, Michael Jackson, the same way he treated his first, Muhammad Ali. Very gently.

Now, if only Don King would handle the English language with similar care, we could all understand what makes the man tick. It's just that those malaprops keep propping up.

"Michael and Ali both have sixth and seventh senses," King says. "Most of us humanoids, like you and me, are double-parked at five. I calculatedly avoid usurping their lifestyles. They are trees. I just want to be a twig."

King's telephone filibuster comes by way of Las Vegas, where he promoted Friday night's World Boxing Council heavyweight championship bout between Greg Page and Tim Witherspoon. These are busy times for King, but he always has a spare moment to assault the mother tongue.

"The fight game is like a tea party compared with show biz," says King, who sort of invents his vocabulary as he goes along. "Boxing is basic. But when you deal with Hollywood, it's one mogul after another. There is no end to the innuendos, insinuations and rumorizings.

"I feel like James Bond chasing Goldigger in the movie. To get to the house, I've got to swim through a pool of sharks and piranhas, spreading elixirs to survive their every nibble. But in the end, it's not the promises, it's the deliveration. And what I give Michael is what I gave Ali. Integrity."

King is sensitive these days, for stories abound that Michael

Jackson wants out. The fabulously successful young man does not want King—the most powerful and, yes, the smartest man in boxing—to organize a 40-city concert tour starting in June. Or so the rumorizing goes.

"Michael signed the contract under his volition," King reminds. "I advanced the family millions of dollars. I was at the hospital, at his bedside in Los Angeles, fretting like the rest of adoring fanatics, when his hair caught on fire during that Pepsi commercial. Which I arranged for him. Which will mean up to an including $5 million or $25 million.

"But, here comes *Rolling Stone* with an article saying Michael demands I check with him before I book him into a city. What's so unusual about that? I do that with a fighter, too. Once again, the press has disembarked on a chase to defame me. A paper in L.A. says I did 4½ years for murder. It was 4 years for manslaughter. Innuendo and insinuation without representation!"

After he was paroled in 1971, the flamboyant King, his porcupine coiffure and hilarious harangues burst forth in Cleveland, his hometown. He organized a charity exhibition involving Ali, who urged King to make a career of it. The sporting public's eardrums have never been quite the same.

"I am honored and privileged to be touched by two people who have been touched by God," said King, who often wraps himself in religion or the flag. "Only in America. These two men are geniuses who captivate people ages 5 to 50, and I am humbled by their awesome presence. I bow to them on every knee at my disposal.

"Michael will be bigger than anybody ever in the recording industry. He not only writes his lyrics and the music, but he performs. And he's a vegetarian. You and I hear a word, that's all we hear. He hears a word, and he hears a tune to go with it. He's not of this earth, is what I mean.

"Ali expressed himself in the ring, with poetry, with gregariousness. They are both compatible, but Michael is shy. He's a recluse. When he's on stage, he gives all he has. When he's not on stage, though, he's with his family or by himself. He spends a lot of time in his room. He takes care of himself. He's a vegetarian, you know."

Besides securing the best deals possible for Jackson, King assumes an otherwise passive role. It was the same way with Ali.

With stars of that magnitude, King figures, bombast must be kept to a minimum—no easy task for a 250-pounder who wears gold chains as thick as garden hoses.

"Artists like Ali and Michael have forever changing moods," King said. "You don't impose yourself on them. If you have a suggestion, you plant a seed for them to water. If you think they're going off course, you give them a nudge like you would to an electric train. Ali's mind was fast-paced. His attention span was one day.

"Michael is extremely more analytical. Very private, with amazing syncopation, devoted to his parents, video games, Disneyland and, of course, E.T. He's into that extra-terrestrial stuff. Michael dances to his own drummer, like Einstein had to do to discover relativity. Michael is a prince, and smart.

"Regretfully, Ali has not found anything to fill the emotional cavity left by his departure from boxing. It's not that he hears bells. It's that he doesn't hear the applause anymore. But Michael can go on doing what he's doing forever.

"And, contrarily to Ali, nobody will walk up to Michael and tell him he's from the Omaha Old Folks Home and get $150,000. No piranhas in Michael Jackson's entourage. And while the press chases Don King's apparition, Michael and Ali know where to come for truth. Just like the great philosopher Henry David Thoreau said."

Well?

SCHOOL FOR SCANDAL

APRIL 8, 1985

And so, now that the college basketball season mercifully has ceased, we discover there was a problem even more serious than Bobby Knight throwing chairs. Some of America's finest athlete-students might have been throwing games.

Normally, hoop devotees would cringe in horror at such a disclosure, but, of course, we all can relax now. Why just the other day, a gaggle of university presidents got together to discuss corruption at their institutions of higher earning. After considerable dialogue, these erudite gentlemen peered over their bifocals and voted in favor of—are you ready?—integrity. Whew. We knew they had it in them all along.

Unfortunately, it took a district attorney in New Orleans to evoke such a response, and to raise the possibility that college basketball in particular—and college sports in general—might be on the verge of exploding any moment now, like a balloon full of water, like Bobby Knight cautioned it would.

You have to be naive to believe that this latest scandal will begin with the mighty Green Wave at Tulane or end with a Carbondale chiropractor's allegations about illegal payoffs at that jugger of nauts, Southern Illinois University. What's required is that more people talk; what's unlikely, though, is that enough people will listen.

Only one week ago, remember, much of the country witnessed a stirring climax to the Final Four. It was a theatrical tournament, even if teams didn't play with the shot clock they played according to all season—the same timepiece that was adopted for next year's event one day after this year's finished. Nevertheless, Villanova's Cinderella slaying of dragon Georgetown was entertaining, as was much of what came before.

Certainly, the financial and artistic results will do little to prompt sentiment to clean up the wickedness that is apparent, and still brewing, in college athletics. Monday night's Villanova-Georgetown championship pulled the second highest rating of any basketball telecast ever, the top dozen of which all have been "amateur" in nature. The National Basketball Association's best showing—last June's Game 7 between Boston and the Lakers—is the best for a pro tiff, but still a dismal 13th.

Add to that the gushy and irrational praises penned and sung by the certain overzealous sectors of the national media— that college basketball is everything sports is supposed to be about, that the Final Four is innocence in short pants, that what we have here "l-l-live from L-L-Lexington" is the World Series and Super Bowl rolled into one, folks. Claptrap, to be sure.

But, given that backdrop, rest assured that college presidents, chancellors and most of the self-serving athletic administrators below them will confront evil and immorality with rhetoric only. Then they will form a whitewash committee and retire from public life, content to do what they always have— choose higher profits over higher ethics.

Georgetown's John Thompson and Indiana's Knight surely are two of the most intimidating coaches in a somewhat sleazy profession, but they won't intimidate anybody into imposing their values—go to class first and the court second—on the masses. The games will continue to be held in huge arenas instead of campus gyms in front of gamblers and scoundrels instead of student bodies.

Until college athletics are de-emphasized so as to be decontaminated, or until college athletes are treated as they should be—assets to be paid over the table rather than under—there will be the Tulanes of 1985, just as there were the Boston Colleges of 1981, just as there were the LIUs, CCNYs and Kentuckys in 1951. Greed and stupidity will thrive forever, climate permitting.

Educators, who claim to be so wed to history, forget that the scandal more than 30 years ago featured strikingly similar elements. Only the names were different. Judge Saul B. Streit, who presided at the 1951 trial, told his courtroom that four players got into school with forged entrance papers, and that one senior's academic "load" consisted of courses in oil painting, public speaking and rhythm and dance. Some of the athlete-students had IQs of 80. Scary, but still true.

And while the madness of college sports continues

unchecked, glorified by everyone from journalists to adults who paint blue Wildcats' feet on their cheeks before the big game, we should remember that one temptation has been added to the 1951 abyss. Drugs are as prevalent around the campus as they are anywhere else in society. Cash needn't be the sole inducement anymore to miss a crucial free throw.

Presidents, coaches and crazed alumni can always back off with the favored excuse: "These kids should know better." Obviously, they don't. Obviously, if a young man at Tulane or any other institution can squander a possible NBA career for a few hundred bucks and a day's worth of cocaine, he needs help. He needs to be taught. But will he be? Not if those Nielsen ratings keep climbing.

So long as Bobby Knight continues to call a phony a phony, he can throw all the chairs he wants. He's not what's wrong with his sport.

GRAPPLING WITH AN HONEST CRISIS

JUNE 20, 1985

Read no further if you are subject to fits of deep depression. Just when your favorite sport and mine, professional wrestling, was threatening to take over the planet, was bidding to become the rage of the '80s, we have had our hearts cut out.

Scandal is a word not to be thrown out lightly, particularly when referring to cataclysmic events such as one grown man in leotards attempting to scratch the eyes from another adult wearing green tights to match his earring, all of which clash somewhat with a robe bathed in pink sequins.

But duty demands that we broach the subject of illicit activities this somber morning in our spectating lives, because the very honor of pro wrestling is being challenged. All along, we thought we were different. Our friends worried about whether their heroes in other sports were shaving points. We knew our heroes were clean, even if they didn't shave their underarms.

At least we thought we knew. And then this. A promoter outside Pittsburgh files suit just the other day against a wrestler. The charge? Winning matches too easily, and too quickly, and generally ignoring directions—not necessarily in that order. Again, read no further if you have broken into a cold sweat.

Robert Milarski is the defendant grappler. Still growing at age 32, he decided to abandon a promising career as a commercial artist for fun and profit in the ring. That was two years ago. Since then, Milarski has won every one of his matches, none of which has lasted more than five minutes.

Not so fast, said plaintiff promoter Newton Tattrie, who took Milarski under his wing, trained him, fed him, coached him.

Tattrie is well qualified, having wrestled for three decades under the *nom de plume* of "Gito Mongol." Tattrie taught Milarski everything he needed to know about wrestling, including how to apply a not-so-full Nelson. That's when Milarski tuned out.

"I like to get in there, do my thing and get out," a perplexed Milarski explained over the phone Wednesday from his home in Pittsburgh. "I'm still learning my trade, but I'm 6 foot 1 and 302 pounds. Strong, man. I can destroy some of these guys they put me up against. Do I have to tiptoe around just to stretch the thing out? Aren't I supposed to do my best?"

Ah, that is precisely Tattrie's point. If you want to get paid by the fiddler, you've got to dance a little. "I want to know if I have the right to tell a guy to take it easy," said Tattrie, who believes that Milarski and his ilk should be actors first and athletes second. Imagine if all matches ended within five minutes. How is a promoter to sell that again next week?

"I see his point," conceded Milarski. "I just want to know what's right. Are me and Gito still friends? Of course, we talk all the time, even though he just sued me. He just wants to know what's right, too."

Perish the thought, but it had been suggested that there is a subplot here. The Pennsylvania Athletic Commission considers wrestling in the same category as boxing. That means the state takes a 5 percent cut of gate receipts. If Tattrie were to convince authorities that wrestling was not the same as boxing, then there would be no tax. But that would mean wrestling is entertainment instead of sport, which it isn't, right. Right?

"Well . . . whatever they decide is okay with me," Milarski mused. "If they tell me to run around for 20 minutes before I pin the guy, I will. But if I do that, I don't want to be breaking the law that says I gotta give my all, just like a boxer. And what I'm doing now, I guess, is breaking my contract with Gito. I don't want to do either. You see the fix I'm in?"

Uh, fix?

"I didn't mean it that way," Milarski said hurriedly. "I've heard all the stories about pro wrestling, about how these things are all rehearsed. But that's never happened to me. All Gito's ever told me is take it easy on this guy because he ain't no good. That other stuff, I don't know about. I'm still just a beginner in this. I only get about $50 a bout."

Milarski is so fearful about being depicted as a rebel that he won't reveal his ring name. He's afraid he'll be blackballed by other promoters when he wants to grunt onward and upward in the profession. Maybe there's an Andre the Giant in his future. Or the Missing Link. Or Hulk Hogan. Or a date with Cyndi Lauper.

"That's where wrestling's demise as a sport began," said Paul Johnson, a general manager of the Rosemont Horizon. "When it made the cover of *Sports Illustrated,* when it became yuppified, I knew it was in trouble. We have many wrestling cards in our building, and we face the same problem as Pittsburgh. Only in Illinois, boxing and wrestling lose 10 percent in tax right off the top.

"I wasn't going to return your phone call. I knew what you were calling about. When I heard the news, I went inside, put my Sgt. Slaughter T-shirt on and endured a few moments of silent mourning. I'm going to have to come down firmly on the side of spectacle. Wrestlers now should be obligated to go more than five minutes. I'm afraid that is the price we wrestling fanatics have to pay for progress. I'm going to be forced to hang up now."

Meanwhile, as we all sulk about our business, think about poor Robert Milarski waiting back there in Pittsburgh to discover what he is, what is right, what his life in fuschia Speedo is all about.

"The guy on the state athletic commission has called this a nuisance suit," he groused. "The guy who runs the Civic Arena said wrestling is a sham. I don't like to hear that kind of talk. I just want to know whether I'm a fish or a fowl? I'm deeply concerned how this will come out. If we aren't a sport, then why is the state commission telling us what to do? Why do sports and politics always have to mix?"

Why indeed. Has there ever been a darker day in American athletics?

MINI-TREND
IN HONESTY

FEBRUARY 20, 1986

Hypocrisy and deceit, staples of our modern sporting swamp, have taken a severe whipping of late. Meanwhile, ethics and fair play, a couple of erstwhile interlopers, have crashed the scene, scoring points and creating all sorts of wonderful shock waves. One can only hope the trend continues, though we should know better than to anticipate a complete overhaul.

First, from Lausanne, Switzerland, came word that the International Olympic Committee will consider admitting professional athletes into hallowed summer and winter Games. Then appeared a second rare ray of cleanliness from another bastion of shamateurism—Athens, Georgia. There an English instructor was awarded $2.57 million in damages for bucking the system. Seems she has this deranged idea that jocks should depart campus after four years with, if not a diploma, some working knowledge of the alphabet beyond the letters X and O.

What next? A drug program that works? A league that takes a hard look at hard drugs? A commissioner who hands down life suspensions instead of rhetoric? Stranger things have happened, but, again, don't hold your breath, or your laughter. We might merely be experiencing a brief fling of morality and righteousness, a movement that will burn out as suddenly as it appeared.

Still, the mere possibility that the IOC would bother to think about dropping the pretense associated with its quadrennial muscle dances is encouraging. This comical group of "leaders"—pledged to the lyrical but flimsy notion that international track meets foster good will and understanding—indeed will vote in October on whether to open the heretofore closed Games to all athletes, pure or paid. This change in policy would be a distant runner-up to the best solution, eliminating the Olympics altogether.

251

Juan Antonio Samaranch, president of the aptly nicknamed "Earls of Dandruff," seldom has been hailed as a paragon of reason, which is to say he's the perfect man to bang the gavel for this outfit—but ever so quietly, so as not to arouse the sleepy. Still, there he was, rattling the committee's stuffed shirts with his recent contention that "for us, a professional is the same as a state athlete."

Although we all know and believe deep in our hearts that sports and politics don't mix, feel free to assume that this theory will not fly easily. The Soviet Union, a champion of forthrightness, indicated it doesn't care, that the more eligible participants, the merrier. That would be a huge plus for the amendment, if only the Soviets weren't so accomplished at saying one thing and meaning another. This is a land, remember, where amateur athletes devote no more than 50 weeks a year to their hobbies.

The specter of Wayne Gretzky and his ilk competing against the Soviet hockey team is undeniably delicious, but premature and far-fetched. And it's not only the foreign federations that could interfere with logic. The National Hockey League, bless its timid soul, would have to act, presumably under the guidance of doughty president John Ziegler. But whether the hallowed NHL schedule could be suspended for, say, three weeks to make way for the hallowed Games wouldn't depend on Ziegler, anyway—even if, by some miracle, he had an opinion on the matter. Because Alan Eagleson, the Toronto barrister who runs the Players Association and the league, tells Ziegler what to do.

Eagleson, like everybody else involved in Samaranch's proposal, would ask a price for progress. Still, of such grist is a dream solution rendered. There might yet be a day when a Carl Lewis can drive his Mercedes right up to the long-jump pit and not be embarrassed, either by his fancy wheels or his well-fortified trust fund. He will show up simply to compete against the world's best, and never mind the false labels. Let the pro-am games begin.

If the IOC is perplexed about how to eliminate absurd camouflage, Mrs. Jan Kemp could supply a workable plan. She's the courageous and bold professor with three degrees who challenged her dismissal by the University of Georgia, claiming that this institute of higher earning, but not necessarily learning, canned her in 1983 because she had the audacity to question preferential treatment for athletes. Her winning testimony included evidence that school officials changed failing grades of nine football players in 1982 so they might partake in that renowned steppingstone to society, the Sugar Bowl.

The NCAA is designated as watchdog for such recurring indiscretions, but while this governing body dozed as usual at the controls, it was left to a 36-year-old woman with some backbone to expose the corruption that exists well beyond the boundaries of the Bulldogs. The university, of course, took umbrage, a logical reaction in that it had precious little ammunition. Well, yes, admitted administrators, the institution does take some indecent liberties with transcripts of certain athlete-students, particularly those in "revenue" sports such as football and basketball.

Some highfalutin promises followed, such as chancellor H. Dean Propst's assertion that favoritism "must be directly addressed without equivocation." But Georgia president Dr. Fred C. Davison's reaction was more predictable. Though saddened, he said his fine academic establishment could not "disarm unilaterally." What's he mean by that bit of gibberish? He means that if his Bulldogs stop conniving, everybody else has to stop conniving, too, or else there won't be no grits on the table. A fine attitude.

Then there was another enlightening message delivered by a lawyer for the college. Said O. Hale Armand Jr., referring to the typical sweathog on scholarship: "We may not be able to make a university student out of him, but if we can teach him to read and write, maybe he can work at the post office rather than as a garbage man when he gets through with this athletic career." Need you know more about the noble aspirations of our nation's educators?

What it all means is this: If the 1988 Olympics are open to professionals, the University of Georgia will be welcome. Can't you see it now? All those groveling alums and boosters, crawling about the streets of Seoul on all fours, babbling "How 'Bout Them Dawgs!!" All in the name of sport. Beautiful.

STARS &
STRIPES &
TEDIUM

FEBRUARY 1, 1987

FREMANTLE, AUSTRALIA—They commenced the world series of synchronized sailing Saturday, and, oh, buoy, what a colossal bust it was. You've seen bigger waves in your bathtub, more whitecaps on a kitchen sink, and you'll find stronger wind in a hot attic. Like so many other big events in sports, this opening race of the America's Cup finals couldn't possibly justify the hype factor. It wasn't worth the wading.

What's alleged to be the most exciting 24.1 miles in athletics instead became a tedious rout, a typical Super Bowl, only this one was watered-down with spinnakers. If it had been a fight, it would have been stopped, except the local boat barely got started. Stars & Stripes of the United States won the first race in a best-of-seven series over Australia's Kookaburra III by 1 minute 41 seconds. It was like having your ace pitcher go to the mound on five days rest in the opener of the Fall Classic, then watching him fail to retire a batter.

At dawn, this town was buzzing with anticipation because the weather was perfect for the home craft. Stiff breezes, the kind that supposedly would benefit Stars & Stripes, were nonexistent. There was a cloud cover, and with it, the usual mild puffs from inland. The "Fremantle Doctor," which ordinarily carries relief from summer's heat with gusts off the Indian Ocean, took the afternoon off from making house calls and sent a nurse instead. Perfect for the Kookaburra, or so the Aussies hoped.

They came early to stake out perches along the harbor, waving their country's flag. They painted their faces and bodies in green and yellow, Kookaburra's colors. They draped bedsheets over the rocks to provide a sendoff for Iain Murray and his crew. "Iain Walks on Water," read one. How prophetic. Hours later, Kookaburra crawled in, beaten to a pulp, so far behind that the boat might as well have drifted off-course toward one of the nearby beaches, where women tend to shed the upper portion of their two-piece bathing suits. It was a slaughter. At least if the Aussies had stopped to catch some fish, they would have had an alibi. None of the losers fell overboard, nobody got seasick. No excuses whatsoever. The Kookaburras simply got their halyards handed to them.

"It's just one race," said Dennis Conner, the humble skipper for Stars & Stripes. "The other boat was very fast, we were just lucky. We've got a lot of racing to go."

Because of the rare still factor, there almost wasn't a race Saturday. The start was delayed 20 minutes by good weather, of all things. For four months here, the skies have been howling. However, not this day. The breezes, or what there was of them, ranged from 8 to 18 knots, well below the prescribed velocity that makes for action. It must have been a bland sight on ESPN, because even to these educated eyes, the pace made the whole bloody mess seem like a pleasure cruise. You'd spill more cups of coffee on the Wendella.

Not that there weren't curious moments. Imagine spending $18 million to bring a boat here, then having your navigator lean off the side with a stick in his hand to knock the weeds off the rudder. Peter Isler, a Yalie crew member for the American machine, was assigned thusly. They come halfway around the globe to remove kelp? Besides, isn't that the job for the sewerman? They use computers to figure out everything from the atmospheric conditions to tacking strategy, and a glob of seaweed throws off the entire equation? What's next for yachting, a battlefield by Perrier?

Then there was the matter of crowd control, another vestige from more conventional sports. There was a huge spectator fleet Saturday, from dinghies to the Achille Lauro, and to hear Conner tell it, he had a more difficult time avoiding all those floating admirers than he did staying ahead of Kookaburra III. He said it was "gross" how close they came. Can you build a restraining wall in the Indian Ocean? On second thought, perhaps Conner should be thankful that enough people care. It's good for the sport, and besides, his mug is scheduled for the cover of next week's *Time* magazine.

"There is tremendous interest in this back in the States," said the 44-year-old drapery executive, stretching the truth a whole bunch in a bit of sailsmanship. "There is really a sport out here. This isn't just something that rich people do. This is actually a complicated endeavor."

It surely did not seem as such. Light weather or no, Conner was ahead by 1 minute 15 seconds at the first mark and 1 minute 20 seconds at the second. He got out of the gate quickly, and took the lead.

As Conner modestly offered, it's tough for the guy who's behind when the winds are forever shifting because when you're ahead, the boat in front has the clear advantage. All Murray could wish for was a fairer situation Sunday, when there would be racing. No lay days for him.

"I don't think today was a true test of the relative merits of either boat," Murray said. "We thought we'd have the edge, but I'm not a great believer in luck. Dennis made the most of his opportunitites today, and he didn't leave us much room."

Australian boat fans are fretting not only about being defeated but about being swept as well. The United States had held the America's Cup for 132 years until Conner, aboard Liberty, lost it to Australia II four years ago at Newport, Rhode Island. Now Conner has returned to get it back for the first time. But he needn't be too flushed by Saturday's triumph, because he led in 1983 by 3–1 before he absorbed the shock of his life.

Win or lose here, though, Stars & Stripes has solved the problem of high-tech seaweed. Just have a guy from the Ivy League beat it to death.

A RACE NEVER LOST, A RACE NEVER OVER

DECEMBER 28, 1986

NEW YORK—In a sports year marred by drugs, deception and even death, a guy who finished last finished first.

Bob Wieland cherishes the purity and joy of athletic competition, so he requires no illegal substance or inflated salary for arousal. A simple blast of fresh air up his nose and it's all systems go, which is why he lined up with the rest of the runners at the New York City Marathon in early November.

Some of the other participants and thousands of spectators looked at him quizzically, but Wieland just looked ahead. He figured it would be a long 26 miles, and was it ever. When he completed his journey, Wieland came in 19,413th in a field of 19,413, or more than four days behind the leaders. Fred Lebow, director of the event, was rousted from his office to make it official—98 hours, 48 minutes, 17 seconds—"a world record for the slowest marathon ever," he proclaimed, smiling.

But the crowd cheered, and Bob Wieland raised his arms triumphantly. It didn't matter then, and it doesn't matter now, that Bob Wieland has no legs.

"June 14th, 1969, in a section of Vietnam they called Hobo Woods," Wieland was saying from his home in California. "I was in the 25th Infantry of the U.S. Army, running up a hill to assist some of my fallen comrades when I detonated an 82-millimeter mortar round. I guess my legs went in one direction and the rest of me went in another direction. I don't know for sure, of course, because I was gone for five days. So far gone, that I was pronounced dead on arrival at the hospital.

"I wasn't breathing, and even after I began doing that again, I wasn't in real good shape. I had malaria, my body temperature was 106 degrees, and my body wasn't that much of a body, either. I had gone from 205 pounds to 87. When I came to, I was alone. I pulled up the sheets and saw what had happened. That did tend to spoil the day, when I realized I'd lost my legs, but I was so happy to be alive, I didn't have time to be depressed. That's the way I've operated ever since. Feeling sorry for yourself takes an awful lot of energy."

There was a provision at the New York City Marathon for the 50 or so handicapped persons—a few yards of grace as it were, a head start. But Wieland balked at the favor and insisted that they get on with the thing, even if it meant his getting trampled a bit. At 8:23 a.m., the gun went off, and this Vietnam vet commenced his trek, swinging his frame to and fro, between those powerful shoulders working in concert with his hands, which have been his feet for nearly two decades.

"I wore what I call my size one Adidas, thick shoe-like things I hold on to, no irritation whatsoever," Wieland explained. "On my lower torso, no wheels. Thick leather chaps, four to six layers, to cushion me against the pavement. Had to change every few hundred yards because they wear out, but otherwise there was no problem."

It was Wieland who took on the Walk Across America in September, 1982, when he departed Los Angeles for Washington—"2,784.1 miles, to be exact."

He was blessed with an occasional helper, but most of the trip was a solo affair. That entailed "walking" a prescribed distance to his van, then driving back to the point where he'd left his wheelchair, then advancing a few more miles by motor, then parking his van, then taking his wheelchair back to repeat the entire procedure. It took him almost four years.

"The marathon in New York was a lot different," Wieland said. "It was shorter, but I did want to finish as soon as possible. I couldn't go at my own pace, and as a result, I barely slept. Maybe five hours in five days. As it was, I fell so far behind that I got a good view of the sanitation trucks picking up from the crowd that had watched the race. It got rainy and cold, and I was lucky they didn't mistake me for a piece of garbage. But, you know, the only time you worry about failing is the last time you try something. I've always considered my situation now preferable to the alternative. Physically handicapped has it all over being physically dead."

On returning from Vietnam, with his spirit intact, Wieland fortified both mind and body. He completed his education, taught strength and flexibility, founded the nonprofit Spirit of America Organization in Laguna Hills, California, and prepared for the rest of his life.

Soon, his arms were as sturdy as his faith in God. In 1970, he was too weak to lift a five-pound weight. In 1977, he bench-pressed 303 pounds at a body weight of 122 pounds.

"That's a world record," Wieland said. "I might have a couple others, except one organization didn't recognize me because I wasn't wearing shoes. That's not important, though. What's important is that they realized I hadn't gotten lost in New York, that the race wasn't over.

"They started getting reports of this optical illusion trudging through places like Harlem and Central Park. A lot of people started following me, and the support was tremendous.

"They gave $25,000 and a Mercedes to the winners, Gianni Poli and Grete Waitz. I remember when I finished, somebody yelled, 'Hey, they gave the keys to the wrong dude!' But that's not what's important. No. C783 finished, tattered and chilled. Bringing up the rear."

Wieland, training now for the Los Angeles Marathon in March, wishes to be thought of as an athlete—nothing more, nothing less.

He is a fan of all sports and, like most of us, cringes at the hypocrisy and lack of fun that the games people play can take on in this cutthroat era.

But, loyal sweat setter that he is, Wieland believes if the money is there, the players should share in it.

"It's not their fault, it's the owners of these teams," he said.

"I'm all for athletes getting what they can get. They deserve it. But if they don't enjoy what they do, and don't work hard at it, well, they could always try doing it without any legs."

Bob Wieland—the Sports Person of a good, bad and ugly 1986—did. And nobody did it better.

A SPECIAL LESSON

AUGUST 6, 1987

SOUTH BEND, INDIANA—You drive here from a hot Chicago, and your car's air conditioning unit is spitting out blasts of warm blanks, and the toll gate jams just when you want to make some time, and you curse life's inconveniences.

It's not your day, you say, and then you see their faces, and you realize it's not supposed to be. It's their day, and it's their week, and if only they could have more days and weeks like these.

You come to the International Special Olympics on the University of Notre Dame campus expecting to feel sorrow for the 4,717 athletes, ages 8 to 83, from 70 different countries, but you wind up feeling humbled by the joy that pervades the place. You know that these people have been missing out on a lot of common pleasures since birth and will until they pass on, but you also realize that maybe you've been so swallowed up by running for airplanes that you've forgotten a few things, too, like what it means to hug someone for finishing eighth out of eight.

You walk into a hotel and there's a mentally retarded kid in his track uniform scouring the lobby for any kind of souvenir that says Fighting Irish or Notre Dame on it. And you see the polite lady behind the desk give the kid a simple post card, and you see his eyes explode in glee, and even though he can't really say thank you, he can't say thank you enough. And you see the lady behind the desk, and you know that she's not tearing about the eyes now because she caught a cold.

You run into a Bill Hickey, who's the director of food services for the university and who has been serving up thousands and thousands of meals daily, and he tells you about the boy he met the other day, the boy from Ireland. Bill tells you that he asked the boy which part of Ireland he was from, north or south? And the boy looked at Bill and said, "What's the difference? We're all the same." And Bill wondered why they can't understand that back in Ireland, where the normal folk shoot at each other in the name of anger and politics.

And then Lefty Smith drops by, the same Lefty Smith who used to coach hockey at Notre Dame, the Lefty Smith who was a prime mover in bringing the Games here. He relates a tale about 1983, when he was at the Special Olympics in Baton Rouge, bidding for South Bend in 1987. And Lefty recalls how the athletes came into a restaurant that first night down there and the customers dropped their jaws into their salads, because they'd never been exposed to the mentally retarded en masse.

"The people in the restaurant were frightened, I think," Lefty says. "They didn't know whether these kids were going to attack them with forks and knives or start throwing food around, or what. But then the kids kept coming back to that restaurant, night after night, with their medals and their ribbons on. And pretty soon, the regulars got to the point where they'd stand up at their tables, in the middle of their meals, cheering for the kids and what they'd done that afternoon. That's exactly the emotion that's swept up this community. I've never seen anything quite like it, and I've been around here on a lot of football Saturdays."

And then you go out into the sunshine and realize what you've lost a handle on out there in the real world, the world of agents who lie and coaches who cheat and college presidents who sanction deceit and athletes who scream when their filet isn't cooked quite right. They staged an opening ceremony the other night, you're informed, and these athletes lined up at 5 o'clock in the broiling temperatures and weren't excused until 11 because ABC wanted to produce a delayed tape that was smashing, which it did and which it was, one night later.

Imagine, a guy from the network was saying, what it would have been like asking real athletes, the normal millionaires, to stand still that long for anything, except perhaps a free car or another commercial endorsement? But the kids, ages 8 to 83, gladly sweated it out in the bowels of the stadium, probably because they aren't dumb enough to complain. They've been sheltered, after all. They haven't learned how to hate or how to be ungrateful or how to practice hypocrisy. And in lieu of drugs, it seems, their narcotics are fresh air, love and companionship.

Mind you, Donna Sue Montgomery, 37, from Kentucky, came to win the 25-meter walk. But when the first-place time was announced as 6.7 seconds, and hers came over as 1 minute 41 seconds, it didn't seem to matter. She got into her wheelchair with a smile and headed over to receive her medal or ribbon, it didn't matter which. They all earn something, including David Diekow of Alaska, who had to be propped up by a volunteer—on vacation time—to accept his prize for fourth and the red rose, which the kid held high in a quivering hand. More than a sporting event, the International Special Olympics is an event, period.

You see a youngster dribbling a basketball toward the basket, an unmolested layup, a sure thing, and then you see him stop short to pick up a fallen opponent from the floor. The two points could wait, but not a helping hand. You see Geary Locke, 23, a local lad, crying because he finished third in his heat, crying because he figured his dad deserved a victory. His dad was Bill Locke, who, perhaps more than anyone else, brought the Games here. But Bill died of a massive hemorrhage three years ago, and Geary wasn't so sure Dad would be proud of him now.

"But I know his father is," said June Locke, Geary's mother. She was there Sunday night when Geary climbed the stairs of the stadium and lit the flame with the torch and said, "Dad, this is for you." And June Locke was there when Geary stopped crying Wednesday, which was when Sargent Shriver, the president of Special Olympics International, presented Geary that very torch to keep.

It was then that June Locke started to cry, because she's a special parent behind a special child. But there are lots of them, lots of special parents. You don't hear any of them shouting to kill the umpire, and you don't hear any of them browbeating a coach to get their son or daughter into the game, and you notice that even the reporters here have developed manners, keeping their microphones and ink-stained elbows out of each other's faces and away from participants' chins.

Must be that this isn't reality with all its attendant cynicism and cutthroat mentality. Must be that this is different, a friendlier spot than the Persian Gulf or the Iran-contra hearings or even the other Olympics, the one where amateurs take steroids to build their muscles and quiet cash to build their trust funds. Must be that this is purer than all the other forms of athletics that call themselves genuine.

"My son Chris is 16," says Sue Coffman, the Area Two Coordinator for Special Olympics, a woman who is doing it on adrenaline this week. "Like any mother, I wish that he was born normal. I wish that it didn't take him six years to learn how to tie his shoes. These children, many of them come here not only to compete, but to develop their sense of responsibility, to be able to tell time, to be able to pack their belongings, to be able to live in a dorm or with a strange family that has taken them in.

"Yes, I wish he was born normal, because every parent of a mentally retarded child wonders down deep what will happen to them, who will take care of them when we die? Will they be okay? Will society look down on them, or will society, through events like these, learn to appreciate them? I wish, yes, but also I would not trade my Chris for any child on Earth. He's so good-hearted and so kind, and he was given to me by God for a reason. If it wasn't for Chris, I would never have gotten involved in something so wonderful as this. And, besides, you look at these kids smile and you wonder . . . what is normal?"

And you drive back to a hot Chicago, and you look through that toll gate now, because you are asking yourself the very same thing. Exactly who is handicapped here? Them or us?

Index